CRIME
INVESTIGATION

CRIME
INVESTIGATION

THE ULTIMATE GUIDE TO FORENSIC SCIENCE

PaRragon

Bath · New York · Singapore · Hong Kong · Cologne · Delhi · Melbourne

This is a Parragon book
First published in 2007
Parragon
Queen Street House
4 Queen Street
Bath BA1 1HE, UK

ISBN 978-1-4054-9872-2

Editorial and design by
Amber Books Ltd
Bradley's Close
74–77 White Lion Street
London N1 9PF
www.amberbooks.co.uk

Project Editor: James Bennett
Design: Joe Conneally
Picture Research: Kate Green

A copy of the CIP data for this book is available from the British Library.

Printed in Indonesia

Contents

Introduction

'We all think of death as the ending. For forensics, it's just the beginning.'

Nancy Haley, Supervisor,
Forensic Toxicology Laboratory,
Department of Health, Rhode Island, USA

CRIME AND JUSTICE SEEMED SIMPLER IN THE EARLY NINETEENTH CENTURY BEFORE MODERN COMMUNICATIONS AND EFFICIENT TRANSPORTATION. Criminals were normally easier to apprehend because they lived in small communities with their victims and any eyewitnesses – the hit-and-run crime would have to wait for a modern infrastructure. And when suspects were arrested and tried, convictions were normally based on public opinion and even resulted from pressures put on the defendant, including torture. This easy justice, however, was often injustice in the years before standard police procedures and scientific evaluations of evidence.

Today's criminals use modern technology including emails, mobile phone messages, and even television appearances. Ian Huntley, who murdered two ten-year-old girls in Soham, Cambridgeshire, was soon on a BBC news programme coolly speaking about the community's shock. However, the investigative tools of forensic science have also advanced at a remarkable pace. Infrared spectrometers identify fibres left by suspects, CT scanners pinpoint weapons in suitcases, and DNA solves 'cold cases' that are decades old. Introduced in the 1980s, DNA testing has been recently refined to obtain results from only a few cells, ten times fewer than conventional DNA testing.

EVERY CONTACT LEAVES A TRACE

To the trained eye, a crime scene is filled with clues that can be obvious or mysterious. They involve physical evidence like fingerprints, hair, blood, fibres, drugs, paint or soil. Arthur Conan Doyle's fictional detective Sherlock Holmes, who first appeared in 1887, emphasized the importance of miniscule evidence. He searched for fingerprints, analyzed blood, and examined documents. The idea that 'every contact leaves a trace' was stated in 1920 by Dr. Edmond Locard, a French police officer and forensic scientist who ten years earlier had established the world's first crime laboratory in Lyon, France. His concept, now known as Locard's Exchange Principle, is the

Left: A forensic scientist collects fibre samples for microscopic examination as part of a criminal investigation. Fibres from clothing and carpets are among the most common items of trace evidence that are recovered.

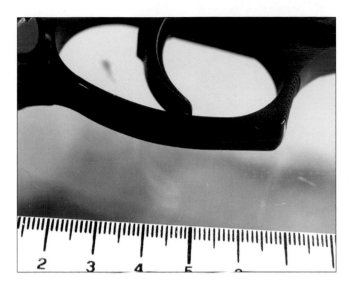

Left: Photographs of this gun, an item of evidence, are needed for use in court. A ruler shows the scale. The gun will also be test-fired to provide bullets and cartridges for comparison with those taken from the crime scene.

Above: Forensic scientist checks for fingerprints on a bottle at a crime scene. His protective suit prevents contamination of the evidence.

key to modern forensic science. In practice, this means physical evidence will be exchanged during any physical contact between a suspect and his victim or the crime scene. A criminal might leave his fingerprints or a hair at the scene, and take away carpet fabric on his shoes.

Such evidence is carefully collected and turned over to forensic scientists who handle such diverse crimes as identity theft, kidnapping, burglary, arson, rape and murder. If someone has died, forensic pathologists calculate the time and cause of death, and a nameless victim can be identified by a variety of methods, which include fingerprints, a dental match, and facial reconstruction in clay or by computer.

The forensic laboratory is often the key to a successful police investigation. The lab results should indicate if a crime was committed and, if so, tests can verify evidence that helps convict the person or persons responsible. Placing a suspect at the crime scene is a basic goal of forensic work. That connection is often a clear sign of guilt, as when fresh tyre marks are found at the scene of an arson attack.

EVIDENCE IN COURT

The name 'forensic science' means science related to crime and courts of law. The word 'forensic' goes back to the Latin *forum* where legal matters were settled. Forensic experts, indeed, are called to testify in court cases by both the prosecution and the defence. The

trail from a crime scene to a courtroom has a sequence that is well established, which can involve specialists in several forensic fields working closely with law enforcement officers. The scientific tools and techniques they use are impressive, but lab results have to be evaluated by highly trained professionals possessing knowledge, experience and intuition.

The following chapters will look at how evidence is collected at crime scenes, the ways of determining the time and cause of death, of identifying unknown victims and suspects, what tools and tests are used in the modern forensic laboratory, the way DNA profiling has revolutionized the fight against crime, how forensic scientists solve white-collar crimes, and what drives a criminal mind. The final chapters present a history of forensic detection and an overview of specialisms in the profession.

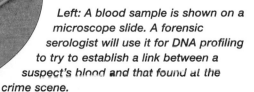

Left: A blood sample is shown on a microscope slide. A forensic serologist will use it for DNA profiling to try to establish a link between a suspect's blood and that found at the crime scene.

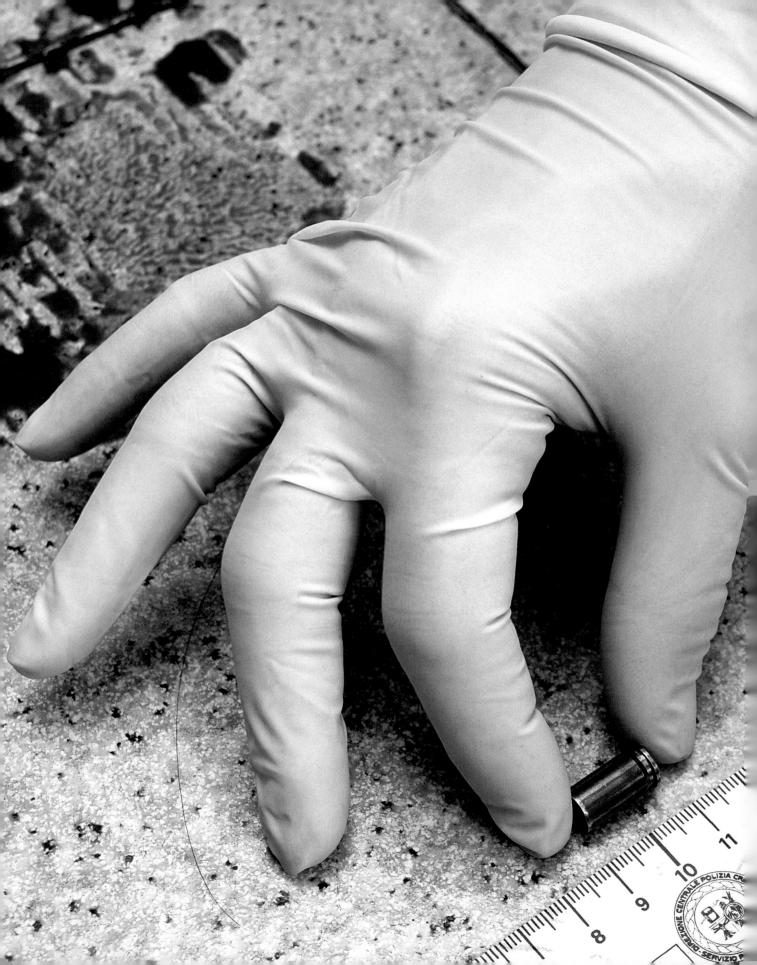

Chapter One

Forensic Science: The Facts

THE INVESTIGATION AND PROSECUTION OF A CRIME DEPENDS LARGELY UPON FORENSIC SCIENCE TO ASSEMBLE THE FACTS THAT PROVE A CRIME OCCURRED AND THAT A CERTAIN SUSPECT OR SUSPECTS COMMITTED IT.

Important evidence collected at the crime scene may include fingerprints, footprints, spent bullets and trace evidence like hairs, fabrics, skin, blood and other stains. However, some of the biological evidence, like DNA, might not be visible to the naked eye.

This evidence will be carefully conveyed to a forensic laboratory to be examined by specialists working in such fields as pathology, toxicology, serology, odontology and DNA analysis. Their forensic tools will range from the familiar microscope to the complex DNA scanner and mass spectrometry instrument.

Evidence bags are required at crime scenes to protect items from contamination as they are collected and shipped to a forensic laboratory.

Among the key evidence that can be retrieved from a scene are cartridge shells (far left) and fingerprints (left).

Forensic Evidence

A crime cannot be solved without evidence. Confessions and circumstantial evidence sometimes prove untrue, but physical evidence can provide an airtight case against a suspect.

Guilty verdicts have been achieved by an expert's testimony that involves a single hair or a piece of fibre. For this reason, a forensic scientist's primary focus at a crime scene is to discover these small pieces, known as 'trace evidence', with other examples of evidence, including skin, gunshot residue and dust.

Fingerprints are sometimes described as trace evidence, as well as the prints of palms and soles at the crime scene. Fingerprints can be removed to be compared to those already on file in a database or to prints taken from suspects. They are also valuable in identifying an unknown victim. Prints made by shoes, gloves and tyres are also extremely useful. In addition, investigators search for marks left by tools, such as those used for breaking into a house.

FIREARMS

If a firearm has been deployed in a crime and recovered, forensic scientists will use chemicals and microscopes to examine the gun and its projectiles. When bullets or shell casings are matched to the firearm of a suspect it is strong evidence.

DOCUMENTS

In a variety of criminal cases, a document examiner provides another type of forensic identification. This involves written evidence like a kidnapper's note, an altered will, account book or lottery ticket, as well as a forged signature on a cheque, or a forged passport. Besides analysing the handwriting, a document expert may be called upon to determine the age and source of the paper and ink.

Of course, evidence can be found away from the primary crime scene. This is why careful searches are made of a suspect's home and vehicle, as well as sites associated with the victim.

Numbered crime scene markers are used to indicate the position of every item of relevance, such as this discarded gun. Each position is logged before the evidence is removed for analysis in a forensic laboratory.

Any hint of contamination will normally make evidence inadmissible.

Because this forensic scientist is wearing protective clothing that cannot cause contamination, this cartridge shell will pass as court evidence.

EVIDENCE CONTAMINATION

Once evidence is found, it must be photographed in its original position and placed in separate clearly labelled bags or containers. These are transported to a forensic laboratory for examination and later may be presented as exhibits in court. All this must be done without the items becoming contaminated in any way whatsoever. This can happen, for instance, if a fibre from an investigator's clothes is transferred onto the victim's clothes, or if the evidential object is dropped on the lab floor. Any hint of contamination will normally make evidence inadmissible in court. The best way to avoid this complications is to set up a 'chain of custody' for those who handle the evidence – the fewer the better – by keeping a documented 'continuity of evidence' record of its movement.

National Forensic Services

The developed nations of the world have established modern and efficient forensic science services that have had remarkable success in working together on international cases.

. . . .

The United Kingdom has a Forensic Science Service (FSS) within the Home Office where it was created in 1991 from regional forensic laboratories. It now oversees those six labs in London, Chepstow, Birmingham, Chorley, Huntingdon and Wetherby. The National Firearms Unit (NFU) is based in Manchester. There is also a Forensic Science Agency of Northern Ireland and four labs in Scotland for the areas of Grampian, Strathclyde, Tayside and Lothian and Borders.

Private companies also offer forensic laboratory examinations and are often employed in court cases by defence and prosecution teams. The UK's largest, LGC, is headquartered in Teddington, Middlesex and has more than 1000 employees. Over

J. Edgar Hoover F.B.I. Building

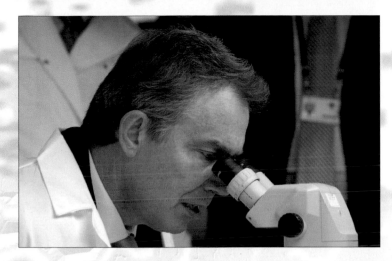

150 years old, it was the Laboratory of the Government Chemist before being privatized in 1996. In 2005 it acquired Forensic Alliance Limited (FAL), then the UK's largest private sector provider of forensic science services. The newly combined group has five laboratories all around the country as well as a specialist firearms facility.

In the United States, the Federal Bureau of Investigation (FBI) Laboratory in Washington, DC, was established in 1932 but back then was known as the Technical Laboratory. It now has a Combined DNA Index System (CODIS), which is a national computerized database available to the 50 individual states, all of whom have their own DNA databases of convicted offenders. The laboratory also runs a Forensic Science Research and Training Center in Quantico, Virginia.

The Royal Canadian Mounted Police (RCMP) has the Forensic Laboratory Services as part of its National Police Services in Ottawa where the National DNA Data Bank is located. The RCMP's forensic laboratories are in Vancouver, Edmonton, Regina, Winnipeg, Ottawa and Halifax, while Ontario and Quebec have their own laboratories.

EUROPEAN FORENSICS

Criminal justice and law enforcement in the twenty-first century has to deal with perpetrators who can communicate worldwide in an instant and, especially in Europe, move effortlessly across borders. To combat this, national agencies of law enforcement and forensic science work closely together, sharing the latest science and technology. The European Network of Forensic Science Institutes (ENFSI) promotes co-operation between the forensic labs from 32 European countries.

A leading provider is the UK's Forensic Science Service (FSS), which has assisted over 60 countries. The first organization in the world that developed a national criminal DNA database, its expertise is available to forensic facilities, police forces and government organization around the world. The service also sends experts to different countries to train forensic scientists in their own laboratories.

The FSS maintains the world's most extensive database containing abstracts of forensic science literature, with more than 70,000 records. This covers problems encountered in analytical laboratories and such various topics as DNA, computer crime, documents examination and arson investigation.

Types of Forensic Specialities

Forensic science is a broad practice that embraces science used for legal purposes, and its practitioners range from physicians to laboratory assistants.

Their speciality may deal with human remains, such as cadavers, bones, hair and teeth, or with inanimate evidence like fingerprints, firearms, detonators, wills and cheques. Some of the major specialities, which may include subspecialities, are:

FORENSIC PATHOLOGY:

This involves autopsies by licenced physicians of bodies that have not yet decomposed. This postmortem examination of the external and internal parts of the deceased is done to establish the cause and time of death. If murder seems evident, the pathologist often visits the crime scene to view the position of the victim. Living victims are also examined in such cases as assault and rape to determine injuries and their causes.

FORENSIC ANTHROPOLOGY:

This is concerned with postmortem examinations of the remains of human bones, usually to identify the deceased and hopefully establish the cause and time of death. This study can determine the age, sex, height and race of a victim, as well as injuries and illnesses.

FORENSIC ODONTOLOGY:

This specializes in the examination of teeth, which are the hardest and most durable substance in the body. When a corpse is badly decomposed, therefore, the best means of identification is often by matching the victim's teeth with dental records. Odontologists also compare a suspect's teeth with bite marks on a victim or on food left at the crime scene.

FORENSIC TOXICOLOGY:

This is the scientific study of poisons and drugs used in murders and other criminal cases, such as date-rape drugs. Tests are also run on the living to determine if such substances caused them to act violently or drive dangerously.

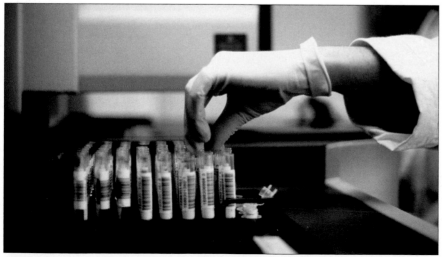

A laboratory technician in France selects a blood sample for testing. The samples are carefully kept in bar-coded tubes to assure the correct identifications.

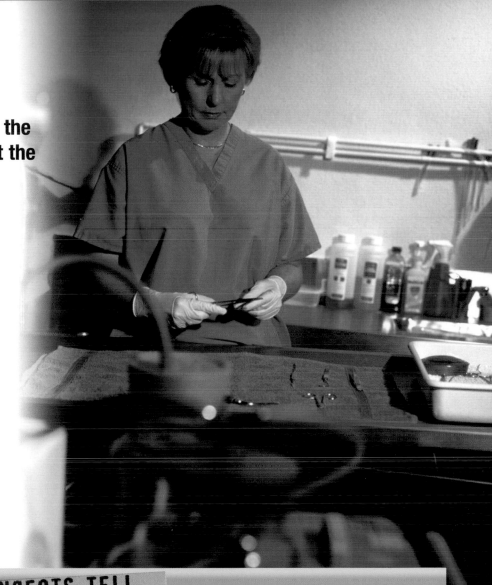

If murder seems evident, the pathologist will often visit the crime scene.

FORENSIC SEROLOGY:

This is the field that examines blood and other bodily fluids, such as saliva and semen. Among the serologist's tests are blood typing and DNA profiling.

FORENSIC ENTOMOLOGY:

This concerns the study of flies and other insects on a corpse, since their known life cycles can be used to estimate a victim's time of death.

WHAT FLIES AND INSECTS TELL

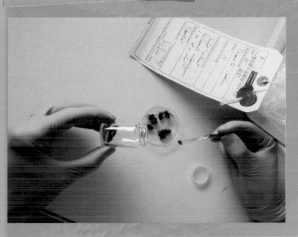

A forensic entomologist uses a technique that dates back to about thirteenth-century China. It was known then that looking at the stages of development and sizes of insect larvae on a body could establish the time of death. Tests on their larvae can also reveal a poison, because they take poison up from human tissue. This is important for toxicological tests because body fluids and soft tissues are soon gone from a corpse.

The type of insects can also indicate a body was moved from the insects' natural habitat, as some flies prefer laying eggs indoors or outdoors, and others always choose shade or sunlight. The concentration of insects on a part of the body may show where wounds are located.

Three Forensic Murder Cases

Forensic investigations have convicted criminals in a variety of ways. Three famous cases involved tooth marks, documents and DNA tests.

TED BUNDY

Theodore 'Ted' Bundy was a charming young American known to have killed 15 women, although he said it was from 40 to 50. On 15 January, 1978, he murdered two female students at Florida State University. Six days later, he was arrested for driving a stolen car, and his identity was revealed as a murder suspect who had escaped from a Colorado jail in 1977.

Ted Bundy (centre) finally faces justice after being charged with the killings of two female students at Florida State University.

A former law student, Bundy defended himself, but was faced by the prosecution's photograph of a bite mark discovered on the left buttock of one of the sorority girls. Dr Richard Souviron, a forensic odontologist, testified that Bundy's teeth matched the bite mark exactly. This was the key evidence that led to his conviction and his execution in 1989.

HAROLD SHIPMAN

British Dr Harold Shipman is estimated to have killed 236 of his patients over 24 years from 1974 to 1998, possibly making him the most prolific serial killer ever. He was only caught after forging a new will for Kathleen Grundy before killing her in 1998. This left £386,000 to Shipman, cutting out Mrs Grundy's daughter. Detective Superintendent Bernard Postles made an intense examination of the will, determining that the victim's name was forged and the phraseology and quality were not hers. The document was typed, and the police matched the imprint of the letters to Shipman's typewriter. Sentenced to 15 consecutive life sentences, he hanged himself in jail in 2004.

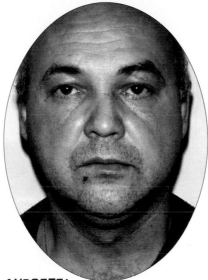

ANDREZEJ KUNOWSKI

Polish-born Andrezej Kunowski, an illegal immigrant in Britain, had sexually attacked some 30 children and young women in both countries. He strangled 12-year-old Katerina Koneva in 1997 at her home in London, and the only evidence was a hair on the girl's cardigan.

Kunowski had previously served 10 years in Poland for 27 sex attacks and was again jailed there in 1995 for raping a 12-year-old. A judge allowed him to go free the following year for a hip operation and he fled to London. In 2002, he was jailed for raping a Korean student. His DNA was taken and matched the sample from Katerina as well as DNA from his final Polish rape. Kunowski was sentenced in 2004 to life without parole.

The paedophile Andrezej Kunowski, seen in this Metropolitan Police arrest photograph, was sentenced on 31 March, 2004, to life in prison for strangling Katerina Koneva.

FORENSIC JARGON

Forensic scientists use their own jargon created from medical, scientific, police and legal terms.

Here is a brief sample:

Blood source: A victim who has bled.

Bull's-eye injury: An injury on a body that has the shape of the weapon used.

Cast-off blood: Blood marks from a victim who has moved or been moved.

Cold hit: A matching of physical evidence with a sample kept on a database.

Crime-scene staging: Changes made in a crime scene by the criminal to cover up evidence.

PERK (physical evidence recovery kit): The scientific kit used to collect evidence at a crime scene.

Trace evidence: Small pieces of evidence left at a crime scene, such as dust, skin, hairs or fabric.

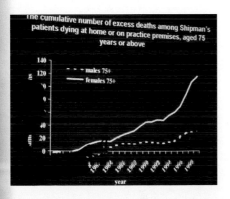

Richard Baker, professor of Quality in Health Care at the University of Leicester, delivers his report on the deaths attributed to Harold Shipman, who was jailed for life for killing about 236 of his elderly patients.

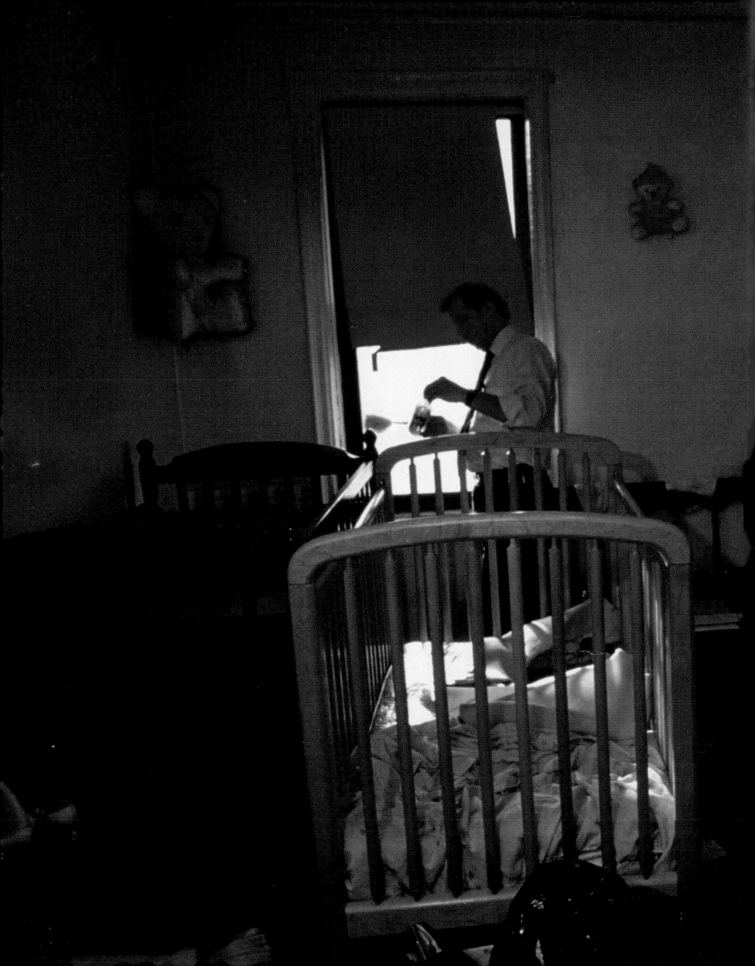

Chapter Two

The Scene of the Crime

A CRIME SCENE CONTAINS THE BASICS OF A CASE: THE VICTIM(S), AND SOME EVIDENCE. This is where the forensic scientist immediately begins to work with others who will be involved in the investigation, such as the police, fire inspectors and witnesses. The forensic officer on the scene is a fieldworker who is variously titled a crime scene investigator, crime scene examiner, crime scene analyst, scenes-of-crime officer, criminologist or some similar name.

A primary crime scene is where a crime takes place, like a murder, while a secondary crime scene is a site related to the crime, such as a burial site or a vehicle used to transport the body. Normally more

Careful measurements must be made of a bullet's path in a car shooting.

evidence is found at the primary scene, but sometimes that site is not known. This was the case when five prostitutes were murdered in December 2006 in Ipswich. Their bodies were found in various rural areas south of the city, but police were unable to determine where they had been murdered. Although no crime scene evidence was available, an arrest was made after interviews with the prostitutes' customers.

The solution to a crime will depend on observing proper procedures. A scene needs to be secured and recorded, evidence found, witnesses and suspects identified and interviewed, and the crime reconstructed.

Time is well spent by forensic investigators at a murder scene (far left). Lifting fingerprints from the interior of a car requires delicate work.

Securing the Scene

When a building is on fire, vehicles collide, or miners are trapped underground, onlookers are drawn to to watch the tragedies unfold. The news media will also rapidly converge on such a site.

This public curiosity can create difficulties, and it becomes a significant problem when a murder or other major crime has been committed. Officials needed to sort out the situation will already occupy the scene. This may include police, forensic scientists, firemen, physicians, ambulance personnel and possibly more specialists, such as bomb disposal experts.

The size of a crime scene can be limited to one room or spread over an extensive area, as happened when more than 1000 police and soldiers had to search 2189 square kilometres (845 square miles) of Scottish countryside in 1988 after a Pan American flight was bombed over the village of Lockerbie, causing the death of 270 people.

FIRST OFFICER ATTENDING

The immediate job for the first policeman on the scene, known as the first officer attending (FOA), is to help any victims who are alive. If

NICOLE SIMPSON AND RONALD GOLDMAN

The murder trial of footballer and actor O. J. Simpson involved the stabbings of his former wife, Nicole Simpson, and her friend, Ronald Goldman. It was a small crime scene: just the walkway leading to her apartment. The first two officers on the scene determined that the victims were dead and, with three more officers, they secured the scene, created a sign-in sheet and, by the time two detectives arrived, there were already 18 officers present. A police photographer joined them but could only take area shots until the civilian forensic scientist arrived.

Detectives then went to O.J. Simpson's house, declaring it too a crime scene. From there the police criminalist collected blood spots and a bloody glove. Despite this and other evidence, Simpson was acquitted in 1995 after a televised trial that lasted more than eight months.

they are injured, they must be medically assisted immediately, even if this destroys evidence. A victim should not be cleaned up, however, until a forensic officer has checked for bloodstains, hair and other trace evidence.

The first authorities on the scene will also detain any possible suspects and eyewitnesses, taking down their statements. They should be kept separate to avoid having trace evidence transferred from one person to another. If someone had reported the crime, they should be interviewed, detained, and denied access to the crime scene. Perpetrators have been known to report their crime to appear innocent and gain entry in

order to confuse the scene. A crime area should also be sealed off from onlookers to prevent evidence from being contaminated or lost. The police will cordon off the site, normally marking the perimeter with tape, and will restrict the areas of access, logging in all visitors and recording what they remove. Tents may be erected to protect the scene from the elements and onlookers.

Above: Scene of crime officers (SOCOs) investigate a shooting. Police tape marks out the boundaries of the crime scene. The SOCOs are wearing paper suits, overshoes and masks to prevent contamination of evidence.

Below: Wreckage of the bombed Pan American airline lies on Scottish soil after 270 lives were lost.

Suspects and witnesses must all be kept separate to avoid trace evidence being transferred from one person to another.

Preventing Contamination

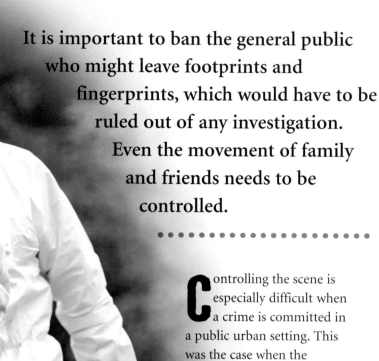

It is important to ban the general public who might leave footprints and fingerprints, which would have to be ruled out of any investigation. Even the movement of family and friends needs to be controlled.

Controlling the scene is especially difficult when a crime is committed in a public urban setting. This was the case when the controversial Dutch filmmaker, Theo Van Gogh, was murdered in 2004 by an Islamic extremist on an Amsterdam street, and occurred on a greater scale with the terrorist bombings of transport systems in Madrid in 2004 and London the following year. In such cases, busy public areas must be sealed off and made secure, often for several days.

PROTECTIVE UNIFORM

Investigators allowed onto a crime scene have to be sensitive to the danger of cross-contamination. They wear a white protective uniform that includes a mask,

HOW INSPECTORS CONTAMINATE SCENES

A recurrent problem with contaminated evidence at crime scenes involves inspectors leaving their own trace evidence, including DNA, at the scene and even on the victim. Many unidentified profiles in DNA databases that were thought to belong to perpetrators have proven to be from officers on the scene.

In a 2003 murder case in New South Wales, Australia, an unknown DNA profile was found on the victim's jumper that did not match the suspect. Then in 2005, the same DNA profile was found after a violent armed robbery. When police who handled both cases were examined, the DNA was matched to a forensic services investigator.

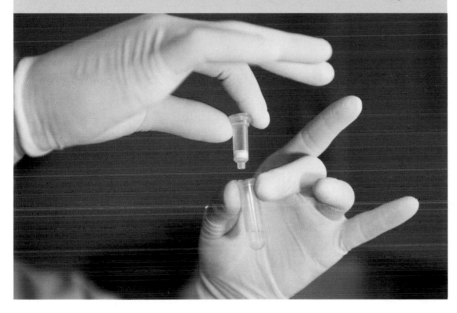

JONBENET RAMSEY

Sympathetic officers are sometimes lenient when confronted with distressed family members. This happened after the murder of six-year-old JonBenet Ramsey in 1996 in Boulder, Colorado. Her father discovered the body in the basement, and police allowed him to carry it upstairs. They also permitted friends to move freely in the house. The evidence was therefore badly compromised, and the case remains unsolved.

The laboratory work on the JonBenet Ramsey murder case included an intense examination of a ransom note, but its author was never identified.

surgical gloves and plastic overshoes. If officials need to pass through part of the scene to reach the focal point, such as a victim, a common approach path will be designated to protect any evidence. A homicide victim and normal objects should not be touched or moved before the forensic scientist arrives at the crime scene. The position of a door or window, for example, could be crucial to solving a case. Officials will also stop anyone else altering the scene, for example, as in the case when a crime survivor or family members wants to try to put a room back in order.

If more than one crime scene exists for a case, such as a victim being murdered at one location and buried at another, a forensic scientist must try to avoid covering both scenes and risking cross-contamination. If only one person is available to examine both areas, he or she should undergo decontamination before switching to the other site.

Recording the Evidence

Sketches, oral tapes, videotapes and notes are taken at a crime scene. A police or forensic photographer, however, who records the overall view, including the surrounding area and small evidential details, does the best documentation.

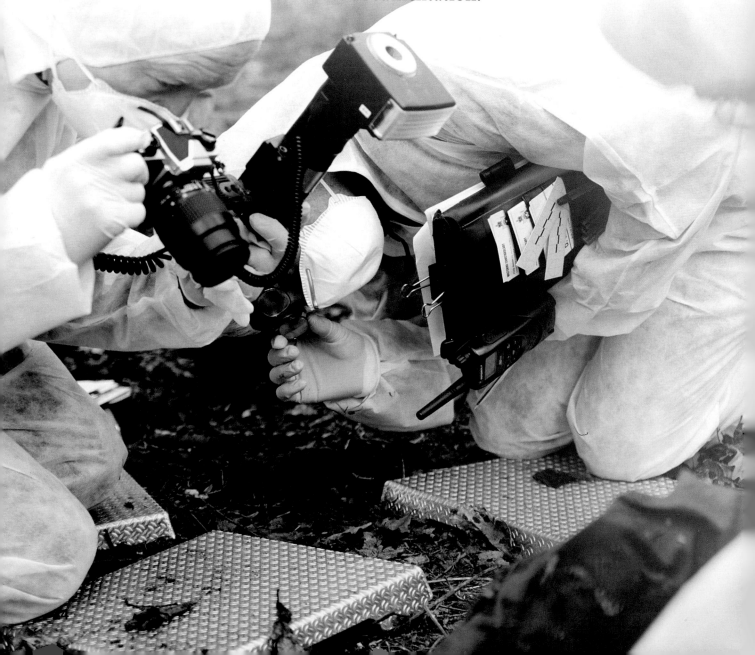

An item of evidence is filmed next to a ruler to indicate the size and again alone, in case the ruler had been covering up further evidence. Other references can be used in the photo to indicate size, such as a pen or coin.

The photographer is usually one of the first allowed through the site, because the undisturbed scene must be recorded before victims are taken to the morgue or hospital, and objects are removed to forensic laboratories. Photos also record fragile evidence, such as latent fingerprints that may be ruined during their recovery, and evidence, like a cigarette stub, that may alter over time. Close-up images will be taken of wounds on a corpse or injured person. After a body has been removed, photos should be taken of the area where it lay.

Recording the scene by video has the advantage of adding comments, but still photographs present the sharpest images and are the easiest to handle in a courtroom.

Each shot is labelled with a number, the location of the scene, the date and time taken and

WHY TAKE NOTES?

Notes are valuable because they can record the sequence of actions taken by officials, whose names and titles are listed along with the times they were at the scene. A written description has the advantage of recording changes at the scene during the investigation. Lists can record several facts about each item of evidence: the object and its description; when and where it was discovered; and by whom. One list can serve as a log of photographs taken, describing them, their location, when and where they were taken and the name of the camera operator.

information about the processing. All this must stand up in court when a clever attorney raises the doubt that someone may have tampered with the prints during the process.

DIGITAL CAMERAS

The advent of digital cameras has introduced the ability to enhance images. This type of camera can remove the background confusion if fingerprints are blurred when overlapping a patterned background, as found on a stamp, bank note, or ticket. Such a change, however, carries the suggestion of manipulation, and some juries may discount the value of that evidence.

SKETCHY EVIDENCE?

Sketching is still used to indicate spatial relationship at a crime scene between objects or with an object and a corpse. Sketches are particularly clear, because unimportant items will not be shown and wounds on a body can be emphasized. Sometimes sketches are the only record available of the undisturbed crime scene, if a body has to be removed before the photographer arrives.

Finding Evidence

A crime scene needs to be searched quickly and thoroughly. If evidence remains after police remove their security restrictions, it will be compromised and unusable.

Most sites remain sealed off for a day or more, but this can vary according to the crime. In Canada, police barred entrance to the international wing of Jean-Lesage Airport in 2007 in Quebec City for three hours after a false X-ray alarm, while the street in a Vienna suburb where Natascha Kampusch escaped eight years of captivity in 2006 was closed for several days.

Investigators use their experience and common sense when probing through a site for clues. The crime-scene manager and scene of crime officers (SOCOs) will be trained in forensics. The police collecting evidence wear protective kits. They may advance in a line across an outdoor area or crawl along an indoor scene shoulder-to-shoulder conducting a fingertip search. A geometric search pattern may follow a spiral route towards or from a corpse,

DR DAVID KELLY

An example of high standards in a crime-scene search involved the death of Dr David Kelly, an employee of the UK Ministry of Defence, who committed suicide in 2003 after being named as the source criticizing the British government's statement on weapons of mass destruction in Iraq.

When his body was discovered in a wood, a Home Office pathologist and forensic biologists looked at the scene. Police teams conducted a thorough four-hour fingertip search 10 metres (33 feet) on either side of the scene's approach path they had established and also searched a radius of 10 metres (33 feet) around Dr Kelly's body. It was then removed and a 30-minute search was made of the ground where it had been. Nothing of significance was found.

while large areas can be divided into quadrants to be searched in a straight line or a crisscross-grid pattern.

If evidence might be both outside and inside a building, the former is searched first due to the possibility of rain and wind ruining the items. The search will also concentrate on the criminal's probable entry and exit paths.

FINDING EVIDENCE IN ISRAEL

In Israel the criminal identification technician (CDT) is responsible for finding the physical evidence at a crime scene, as a complement to an investigator's work. In this initial examination, field kits are used to seek evidence such as fingerprints, footprints and bloodstains. The CDT also documents the scene of the crime with photographs and drawings. The technician then transfers the evidence to laboratories located at the national facility in Jerusalem for tests. On some occasions, the CDT is asked to testify in court about the evidence found at the scene and to provide expert opinions submitted to the court as evidence.

Right: Israeli forensic experts examine the scene of a suicide bombing which killed eight people in Tel Aviv in April 2006.

Collecting Evidence

First, evidence that is fragile or in danger of contamination, such as fibres and hair, must be attended to. This trace evidence can be collected from areas like carpets and floors, furniture and car seats, using a special vacuum, tweezers, clear adhesive tape or by hand.

Clothes and other textile products can be simply shaken or brushed to recover hairs. In all cases, wearing surgical gloves will avoid any transference of an investigator's DNA to the evidence.

Fingerprints are among the best evidence that can be recovered. They are a personal signature, and have been accepted in court cases for more than a century.

Argentina saw the first person convicted of murder by the use of fingerprints, Francisca Rohas, who killed her two sons in 1892 and cut her own throat trying to blame the crime on an attacker who had broken in.

Visible prints are classified as either patent prints, such as those stained with blood, grease and paint; or as plastic prints, which are impressions in some soft material like putty, soap and dust.

Others indicators of a suspect's presence at a crime scene are footprints and tyre tracks. If both are left in soft ground, they can be photographed, cast in plaster, lifted and then compared with known shoes and tyres belonging to a suspect. If shoe prints are found on a floor or other hard surface, they can be detected the same way as fingerprints are, by applying a powder. Such shoe marks can be lifted by a fabric covered with a sticky gel or by using an electro-static device.

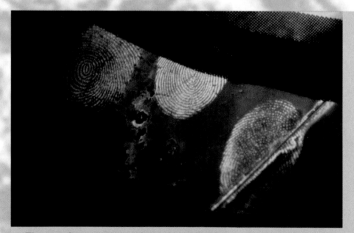

Fingerprints on a scarf are revealed here using a laser technique. The fingerprints are dusted with a chemical that fluoresces when exposed to laser light. This technique is useful because it works on porous surfaces.

LATENT FINGERPRINTS

Latent prints, which are invisible, are still detectable because light can reveal any sweat or oil on a surface left behind by fingers. When an angled beam of ultraviolet light, or a laser, is shone over the prints they will fluoresce, or glow. Latent prints can also be made visible by applying a powder, often carbon black, white or grey aluminium to the prints, using a soft brush. If marks have been absorbed on porous surfaces like paper, magnetic powder can be applied by an applicator that does not touch the surface. All prints are then carefully lifted by a transparent tape and mounted.

Scales are placed over a can of fizzy drink to be photographed at a crime scene. The can has been dusted for fingerprints.

CRIME-SCENE TOOLS

GENERAL-PURPOSE SCIENTIFIC TOOLS

- **Exposing evidence:** magnifying glass, torch, and laser, infrared, and ultraviolet lights

- **Recovering prints:** aluminium and black powders, black and grey magnetic powders, soft brush, magnetic applicator, gel fingerprint and footprint lifters, clear lifting tape, white latent print cards

- **Collecting trace evidence such as hairs, fibres, and fluids:** tweezers, utility knife, scissors and cotton swabs

- **Making casts of tyres, footprints and tool marks:** casting plaster, mixing bowl and spatula

- **Packaging evidence:** permanent pen, evidence labels, plastic and paper bags and glass tubes

Forensic researchers wear special glasses to see the faint glow of fingerprints (shown in green) that are triggered by a flashing fluorescent lamp.

Protecting Evidence

Careful packaging must be used to protect any evidence. Plastic and paper bags, plastic bottles and envelopes are used for dry trace evidence, while airtight containers are normally used for liquids.

To avoid damage and deterioration by mould and mildew, moist biological evidence should be dried before packaging, or put into containers that are not airtight. All biological stains deteriorate with time, so items of clothing are dried before being packaged in separate bags, and are handled carefully to avoid disturbing trace materials. Blood samples at the scene can be put into a glass tube, sealed and placed in a bag. Hair samples are put into an envelope, which is then sealed.

All containers are labeled with a case or exhibit number, the item's identity, the date, time and location

KEEPING DNA

Police forces are reconsidering policies on storing evidence now that DNA can reach into the past to find perpetrators or free the wrongly convicted.

In 2004, a Canadian review committee wanted to test DNA on hair used to convict two men of killing a 16-year-old girl in 1990. However, the police had destroyed the single strand of hair because the law did not require them to keep evidence beyond 30 days after appeals had been exhausted.

In the USA in 2006, a bipartisan Constitutional Project committee recommended that DNA evidence be retained and tested for as long as it could 'establish innocence or avoid unjust execution'.

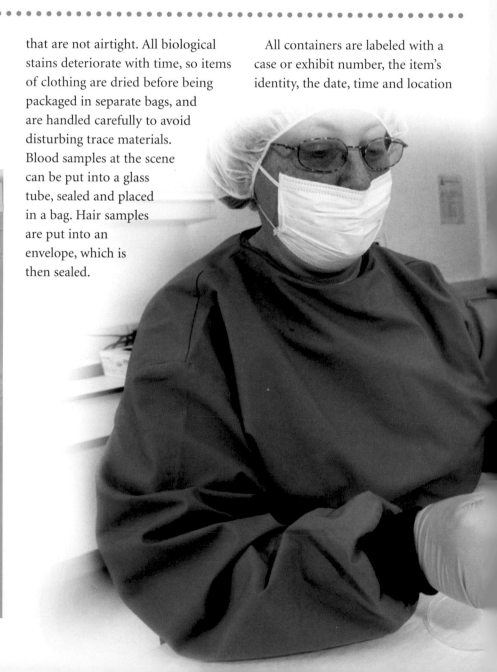

it was found, and the initials of the inspector who found it.

Even after all the precautions of safe packaging have been taken, evidence may be ruled inadmissible in court if a record is not available showing that the items were kept secure during their journey from the crime scene to the forensic lab and then the courtroom. This list, called the 'chain of custody', is the record of every person who handled the evidence and had put their initials and the date on the container. This assures that the evidence has not been removed, added to, replaced or altered.

OVERLOOKING THE BROKEN CHAIN

It is important to maintain the chain of custody, but judges sometimes overlook a broken chain. This happened in 2004 in Michigan when a court of appeals heard a defendant's claim that the chain of custody had been broken when cocaine supposedly seized from him was left, unsealed and unmarked, overnight in the police officer's car.

The court ruled the break had happened, but said there was no evidence of mistaken exchange, contamination or tampering, because the officer testified the package had remained inside his locked car in the locked glove compartment until the following morning when he sealed it and placed it in an evidence locker.

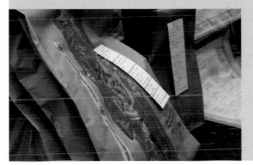

These labelled paper bags contain forensic evidence. Paper packaging is used to prevent condensation and contamination from bacterial growth.

Evidence may be ruled inadmissible if a record isn't kept showing that the items were securely stored.

A forensic scientist (left) removes a cigarette stub from a sealed bag of evidence collected at a crime scene. A vial of hair sample (above) rests on a record sheet that has been sealed with wax to prevent tampering.

Reconstructing the Crime

A primary goal of police and forensic investigators at a crime scene is to reconstruct the crime. They define what the crime was, the sequence of events, who was present and their positions and actions.

This involves getting a feel for the scene and the evidence, interviewing any witnesses, suspects, and surviving victims, and then using scientific methods and logical reasoning. Criminal profiling will be added to understand why the crime happened and what this reveals about who may have done it.

RECONSTRUCTIVE EVIDENCE

Clues as to what happened are known as reconstructive evidence. The direction of shoe prints, fingerprints or tool marks on a window or door, the position of blood splatters and bullet trajectories and the victim's wounds, which can indicate the positions of the attacker and victim, can all be used to piece together the crime.

A deceased individual slumped in a dining-room chair with a wound to his temple and a gun resting on the floor below his outstretched arm may seem to be a clear case of suicide. However, an examination uncovers wounds to the back of his head, scuff marks indicating a struggle and traces of skin under the victim's fingernails. Therefore, the original assumption of suicide quickly changes into a murder investigation. No fingerprints are uncovered on the gun but latent prints are on the door of a cabinet containing silver pieces. Investigators propose their theory: the victim surprised a burglar intent on stealing the silver. They struggled until the assailant struck the victim down, shot him and arranged the suicide scene, being forced to leave the silver behind.

This is an example of a staged crime scene, where the perpetrator leaves false clues to mislead investigators. Such cases could also

Forensic investigators can calculate bullet trajectories by creating a three-dimensional computer reconstruction of a crime scene.

RECONSTRUCTION CLUES

When retired Group Captain T. P. Singh, his wife Shibani, and sister Ajit Kaur were murdered together in 2006 in Chandigarh, India, forensic experts helped police reconstruct the crime. Tracks showed that the perpetrator killed the man followed by his wife and sister, which indicated one or a few assailants. The wife had thrown a flower vase at the assailant(s) and her hair had been pulled, indicating she had fought back. Two gunshots were found in the man's body, showing he had tried to escape. His sister was hit on the head, so she was caught unawares. Four blood types were collected, and the case is ongoing.

include a husband killing his wife with several blows and then positioning her body at the bottom of the stairs to indicate an accident, an arsonist who sets a fire to consume the body of a murder victim or a person involved in insurance fraud, hiding their own valuables and staging a burglary by scattering contents from drawers and breaking a window.

The BBC 'Crimewatch' programme re-enacts (above) the stabbing of Abigail Witchalls in Surrey in 2005, and a gendarme (left) checks a dummy used to recreate the 1999 murder of Isabel Peake in France.

The Modus Operandi

As well as evaluating the physical evidence, criminologists also reconstruct a crime by looking at the perpetrator's *modus operandi* (MO), which is his or her normal way of committing the same type of crime.

JUERGEN BARTSCH

Serial criminals normally repeat the same sequence of actions. Juergen Bartsch, a young homosexual, killed four boys in Essen, Germany, from 1962 to 1966, each time luring a slim, dark-haired victim into a cave or similar type of shelter. He also mutilated their bodies in the same manner, including decapitation, castration, gouging out their eyes, and cutting open their bodies to empty the abdominal area. He was estimated to have attempted more than 100 further homicidal attempts. Bartsch was caught in 1966 and remained in a psychiatric hospital until his death in 1976.

This involves decisions like the weapon preferred, the method of entry, whether the perpetrator disconnects the telephone and whether items are taken after a victim is attacked or killed. Each criminal also has a signature comprised of actions done in addition to those needed to commit the crime. For example, an offender may always talk quietly to the victim, inflict torture or write messages on a mirror.

Investigators will also look closely at the victim and the timing of events leading up to the crime. Family and friends will be interviewed concerning the victim's background and personal relationships, while searches are made of medical, education and employment records, including police files if relevant. If there is a question of possible suicide, profilers will determine if there were alcohol, drug or other problems.

Each criminal has a signature comprised of actions made in addition to those needed to commit the crime.

CAROLINE DICKINSON

The case of the 13-year-old British schoolgirl, Caroline Dickinson, raped and murdered in France in 1996 while on an activity holiday with her school, demonstrates how a perpetrator's method of operation will lead him to the same type of scene to commit a crime. Caroline was killed in a youth hostel dormitory, and five years later Francisco Arces Montes of Spain was arrested in Miami, Florida, for a lewd act in another youth hostel dormitory. DNA tests in the USA matched the sample collected at the French scene. Montes was extradited to France, convicted in 2001 and later confessed.

Files at Interpol were searched after the murder of schoolgirl Caroline Dickinson in a French youth hostel room (left).

RE-ENACTMENTS

Police, victims, criminals and even actors sometimes act out a crime during an investigation or confession. When four young men were killed in northern Rio de Janeiro, Brazil, in 2003, police said they were drug dealers, but a reenaction of the event proved them to have been innocent bystanders.

In Waihou, New Zealand, in 2005, a woman charged with murdering her husband in 1988 showed police how she dragged him to a shallow grave and even how his body landed on top of her after she fell into the hole she had dug.

Handling Witnesses and Suspects

Because the human memory is a fragile entity, it is best for witnesses to a crime to be identified and interviewed at the scene of the crime. Yet, even at the scene, memories have proved to be fairly unreliable.

Witnessing a crime can place an individual in an excitable state. And being probed by the police will add a great deal of stress, especially if the witness is worried about being a suspect.

Before forensic science, witnesses were often the only way of linking a suspect to the crime. If today's courtroom testimony by a crime-scene witness contradicts that of an 'expert witness' who has conducted forensic tests, the jury will inevitably believe the latter. A lawyer will have a much easier time disputing an ordinary person's eyesight than the results of a DNA profile.

DETAINING WITNESSES

Police powers to detain witnesses at a crime scene vary considerably. In Uzbekistan, investigators can detain anyone they deem to be a 'witness' and that person does not have the right to a lawyer during detention which can be extended by the prosecutor without consulting a judge. Any answers obtained from such a witness can be used as evidence in a court case. In the USA, however, powers to detain witnesses are in doubt and often unresolved in the various states. Witnesses cannot be arrested under the Fourth Amendment's prohibition against unreasonable search and seizure, but they can be detained if 'special needs' or 'suspicion-less detention' is crucial to a case.

THE NEW YORK SOLUTION

True suspects at the scene can be arrested and taken to a police station for interrogation. The difficulty is in separating suspects from innocent witnesses. In 2005, the New York Police Department (NYPD) launched a Real Time Crime Center constantly staffed by officers. They immediately access information about a crime scene and potential suspects and send the results by e-mail, fax or telephone to first responders on the scene. The following year, the city announced it will invest nearly $500 million over five years to build a Citywide Mobile Wireless Network so officers can instantly download identifying data like fingerprints and mugshots, which will allow them to detain suspects at the scene.

Right: As members of the emergency services work in the background, a policeman interviews a witness to a car crash.

Above: New York officers interview customers leaving a Harlem restaurant after a shooting in 2005 injured two bystanders.

WITNESSES VS DNA

Linda Razzell, a 41-year-old mother of four, went missing in Swindon in 2002, and bloodstains were later found in the car of her estranged husband, Glyn. Her body was never found, but six witnesses called police to say they had seen her after the disappearance. One, a friend who knew her well, said they made eye contact, and she was sure it was Linda.

Although this information was presented during the court case in 2003, the jury was more impressed with DNA tests that identified the blood in the car as hers. Glyn Razzell was convicted and sentenced to life imprisonment

Linda Razzell had already taken her husband to court twice for assault and feared that he would kill her.

Witnesses Who Made a Difference

All types of crimes are regularly solved through witnesses. Having viewed a crime, many people give confused accounts. But law enforcement depends heavily on eyewitnesses, so one of the police's first acts after a crime is to make an appeal for the public's assistance.

Several people, who identified the perpetrators but unfortunately missed the opportunity to intervene, witnessed one of England's most shocking crimes. James Bulger, a two-year-old from Merseyside, was abducted in 1993 from a shopping centre when his mother's attention was diverted. Within two hours he was dead, his body found on a railway track after he had been violently attacked with stones, bricks and a metal object.

James was seen on a camera with two boys, and several witnesses saw the three on their two-mile trip to the crime scene, all assuming they were brothers or friends. Some noted injuries to James' head, some described him as crying and extremely distressed, but others said he was laughing. One witness said the two older boys were dragging him and one kicked him in the ribs. A woman who queried them was told they had found the toddler and were taking him to the local police station. Even more witnesses saw the three at a railway bridge. The 10-year-old abductors, Jon Venables and Robert Thompson, were convicted by this conclusive evidence in 1993, and imprisoned in an institute for young offenders until they were released in 2001.

SHARP EYES

Another abduction case in the USA in 2007 had a happier ending when information from a sharp-eyed observer led to the rescue of two young boys, one of them held captive for more than four years. Michael Devlin, 41, grabbed Ben Ownby, 13, as he left his school bus in a suburb of St Louis, Missouri, but one of Ben's friends leaving the bus saw a dilapidated white truck speeding away and gave a detailed description to the police. Four days later, officers had traced the vehicle to Devlin and were surprised to find both Ben and Shawn Wilcox, who had been kidnapped by Devlin in 2002 when he was 11 years old.

Police are especially trained to interview witnesses, many of whom may be traumatized by a crime or worried that they may be suspects.

'PEELING AN ONION'

Although they generally arrive at the crime scene after the police have secured it and are in the process of conducting interviews, forensic investigators can also question victims, witnesses and suspects.

A crime scene analyst with the Las Vegas Metro Police Department noted, 'My job is to ask what the story is. It's like peeling an onion – I take it one layer at a time. I listen to everybody and then look at the evidence to see what it says, and if it denies or corroborates somebody's story. I'm not on anybody's side – not even the side of the detectives against the arrestees. My job is to find the truth through the evidence and to document that truth.'

Police (far left) investigate the railway track where James Bulger's body was found. A surveillance camera caught images of Bulger holding hands with Jon Venables as he was abducted from a shopping centre near Liverpool.

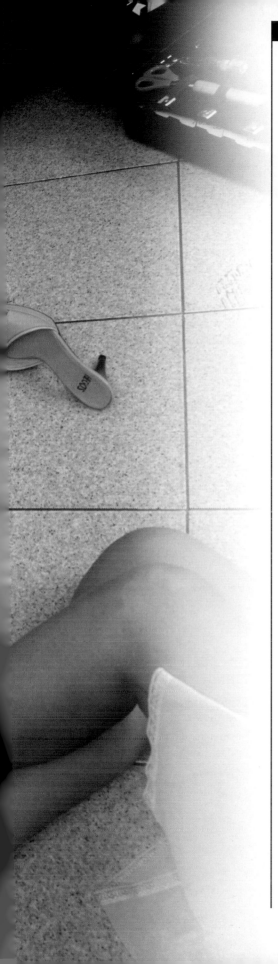

Chapter Three

Details of Death

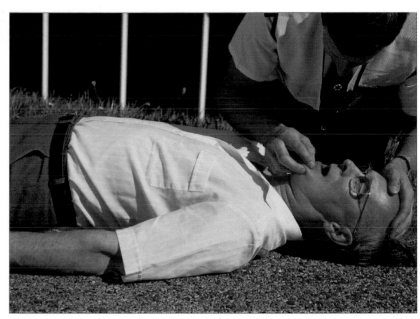

OST DEATHS OCCUR BY NATURAL CAUSES, BUT THEY CAN ALSO BE THE RESULT OF AN ACCIDENT, SUICIDE OR HOMICIDE. Only the last will turn the place of death into a crime scene, and forensic scientists must determine as quickly as possible if murder has been committed. A pathologist's examination is superficial at this point, but checks will be made for rigor mortis and for fluids or marks on the body. Finding other clues will involve examining the position of the body and patterns of bloodstains. The immediate surroundings will be examined for marks, blood specks and items that may have been used in the crime.

A man is found unconscious under suspicious circumstances. The first priority is resuscitation, but if this fails, the location will become a possible crime scene.

The skull of a murder victim in a forensic laboratory is numbered along with other bones for identification.

41

Checking for Life

When a body is discovered, the priority is to check for vital signs, such as a pulse, heartbeat and breathing. A medical examiner will use a stethoscope to attempt to find a faint heartbeat.

A CORONER AT THE SCENE

Disagreement exists as to whether a coroner is actually needed at a crime scene, because some believe a coroner hinders the work. During the inquiry into Dr Harold Shipman's murders (see Chapter 1), the forensic pathologist Dr Peter Acland said a coroner at the scene of death could contaminate evidence and make decisions that complicate the investigation. Dr Acland added that he had never known the involvement of a coroner to benefit a crime-scene investigation.

Michael Burgess, representing the Coroners' Society, added that he saw potential problems with a coroner being physically present at the death scene. However, he said that a coroner or someone separate from the police should be there with the power to authorize an autopsy of the body.

Michael Stone, arriving at the High Court in London on 18 January 2005, was found guilty of murder.

Any slight indication of life calls for resuscitation or other critical medical treatment, and this takes priority over the arrest of a suspect and the possible contamination of evidence. This has been obvious during terrorist attacks like the Madrid bombings of 11 March 2004. Badly injured victims can seem lifeless, so great care must be taken in examining a body for life. When a man brutally attacked Dr Lin Russell and her two daughters, Megan and Josie, with a hammer in 1996 on an isolated lane near Canterbury, in Kent, one of the two police officers first on the scene, Constable Richard Leivers, checked for signs of life and found none. Dr Shaun Russell, the husband and father, was told of the discovery and informed that all of his family had died. However, as the police surgeon, Dr Michael Parks, arrived at the murder scene, Constable Leivers noticed that the body of nine-year-old Josie moved.

'I had ascertained that the female adult was cold and had no signs of life,' Dr Parks reported. 'I immediately diverted my attentions to the child. She moved when I touched her and felt warm. I reassured her and after a brief period of reflection I asked PC Leivers to pick her up. She was semi-conscious and had clear head injuries.'

The girl had lain barely alive next to the dead bodies of her mother and sister for an hour. Although Josie Russell suffered severe head injuries, she made an amazing recovery. Her interview by police was videotaped and presented as evidence at the trial of Michael Stone, who was convicted of the murders in 1998 and given three life sentences.

Resuscitation or other critical medical treatment takes priority over the possible contamination of evidence.

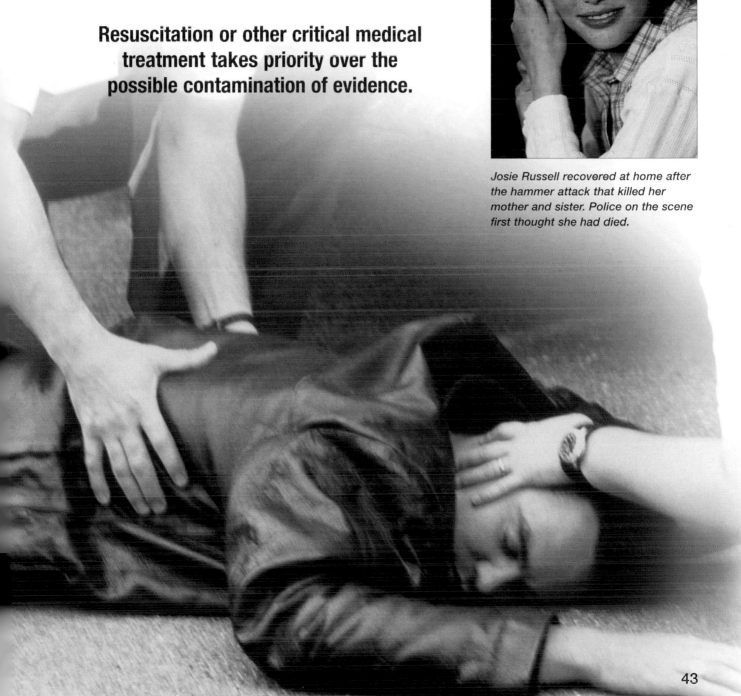

Josie Russell recovered at home after the hammer attack that killed her mother and sister. Police on the scene first thought she had died.

Resuscitation

Police and emergency services are well equipped to treat crime victims, and it is the duty of the first officer attending to give aid immediately to anyone still alive.

An ambulance should be called if the victim is unconscious or slipping in and out of unconsciousness or has difficulty in breathing, is experiencing a heavy blood loss, a deep wound, such as a stab wound, severe burns or another serious trauma.

When victims might have neck injuries, they are placed on their backs, and an officer then checks if the chest is rising and falling. If no breathing is detected, the officer can give mouth-to-mouth resuscitation. If the victim is breathing, he or she is placed on their side with the lower arm stretched out in front of them and the hand of the upper arm under their cheek.

It is important to make sure oxygen is circulating to the victim's brain, so the officer checks for blood circulation by pressing two fingers lightly to one side of the victim's windpipe to feel for a pulse in the neck. If a pulse of at least one beat per second exists, mouth-to-mouth resuscitation continues. If there is no pulse or a slow one, an officer starts cardio-pulmonary resuscitation (CPR), which is a continuation of

Left: Paramedics treat a woman with a suspected neck injury by holding her head and using a rigid cervical collar and oxygen mask.

Right: First aid for a stopped heart involves chest compressions and mouth-to-mouth resuscitation.

the rescue breaths combined with chest compressions.

Often two officers will be on the scene to attempt to revive a victim and summon medical help. If a member of the public arrives first, comfort and some first aid should be given to the victim and emergency calls made.

If there is no pulse, or a slow one, an officer starts cardio-pulmonary resuscitation.

HOW RESUSCITATION EVOLVED

Early forms of attempted resuscitation were not pleasant. The ancient Egyptians have recorded their efforts of hanging patients by the feet and applying pressure to the chest. Other early methods included placing hot ashes on the chest, whipping the victim, rolling him over a barrel, and stretching him over a trotting horse.

In 1767 in England and Europe, a bellows was used to blow smoke into a patient's mouth and even rectum. That year, the Dutch Humane Society issued guidelines that included 'insufflation of smoke of burning tobacco into the rectum' but also 'mouth-to-mouth ventilation'. An English physician, Charles Kite, published in 1788 'An Essay on the Recovery of the Apparently Dead' that first recommended electrodes to shock the body. Nevertheless, more basis ideas continued to flourish in Europe in the late nineteenth century, such as stretching the rectum and, in France, stretching the tongue. Mouth-to-mouth resuscitation was first promoted on a large scale in the U.S. military during World War II, and the use of CPR became standard in the 1960s, introduced by the US doctor William Kouwenhoven.

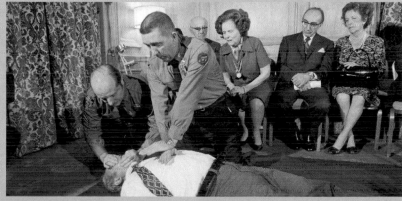

A demonstration of CPR by the New York Police Department is watched by one of its pioneers, Dr. William Kouwenhoven, in 1973.

Examining a Body at the Scene

A forensic pathologist examines a body found at a possible crime scene before it is removed to the morgue. The first examination may be done with the corpse in situ, or it may have to be moved for a proper examination.

This is why the original undisturbed position of the body is photographed, videotaped or sketched first.

The pathologist carries only a notepad and pen to the scene, but the crime scene manager or medical examiner provides any other necessary items, such as a thermometer, swabs for the removal of a sample of any fluids or marks on the body or clothes, and containers for storing evidence.

The examination will concentrate on determining the time of death – this may be a vital clue in linking the murder to a suspect. The time of death, never an exact figure, will be more difficult to judge after the body is removed, an action that will also eliminate signs of rigor mortis.

It may be necessary to remove the deceased's clothing to check for discoloration of the skin. A dead person's skin in the lower regions begins to take on a pink-red colour, or lividity, due to blood settling. This begins some 30 minutes to two hours after death and is complete by eight to 12 hours. This is caused by gravity, so a corpse lying on its left side has lividity on its left shoulder, arm, hip and leg. The overall skin also takes on a greenish tint after 48 hours because of bacteria. This becomes a marbled look after four to seven days. Dark skin, however, will not show these colours.

The temperature of the cadaver is measured with a rectal thermometer. After death, the temperature of the body's trunk will generally fall about .8°C for each hour.

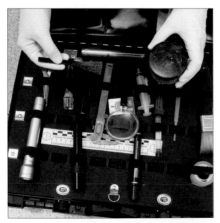

A forensic investigator, gloved to avoid contamination, removes a container of fine powder from a crime scene kit for fingerprint work.

CADAVERIC SPASM

Sometimes a corpse will have a kind of instant rigor mortis called 'cadaveric spasm'. This happens when the muscles were being used with great exertion while dying, as during a struggle or while running hard. This is why the victim might have a death grip on a weapon. A cadaveric spasm, of course, can add confusion to the time of death.

RIGOR MORTIS

A pathologist at the crime scene will check for this stiffening of the body by carefully trying to move the arms and legs, neck, jaw and eyelids. Rigor mortis normally occurs from 30 minutes to three hours after death, taking hold first in the eyelids, jaw, and neck, then progressing downwards. The whole body is affected within eight to 12 hours, the stiffness continues for up to 18 hours, and is gone after a further six to 12 hours. Sometimes at low temperatures, rigor mortis will not even be present.

It is extremely important for a pathologist to investigate the body of a crime victim as soon as possible after discovery. By the time a body reaches the morgue, vital information will have been lost.

The Decaying Body

A corpse is sometimes found several weeks after the victim has died, and this poses problems for a pathologist estimating the time of death. Help will no longer come from rigor mortis, body temperature, and lividity, so the rate of decay will have to be used.

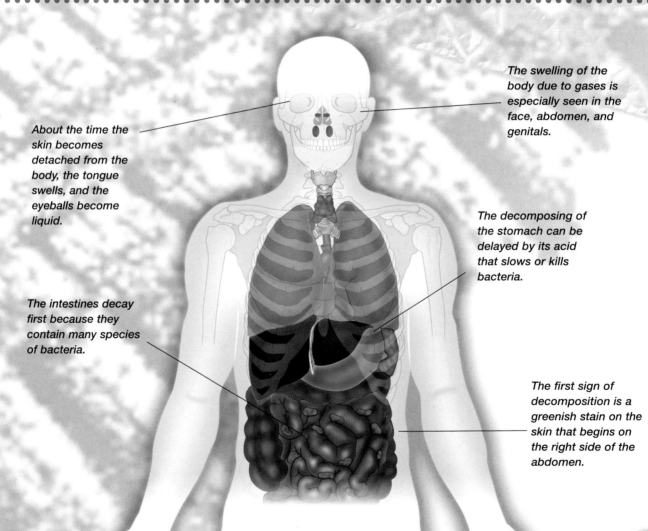

About the time the skin becomes detached from the body, the tongue swells, and the eyeballs become liquid.

The swelling of the body due to gases is especially seen in the face, abdomen, and genitals.

The decomposing of the stomach can be delayed by its acid that slows or kills bacteria.

The intestines decay first because they contain many species of bacteria.

The first sign of decomposition is a greenish stain on the skin that begins on the right side of the abdomen.

Forensic pathologists can trace a body's decay through the organs and other soft tissues. Near the end of decomposing, the body assumes a greenish-black colour.

The sequence of decay begins with a greenish discoloration of the skin in the abdomen area.

Even the rate of decay can change according to the surrounding temperature and humidity, because, for example, a body in the open also decays faster than if it were buried or were immersed in water. More complications arise if the murderer waited a period of time before burying the victim, or if he moved it later.

Bacteria and the chemical breakdown of the body's cells and tissues, known as autolysis, cause postmortem decomposition, or putrefaction. These processes begin immediately after death, but they may not be visible until two or three days have passed. The sequence of decay is unpleasant, even for a veteran forensic scientist. It begins with a greenish discoloration of the skin in the abdomen area, and this spreads to the upper body and head. After three days, gases from the decomposition cause bloating, with the swelling appearing first in the face. The skin then begins to marble, showing a pattern of blood vessels, which resemble a web, near the surface. The skin also develops blisters filled with liquid or gas; when they burst, the skin loosens. Fluids of decomposition drain from the mouth and nose, and the body soon splits open.

Many factors can influence a corpse's rate of decay, including the victim's weight. For example, overweight people decay faster, so the process is not as reliable as tests conducted on someone who is recently deceased.

SKELETALIZATION

When a body's soft tissues have completely decomposed, the forensic anthropologist is left with only bones to work with. This length of this skeletalization process depends on the climate. For example, it might take up to two years in France, but only take a few weeks in the heat of Kenya. A complete skeleton will normally reveal the gender and race, as well as the general age and height of the deceased. Forensic odontologists can also help estimate the age at time of death by the development of teeth and their amount of wear.

The cause of death may be indicated by trauma, such as a hole in the head, or by natural causes like disease. Forensic experts are seldom interested when a victim's bones are older than a century, because the murderer will likely be dead.

A skeleton is arranged in a forensic lab, with the bones numbered for accurate reference. These are the remains of a person abducted and murdered during the military rule in Argentina between 1976 and 1983. The hole in the skull is testament to a violent death.

THE DECAY OF INTERNAL ORGANS

Forensic pathologists can sometimes give a better estimate of the time of death by checking the internal organs, which decay in a known sequence. Bacteria attack the intestines first, and then decay moves to the liver, lungs, brain, kidneys, stomach (food and acid there can retard the growth of bacteria), and lastly the prostate or uterus.

Signs of Violence

Although conclusive proof of a violent crime can be obtained in a forensic laboratory, a forensic pathologist will make a careful examination of a corpse at the scene of death.

Below: This three-dimensional CT scan shows the fractured skull of a man involved in an assault. Direct brain damage and even death can result from such injuries.

Obvious signs include wounds made by gunshot and by blunt and sharp instruments. Cutting, stabbing and puncture marks are examples of defensive wounds that are normally found on the back of the victim's hands, inside the palms and the inner side of the forearms. Scrapes and bruises can also suggest a struggle.

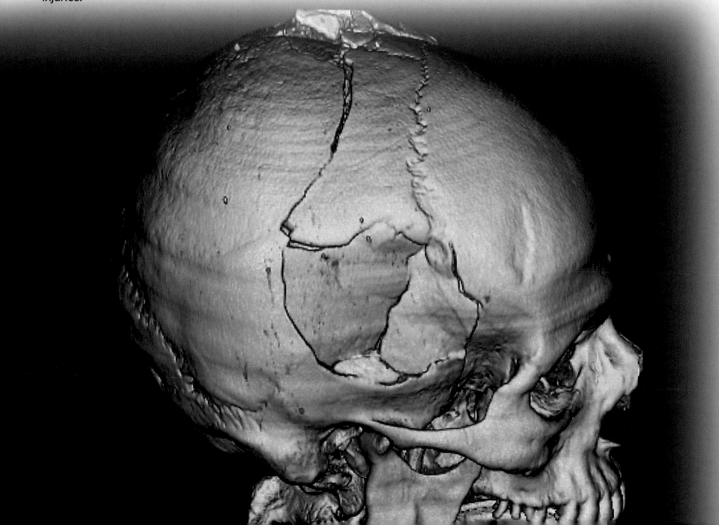

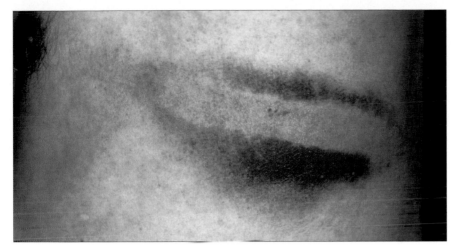

Bruising such as this could be the result of a beating with a club or baseball bat, and will be investigated carefully by a pathologist.

Violent marks on the body can also disprove an apparent suicide or accident victim. When the wife of a traffic policeman was found dead in front of her house in Cholurpalya, India in 2004, it was ruled she committed suicide jumping from the balcony. However, a post-mortem report found she had been strangled, and police arrested her husband and his father.

Other marks indicating violence include those made by ropes, tapes, bandages or other devices used to bind a victim, marks of a blindfold or gag and those associated with torture, such as cigarette burns.

In some cases, despite having obvious marks and trauma, victims may deny they were assaulted, either to protect the perpetrator, such as a spouse, or out of fear of further violence. Police violence can be especially intimidating. The Asian Human Rights Commission has highlighted this, such as the case of R. Don Nawaratne Bandara of Panadura, Sri Lanka. They say he was severely tortured by police in 2001 but withdrew his case against them because he feared for his life. The UN International Criminal Tribunal for the Former Yugoslavia also encountered many victims who refused to testify, citing their own safety. Its first case was dropped after a woman withdrew a rape charge because she could not be anonymous.

TYPES OF WOUNDS

Forensic examiners encounter many different types of wounds, or lesions, and traumas caused by physical assault.

Some of the common names are:

Abrasion: an injury in which the skin is scraped off

Concussion: a serious brain injury caused by a hard blow to the head

Contusion: a bruise in which the skin is not broken

Fracture: a break, crack or shattering of a bone

Laceration: a cut that is deep enough to need stitches

Trauma: a wound or a physical or emotional shock to the body

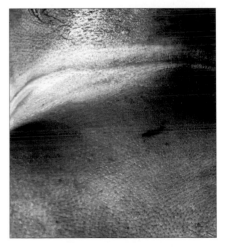

A murder victim has strangulation marks on the back of his neck caused by a thick cord. The appearance of the skin helps determine the time of death.

A LACK OF MARKS

Just the indication of overturned objects is sometimes enough to indicate foul play. When police in Hawaii discovered the body of a 40-year-old woman in 2000, there were no apparent physical marks of violence on her body, but the nearby scene indicated a struggle, so they tentatively classified her death as a homicide. This initiated an immediate investigation, which led to an arrest.

Signs of Abuse

Officials investigating a child's death have on occasion made discoveries of abuse. Maltreatment and a lack of proper care of children turns many death sites into crime scenes.

Each week in England, one to two children are killed by their parent or a caregiver and 16 per cent suffer serious maltreatment by parents; in the US an estimated 1500 children died in 2003 of maltreatment, three-quarters of these under the age of four. Child abuse has become less secret and reported cases are soaring. For example, in Japan in 2006, police investigated 297 cases, an increase of 33.8 per cent over the previous year.

GRIM DISCOVERY

In central Germany in 2000, the body of a child was discovered during an attempted eviction for rent arrears. The mother, a heroin user and prostitute living with her uncle, could not remember when she had last seen the child. She informed her uncle the child was with the grandmother, but also asked him how long someone could survive without food. Police at the crime scene found doors and windows tightly closed. The child's corpse was taken to the Institute for Legal Medicine at the University of Leipzig within one hour of its discovery. There were signs of malnourishment, and a forensic entomologist examined maggots on the body and estimated that the child had died about 14 days earlier. The estimate would have been more exact had the forensic expert been at the scene of the crime.

A wound caused by a cigarette burn in a child's skin is classified as a non-accidental injury.

VICTORIA CLIMBIE

When eight-year-old Victoria Climbie died in North Middlesex Hospital in London, the Home Office pathologist Dr Nathaniel Carey found 128 separate injuries and scars, many from cigarette burns, and declared this 'the worst case of child abuse I've encountered'.
Victoria's parents had sent her from the Ivory Coast to live with her aunt, Marie-Therese Kouao, who ended up staying with Carl Manning in Tottenham, in north London. The girl was twice taken to the hospital's casualty department with injuries but the aunt's excuses were accepted. On the third visit Victoria died of malnutrition and hypothermia, and Kouao and Manning were found guilty of murder and both sentenced to life. An official inquiry found that agencies could have intervened on 12 occasions and possibly saved the girl's life.

Child abuse has become less secret, and reported cases are soaring.

ABUSE OF THE ELDERLY

Adult abuse is often directed towards frail and vulnerable elderly people, with nursing homes becoming crime scenes. Currently, laws are being put into place to allow forensic scientists access to nursing homes to investigate deaths. In Arkansas, for example, legislation in effect since 1999 has led to more than 2000 investigations into deaths in long-term care facilities. One worker at such an establishment in Aldershot abused eight elderly women in his care from 1991 to 1996. More than 100 complaints were made before he was dismissed. They included allegations that he force-fed a 96-year-old patient and poured cold water over a 78-year-old woman.

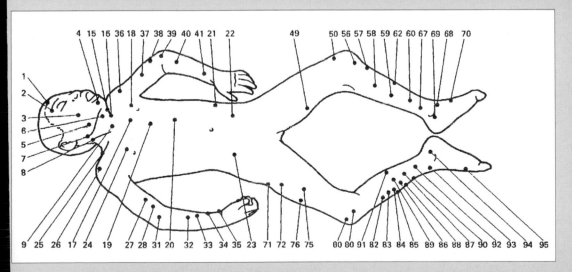

A diagram of the multiple injuries received by eight-year-old Victoria Climbie demonstrates the brutality she suffered before dying. Such striking evidence has been successfully used in court cases to show the extent of a child's abuse.

A forensic pathologist checks medical instruments in the laboratory before an coming up with an analysis.

Chapter Four

Analyzing Evidence

• •

THE FORENSIC SCIENCES ALL COME TOGETHER IN LARGE LABORATORIES, SUCH AS THOSE OPERATED BY THE FEDERAL BUREAU OF INVESTIGATION (FBI), THE FORENSIC SCIENCE SERVICE IN THE U.K. AND THE ROYAL CANADIAN MOUNTED POLICE.

The FBI has the largest biometric database in the world, containing the fingerprints and criminal history records of more than 47 million people. Its laboratory specialists conduct more than one million examinations every year.

Britain has the largest DNA database in the world with more than four million samples, 50 times that of France. The UK's Home Office agreed in 2007 to give free access to European police to this and its fingerprint database. At the same time, the European Union is creating a network to share the national crime records of its 27 countries.

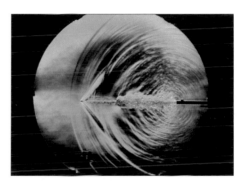

Special photography records a rifle bullet at the apex of a shock wave with the propellant gas preceding it.

Major laboratories have scientists who examine the physical evidence of DNA, fingerprints, hair, teeth, blood, drugs, poisons, fibres, paint, glass, firearms and bullets, explosives, soil and grass, tyre impressions and tool marks. Among the sophisticated analytical techniques are gas chromatography, which identifies chemical compositions, and mass spectrometry used by toxicologists. Accurate readings are assured by an array of diagnostic instruments, such as the powerful electron microscope and the infrared spectrometer.

An FBI officer examines and bags evidence found at a crime scene.

The Forensic Laboratory

In a large forensic crime lab, white-coated scientists and technicians bend over an array of complicated instruments, some scan computer screens, while others handle hazardous specimens using glove-boxes.

The object of all this lab activity is to verify that a crime has been committed and to connect criminal evidence to a suspect. This normally requires close co-operation between basic local police labs and larger regional and national ones where separate departments exist for each speciality. Britain's Forensic Science Service, for example, works primarily for the 43 police forces in England and Wales.

In 2007, it launched its new Footwear Intelligence Technology System, which is accessible to all police forces and contains some 13,000 images of shoe-print types commonly found at crime scenes.

ASSESSING A SAMPLE

Lab work often begins with a scientist briefly assessing a collected sample to identify it and determine if more expensive tests are required. Expertise will help decide if a stain is blood, a metal fragment comes from a bomb, or if a hair is human or animal. Samples are then sent to specialized divisions for testing and analysis. In Canada's Forensic Science Services, departments exist for biology, chemistry, explosives, toxicology, firearms and trace evidence, and there is also a bureau for counterfeit and document examinations. The evidence will be physically handled by scientists and their lab assistants, such as analysts and technicians. To avoid evidence contamination, every sample is stored and logged to follow its progress through the various departments.

FORENSIC PIONEERS

Edmond Locard (1877–1966) established the world's first forensic laboratory at Lyon, France, in 1910. He had been an assistant to the famed physician Alexandre Lacassagne (below), who was himself called 'the father of forensic science'. Locard was famous for his idea that 'every contact leaves a trace', now known as the Locard Exchange Principle. Two years after opening his crime laboratory, Locard used it to solve a case in which a bank clerk murdered his girlfriend. The man seemed to have a perfect alibi but confessed after Locard found minute scrapings of skin under his fingernails containing the pink dust of the woman's face powder.

Students receive first-aid instruction at the Police College in Hendon, England in 1934. The college was the brainchild of Hugh Trenchard, the Metropolitan Police commissioner. It opened that year and included a forensic lab.

The Locard Exchange Principle states that 'Every contact leaves a trace'.

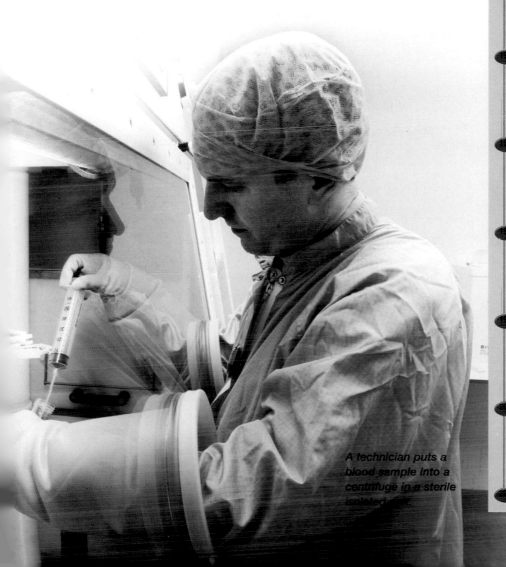

A technician puts a blood sample into a centrifuge in a sterile isolated unit.

FORENSIC SCIENCE LABORATORY TIMELINE

1910 Edmond Locard opens the world's first forensic laboratory in Lyon, France

1923 The Los Angeles Police Department establishes the USA's first forensic lab

1932 The Federal Bureau of Investigation (FBI) in the USA launches its Technical Laboratory in Washington, DC

1935 The Metropolitan Police Laboratory is established at Hendon Police College in London

1936 The Royal Canadian Mounted Police's original forensic laboratory opens in Regina

1957 India establishes its first Central Forensic Laboratory in Calcutta

1975 Ireland's Forensic Science Laboratory opens in Dublin

1991 The United Kingdom's Forensic Science Service is created in London

2005 The South African Police Service establishes its new Criminal Record and Forensic Science Services lab

2006 Pakistan's first forensic laboratory opens in the National Police Bureau in Islamabad

The FBI Laboratory

Through its crime-fighting success, outreach programmes, enthusiastic government support and high-profile portrayals in the movies and on television, the US Federal Bureau of Investigation (FBI) has had a worldwide influence in forensic science.

The FBI began in 1924 under the name of the Bureau of Investigation, and that year began its fingerprint file. A Technical Laboratory was established in 1932 to provide services to federal, state, local and foreign enforcement agencies. In 1967, an electronic database, the National Crime Information Center (NCIC) became operational.

PIONEERING LAB

In 1978 the laboratory pioneered the use of laser technology to detect latent fingerprints at a crime scene. A Computer Analysis and Response Team (CART) came into operation in 1991 to examine computers for investigations, and the next year a database of unique markings from bullets and shell casings was begun. The Hazardous Materials Unit was

established in 1996, and a year later the National DNA Index System (NDIS) was added so forensic science labs could share DNA profiles. A special unit of the laboratory, the Evidence Response Team (ERT), enters a crime scene to collect evidence and take it back it to the lab. Each of the bureau's 56 field offices has an ERT that may range from eight to 50 members. Besides

KOSOVO WAR CRIMES

FBI forensic scientists leave their laboratory when major work is needed in the field. In 1999, answering a call from the International Criminal Tribunal for the former Yugoslavia, the FBI deployed a 65-member forensic team to Kosovo to document crime scenes, collect evidence at massacre sites and perform

forensic exams on the deceased.

One FBI team processed sites in Gjakove and Peje, recovering seven bodies, along with the remains of numerous others. They also discovered bullets, cartridge cases and fragments of hand grenades. Field autopsies found the cause of death of all the victims to be multiple gunshots. Another forensic team went to 21 sites to exhume the bodies of 124 victims. Field autopsies again determined the cause of death to be multiple gunshots, with victims ranging from a two-year-old boy to a 94-year-old woman.

domestic operations, they have investigated international crimes, such as the US Embassy bombings in East Africa.

J EDGAR HOOVER

J Edgar Hoover (1895–1972) headed the FBI for 48 years from 1924 to 1972, becoming its longest-serving director. Especially interested in forensic science, he established the laboratory in 1932 while his agency was fighting against organized crime. He also sent his agents around the country to hear noted forensic scientists.

Hoover, born in Washington, DC, gained a law degree from George Washington University in 1917 and was a special assistant to the US Attorney General before joining the FBI as assistant director in 1921. Three years later, he was elevated to the bureau's top position and began programmes to make US law enforcement more professional.

An FBI team (above) load evidence into their vehicle after Eric Rudolph, the Atlanta Olympic bomber, was captured on 31 May 2003. Fingerprints (insert) of some 47 million people are on file in the FBI laboratory.

Laboratory Specialists

The job of the forensic pathologist in an investigation is generally considered to be the most important because a knowledge of, and familiarity with, most medical fields is required.

This physician, who may be in charge of the forensic laboratory, works closely with the police and has a good understanding of the law. He or she is normally involved in most aspects of a case, including the crime-scene investigation.

The forensic odontologist, or dentist, is especially valuable in identifying remains that have decomposed or have been virtually destroyed. The lab work involves matching the victim's teeth with dental records and X-rays. In disasters, dental identification is often the primary method of identification. This was used, for example, in the 1977 collision of two Boeing 747 jumbo jets in the Canary Islands, which resulted in 583 deaths.

THE TOXICOLOGIST

A forensic toxicologist determines if victims have ingested poisons or drugs. Tests are normally done with preserved samples of body fluids, stomach contents and organ parts.

THE DINGO DEATH

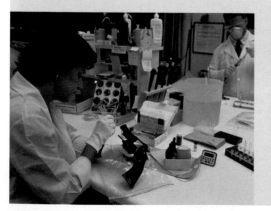

Before DNA profiling arrived, serologists often had difficulty defending their conclusions. This happened in a high-profile case in 1980 in Australia, when the nine-week-old daughter of Lindy and Michael Chamberlain was, according to the mother, carried away by a dingo, a type of wild dog. Apparent bloodstains were discovered in the Chamberlain's car and a forensic scientist identified them as the infant's. This helped send Lindy to prison.

When the baby's jacket was found in 1986 in a dingo's cave, the conviction was quashed, and a Royal Commission concluded that the car's 'bloodstains' were probably spots sprayed on at the factory to absorb noise. But by then, Lindy had served six years in prison.

Scientists in the FBI's serology lab examine traces of blood that can solve controversies like the stains found in the dingo case.

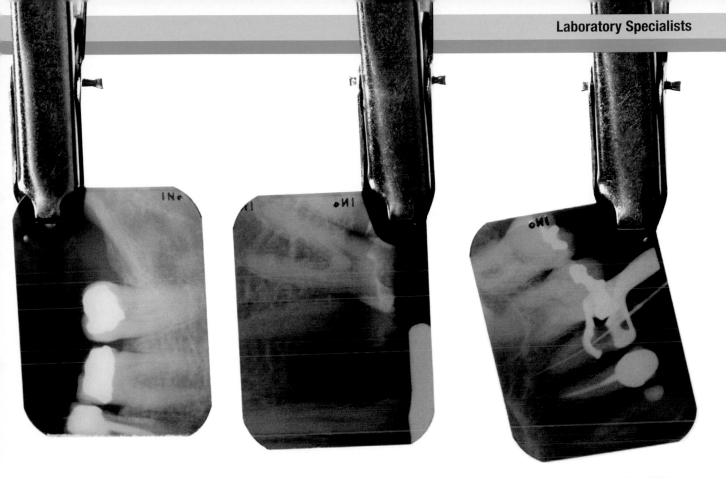

The specialist also examines the coroner's report and postmortem results. Proving foul play did not take place may take time, as in the 2007 deaths of the former Playboy model Anna Nicole Smith and her son, who were both taking medicinal drugs.

A forensic serologist uses blood and other bodily fluids to link a crime suspect with samples at the scene. An inexpensive ABO blood-typing test can compare blood groups quickly, but is mostly unreliable in ruling out a suspect. DNA profiling must be used to conclusively establish an incriminating link. DNA testing is also used on semen recovered in a rape case and on saliva, which could be left on stamps or bite marks.

ALEXANDER LITVINENKO

Identifying a poison can be difficult. When Alexander Litvinenko, a former Russian spy living in London, became terminally ill in November 2006, doctors thought the cause might never be known. Professor John Henry, a toxicologist helping to treat him, suggested that damage to Litvinenko's bone marrow and blood cells suggested

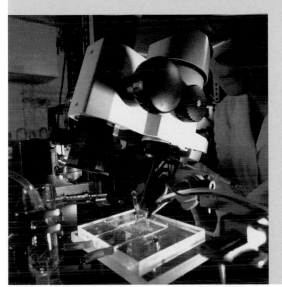

poisoning by radioactive thallium. Radioactivity was eventually identified in the form of polonium. Litvinenko, a critic of Russian President Vladimir Putin, had apparently been assassinated.

Toxicologists (left) identified the poison that killed Litvinenko. Another specialist, the forensic odontologist, examines X-rays of teeth (above).

Two Specialist Murder Cases

Although numerous police officials and investigators are involved in a murder, the evidence in a case will tend to point towards one or more forensic specialities.

The first time a Scottish jury considered bite marks as evidence was in the 1967 murder of 15-year-old Linda Peacock, whose body was found in a cemetery in the small town of Biggar. The mark was on one of her breasts, and Dr Warren Harvey, Scotland's top forensic odontologist, was placed on the case. One mark, fortunately, was unusual, appearing to come from a jagged tooth. Dental impressions were taken from 29 youths in a local detention centre, and only one matched. Gordon Hay, 17, had a rare disorder that created pits in his canine teeth that left the incriminating marks. He was found guilty of murder and sent to prison.

The work of New York City Medical Examiner Dr Milton Helpern and his aide, toxicologist Dr Charles Umberger proved key to solving the 1965 murder of the physician

TESTING FOR DRUGS

Laboratory toxicologists have several methods to screen for drugs. Gas chromatography (right), the main tool, uses the speed of vaporized samples moving at different rates through a narrow tube. This process separates and identifies alcohols and compounds like acetone and isolates substances that will dissolve in alkaline solutions, such as anti-depressants, tranquillizers and synthetic narcotics.

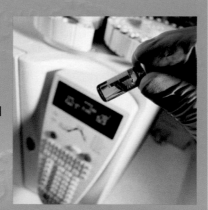

A urine immunoassay kit has antibodies that combine with drugs in a urine sample to produce a particular colour. This will identify cocaine, opiates and methadone, as well as barbiturates and aspirin.

Dr Carmela Coppolino in Florida. Her husband, Dr Carl Coppolino, an anesthesiologist, had injected her with the paralytic drug succinylcholine chloride.

A physician friend of Coppolino's wrongly ascribed the death to a heart attack on the death certificate because the murderer said his wife had suffered chest pains. Three weeks before her death, he had increased her life insurance from $10,000 to $55,000. Although the drug was thought to be undetectable in the human body, Dr Umberger had taken months to isolate it in the brain tissues of the victim. Coppolino was convicted of second-degree murder and served 12 years in prison.

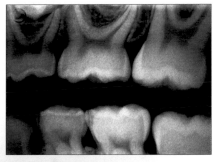

Dental X-rays have been used to solve cases that involved bites, such as the death of Linda Peacock.

Only one of the 29 suspects had a rare dental disorder, which created pits in his teeth, leaving incriminating marks the victim.

Dr Carl Coppolino was convicted of ... his wife, Carmela, in 1965.

TOO MUCH EVIDENCE

Forensic labs throughout Canada were overwhelmed with evidence in the case of Robert Pickton, a pig farmer charged in 2002 with killing six women and facing a total of 26 murder counts. More than 200,000 DNA samples had been tested by February 2007. This followed a 20-month search of his 7-hectare (17-acre) farm, an area so large a mobile lab was set up on the farm for preliminary tests before evidence was sent to the six Royal Canadian Mounted Police labs, where additional staff were hired to process the items. Although Pickton's trial began in January 2007, the forensic testing continued, because the trial was expected to last a year.

Fingerprints

Fingerprints will always be an uncontested form of identification because no two are alike and a person's prints do not change throughout life.

THE NIGHT STALKER

Richard Ramirez, 25, became known in Los Angeles as 'The Night Stalker' when he terrorized the city from June 1984 to August 1985. He sexually attacked and murdered more than a dozen victims, with almost as many surviving other attacks. After the last attack, a teenager wrote down his car's registration. The vehicle was located and fingerprints taken. The LAPD had a new AFIS system and matched Ramirez's prints within minutes. Ramirez was convicted and given a life sentence.

The first courts to convict a suspect by fingerprints were in Argentina in 1892 and in England in 1902. Then in 1903, the New York State Prison system began using them for criminal identification. Today fingerprinting remains a major source of identifying criminals, boosted by online databases containing millions of prints of known criminals.

Fingerprints are now being scanned electronically into databases, gradually replacing the traditional ink-and-card process. The computerized system, called the Automated Fingerprint Identification System (AFIS), is extremely fast, with computers now able to search through 500,000

FINGERPRINT PATTERNS

The UK, US, and most other English-speaking countries use the Henry System for classifying 10-print collections, developed in 1899 by Sir Edward R. Henry with the British police in India. Three basic types of ridge patterns classify fingerprints:

Arches: these ridges, making up about five per cent of all patterns, rise above one another in the centre like an arch. There are plain arches and tented ones that rise more sharply.

Loops: these patterns, about 60 per cent of all patterns, are ridges that double back on themselves.

Whorls: these resemble small whirlpools revolving around a point, and make up some 35 per cent of patterns. There are four types of whorls.

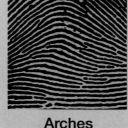

Arches

Loops

Whorls

prints in less than a second. The system scans prints and plots the positions of ridge characteristics, then compares this with prints in the database. It suggests possible suspects, but the fingerprint expert still makes the final decision. The AFIS is especially valuable in scanning partial prints, using digital enhancement for better contrast and sharpness. It is also able to suggest a match between the broken pattern taken at a crime scene and a complete one on the database.

Australia was the first nation to establish an automatic system. Its National Automated Fingerprint Identification System (NAFIS) was set up in 1986 and now holds 2.6 million 10-fingerprints. The FBI developed their system in 1991 and today has 47 million such prints, while Britain's system, bearing the same name as Australia's, linked all its forces in 2001 and now has more than five million prints.

In 1986 Australia was the first country to establish an automatic fingerprint ID system.

The identifying characteristics of fingerprints have become standardized.

The History of Fingerprints

The first use of fingerprints for solving crimes is lost in the early mists of history. Certainly, in 100 CE the Roman attorney Quintilian proved a blind man innocent of murder who had been framed by someone else's bloody palm prints.

A more exact classification of prints was needed for complicated cases. Finger ridges were described in 1684 by the English botanist and physician Nehemiah Grew. Four British men also developed modern fingerprinting. In 1880, two published their interest in using them for identification: the Scottish physician Henry Faulds, then working in a Tokyo hospital, used printer's ink to record prints and thought about using them to identify criminals; William Herschel, a civil servant in Bengal, India, reported he had used them for identification since 1860.

The English scientist Sir Francis Galton *(pictured right)* suggested the system of grouping fingerprint patterns into arches, loops and whorls. Then in 1899, Sir Edward R. Henry developed today's modern classification system with subdivisions of Galton's pattern types. He was put in charge of Scotland Yard's new fingerprint branch in 1901. Juan Vucetich of Argentina also devised a classification system in 1904 that became used in Latin American and Spanish-speaking countries. In 1924, the FBI began what would become the world's largest fingerprint database, using the Henry system but adding numerous sub-classifications for more accuracy.

JAN PURKINJE

One of the first scientists to classify fingerprint patterns was Jan Purkinje (1787–1869), who was born in Libochovice, Bohemia (now part of the Czech Republic). In 1823, the same year he became professor of physiology and pathology at the University of Breslau, Purkinje classified fingerprint patterns into nine varieties: transverse curve, oblique loop, ellipse, central longitudinal stria, almond whorl, circle, oblique stripe, spiral whorl, and double whorl. Purkinje received a modern compound microscope in 1832 to examine tissues. He discovered the sweat glands in 1833. At the university, he established in 1839 the world's first department of physiology and in 1842 the first official physiological laboratory.

Today's classification system of fingerprint arches, loops and whorls was developed in 1899.

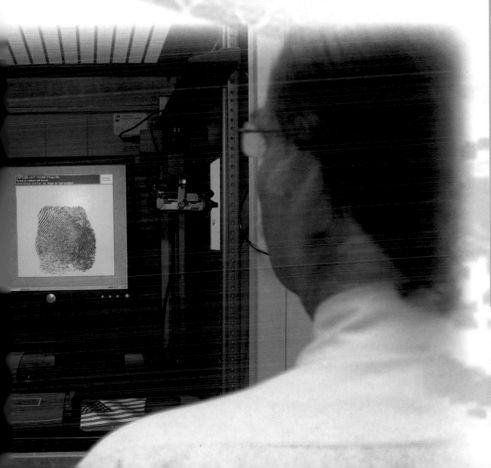

TRAINING

Fingerprint experts in the UK undergo a rigorous training programme lasting several years. They are trained and qualified by Centrex National Training Centre, a Home Office department, which is independent from any police force. Its head is Mike Thompson, a fingerprint expert with over 32 years of experience. He said the centre emphasizes court testimony. 'Our training', he noted, 'makes clear to the fingerprint officers that their first duty is to the court and to explain in easily understood language how they reached their findings.'

The new digital fingerprinting system at the police station in Auburn, New York, is the latest refinement in capturing prints without using ink.

Trace Evidence

The trace evidence unit of a forensic science lab is the most diverse discipline. Any unknown material that cannot be placed in a specialist unit must go to the trace evidence unit for an attempt to identify it.

An examiner will have to investigate a range of items that will include hair, fibre, glass, paint, explosives, footwear and tyre impressions and arson debris. Personal items may include cosmetics, like lipstick, mascara and nail polish.

The FBI's Trace Evidence Unit maintains reference collections of human and animal hairs, natural and man-made textile fibres, fabrics, feathers, woods and seeds. Besides testing and matching nonhuman evidence, the Unit also helps identify

THE VALUE OF HAIR

Many cases are solved because hairs have been transferred between a victim and perpetrator. One individual hair can lead to a conviction. Hairs can survive years after a body has decayed, and they hold many secrets within one thin shaft and follicle. They can be a source of DNA, including valuable mitochondrial DNA (mtDNA) passed through maternal generations. Hair also records poisons like arsenic, and past drug use, including alcohol and nicotine. As well, general racial types can often be determined from samples.

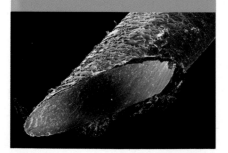

EDMOND LOCARD

The French forensic scientist Edmond Locard (right), the first to declare that 'every contact leaves a trace', gave a dramatic description of how trace evidence entraps a criminal:

'Wherever he steps, whatever he touches, whatever he leaves, even unconsciously, will serve as a silent witness against him. Not only his fingerprints or his footprints but his hair, the fibres from his clothes, the glass he breaks, the tool mark he leaves, the paint he scratches, the blood or semen he deposits or collects. All of these, and more, bear mute witness against him. This is evidence that does not forget. It is not confused by the excitement of the moment. It is not absent because human witnesses are. It is factual evidence. Physical evidence cannot be wrong, it cannot perjure itself, it cannot be wholly absent. Only human failure to find it, study, and understand it can diminish its value.'

human remains by examining trace samples of teeth and bones.

MICROSCOPES

Various microscopes provide the power to identify and compare trace evidence. A scanning electron microscope (SEM) is used to view surface details that are 100,000 times smaller than the breadth of a hair. Light microscopes can view inside an item of evidence and are normally used to identify hairs. Comparison microscopes have duplicate systems, actually two compound light microscopes, so that two samples can be viewed in a single eyepiece. It is used, for example, to match bullet casings.

'Wherever he steps, whatever he touches, whatever he leaves, even unconsciously, will serve as a silent witness against him.'

A forensic expert examines the sole of a shoe searching for soil or any other residue.

Trace Evidence in Two Cases

The first court use of trace evidence was recorded in England in 1784 when John Toms was convicted of killing Edward Culshaw in Lancaster.

Police investigating a bullet wound in the victim's head found crushed paper used to keep the powder and balls in the muzzle. This was a torn piece of newspaper that matched a piece of newspaper found in the pocket of the murderer.

The use of evidential fibres was expertly done in the US in the arrest and conviction of Wayne Williams, who murdered more than 25 males, including children, in Atlanta, Georgia, from 1979 to 1981. One victim had a yellow-green fibre in his hair that matched a carpet in Williams' home, but FBI forensic scientists had to rule out other houses having such a carpet. They traced the fibres to a textile company in Boston to find that the owners of only 82 houses in the state of Georgia had bought that colour.

One victim also had a single rayon fibre on his shorts that resembled carpeting in Williams' Chevrolet station wagon. The FBI had the company help them calculate that there was a one in 3,828 chance of the victim being in contact with a vehicle having this carpeting. During the court case, 28 fibre types from 12 victims were linked to Williams. He was convicted and received two consecutive life sentences.

A coloured scanning electron micrograph shows synthetic fibres woven for clothing material.

MIKE GRIEVE

Born in Buxton, Derbyshire, Mike Grieve (1942–2002) became one of the world's best forensic fibre experts. He began the fibre section at the Metropolitan Police Forensic Science Laboratory while working there from 1964 to 1967. Five years later he moved to the US Army Criminal Investigation lab in Frankfurt, Germany, and once more began a fibre section. In 1992 he joined the Forensic Science Institute of the Bundeskriminalamt in Wiesbaden, Germany, and one year later, with Ken Wiggins, established the European Fibre Group.

Grieve lectured on the importance of fibres as evidence in criminal cases and wrote *Forensic Examination of Fibres* (1999), which has been called 'the fibre examiner's bible'. The European Network of Forensic Science Institutes posthumously awarded him the Distinguished Forensic Scientist Award in 2003, calling him 'the best forensic fibre expert in the world'.

One victim had a yellow-green fibre in his hair that matched a carpet in the suspect's home.

The serial killer Wayne Williams was convicted by carpet fibres from his house and vehicle.

TYPES OF FIBRES

More than 100 billion pounds of fibre are produced each year. Forensic scientists place them into classifications, noting their materials, weaves and colours. This 'class evidence' is divided into two main groups: Natural fibres include those that come from vegetable sources, such as cotton (pictured below in yellow), sisal and flax. Among the cotton fabrics are crinoline, muslin, gingham, organdy, calico, seersucker and velveteen.

Artificial fibres include natural polymers like Rayon, Cellulose and rubber, and synthetic polymers like polyester (below in green), polyethylene and Terylene.

Firearms

In the noisiest section of a forensic lab, guns recovered from a crime scene, or a suspect, are fired to reproduce the unique marks, grooves and scratches evident on spent ammunition found at the scene.

T he lab firearms examiner loads and fires the unknown gun into a box of gel or water tank, and then uses a comparison microscope to try to match the striation marks to the ammunition evidence. A computer database can also be checked for matches with evidence from previous crimes.

DISGUISING FIREARMS

Firearm specialists also deal with other problems in the lab. Some criminals file off the serial numbers of guns, but the metal will retain the original indentions below the surface. Lab technicians can raise these by magnetizing the gun, using an etching solution, or placing the

gun in an ultrasonic bath.

Links can even be drawn if no firearm ammunition is found. Traces of gunpowder, called gunshot residue (GSR), can cling to the

NIBIN

The USA has one of the best forensic databases for recovered bullet and cartridge cases, known as the National Integrated Ballistics Information Network (NIBIN). It was established in 1997 by

combining the databases of the FBI, called 'Drugfire', and the Bureau of Alcohol, Tobacco, Firearms and Explosives (ATF). Ever since it came into operation, NIBIN has recorded some one million samples from crime scenes. Through NIBIN, which is maintained by the ATF, the computerized images can be compared rapidly with images in the systems of some 220 federal, state and local law enforcement labs. When firearm examiners begin a search, a scanner automatically shows a digital image of the items, looks for matches and then displays them on a monitor.

perpetrator's clothes, hand, arm, hair and face. Samples can be taken from the suspect, and a scanning electron microscope used to locate these tiny particles on hair or fibre. Residue on clothing can also reveal the distance between the shooter and victim, since the spread will be wider from a farther distance. Test firings on similar fabrics will give an accurate estimate of the distance.

MARKINGS ON SHELL CASINGS

After a bullet has been fired, a shell casing is left as evidence. A firearms examiner can compare a variety of marks left on the metal:

Striations: The barrel of each weapon leaves its unique pattern of marks that are used in comparisons. Striations run parallel to the length of the bullet.

Firing pin: Dents will be made by a firing pin in the soft metal base of a casing. Seeing where the firing pin struck helps identify the type of gun used.

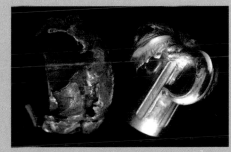

Rifling: These are spiralling grooves inside the barrel, which are used to spin the bullet. Their angle and direction, clockwise or anti-clockwise, help identify the type of weapon and match the shell to a gun.

Two spent hollow bullets show their distinctive striations and markings. These can be used to identify a gun.

Some criminals file off the serial numbers of guns, but the metal will retain the original indentions below the surface.

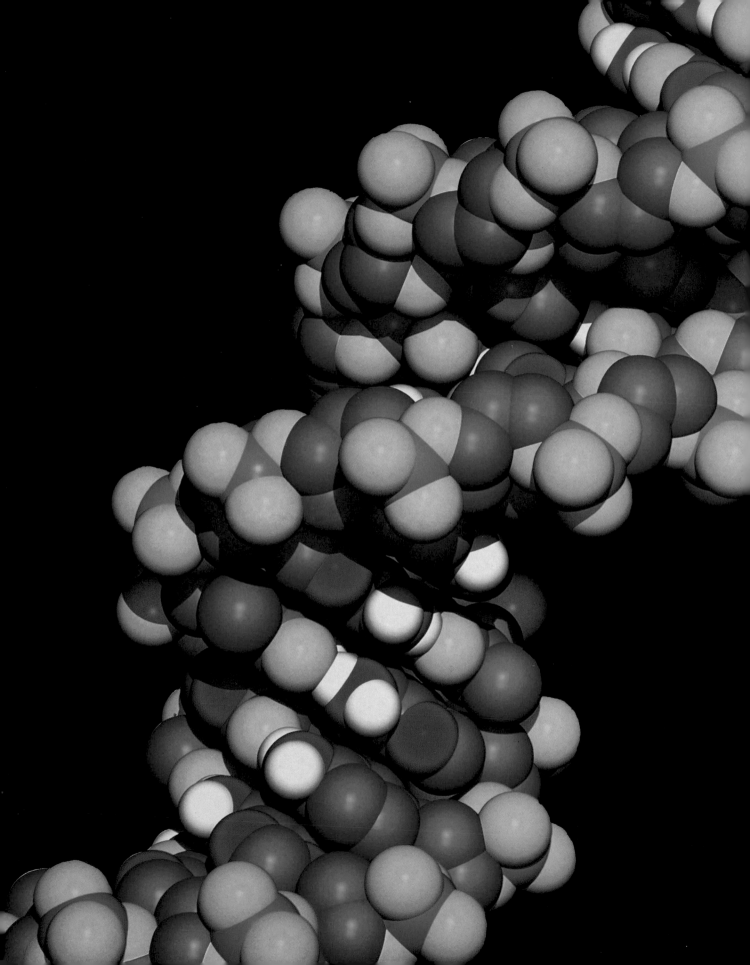

Chapter Five

DNA and the Criminal

● ●

DNA tests are the most trusted evidence in legal history. A better chance exists of finding and matching DNA to a suspect than using fingerprints, because criminals can avoid leaving prints by wearing gloves or wiping away the incriminating marks. DNA, on the other hand, can be extracted from microscopically small trace evidence that a perpetrator cannot even see. Today in

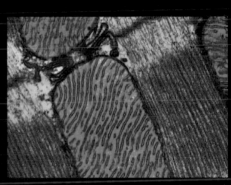

Mitochondria in a heart muscle are coloured blue in this transmission electron micrograph (TEM). Mitochondria DNA (mtDNA) is a more abundant DNA type.

Britain, for example, 70 per cent of all forensic tests are DNA ones.

Two scientists, Britain's Francis Crick and the American James Watson, identified the double helix structure of DNA in 1953. In 1984 the British geneticist Alex Jeffreys discovered genetic fingerprinting, and this led two years later to the first court case in which a DNA sample convicted a suspect, the murderer Colin Pitchfork. In 1987, DNA evidence was allowed in a US court case.

Advances continue to be made in DNA recovery and testing. The 1990s saw the emergence of mitochondrial DNA (mtMDA) testing in forensic casework, which is valuable when the biological evidence is degraded or small in quantity. As well, mtMDA lasts so long that accurate tests can be made on ancient skeletons. Another new technology, developed by the UK's Forensic Science Service, is DNA Low Copy Number (DNA LCN) testing, which can be used to obtain profiles from samples containing only a few cells.

Computer artwork on a strand of DNA shows colour-coded atoms: carbon (blue), oxygen (yellow), hydrogen (white), nitrogen (magenta) and phosphorous (orange).

What is DNA?

Deoxyribonucleic acid, or DNA, is a two-metre (six-foot) long spiral within every nucleus of our body's cells, which number about 60 trillion. It is located in the nucleus, so it is referred to as nuclear DNA.

It has a double helix structure that looks like a twisted ladder formed into long strands called chromosomes. Inside the spiral are three billion connecting rods that add the 'rungs' to the ladder. Known as bases, these are of four different types, which are known as guanine (G), cytosine (C), thymine (T) and adenine (A). The order in which they are positioned along the strand is unique in each person, with the exception of identical twins.

Pairs of bases form the double helix, with C only pairing with G and A with T. This never varies, so when DNA replicates itself, all new strands are exact copies. One person's DNA has six billion bases that create three billion base pairs.

A small section of the DNA spiral contains our genetic code, the genes that give us our looks and characteristics, such as curly hair or blue eyes. However, forensic scientists are only interested in the large remainder portion of the spiral. Although it seems to do little and is called 'junk' DNA, the short sequences of the base pairs repeat themselves, and this varies greatly among people, allowing individuals to be identified.

Besides nuclear DNA, another type in most cells is mitochondrial DNA (mtDNA), so named for being located in another part of the cell, the mitochondrion. It is arranged in a circle much smaller than the linear nuclear DNA. While nuclear DNA is inherited from each parent equally, mtDNA comes only from the mother, which is vital for tracing direct ancestry.

SIR ALEC JEFFREYS

DNA fingerprinting was discovered and named by the British geneticist Alex Jeffreys on 10 September 1984 in his lab in Leicester University. He was alone in the darkroom when an X-ray image in the developing tank suddenly gave him the idea that each person has a unique DNA pattern and that this could be used for criminal cases. Born in Oxford in 1950 and graduating from the university there, Jeffreys was knighted in 1994. He remains amazed at his own discovery. 'It is the most powerful criminal investigation tool there is', he said. 'If you had told me all that 20 years ago, I would not have believed it.'

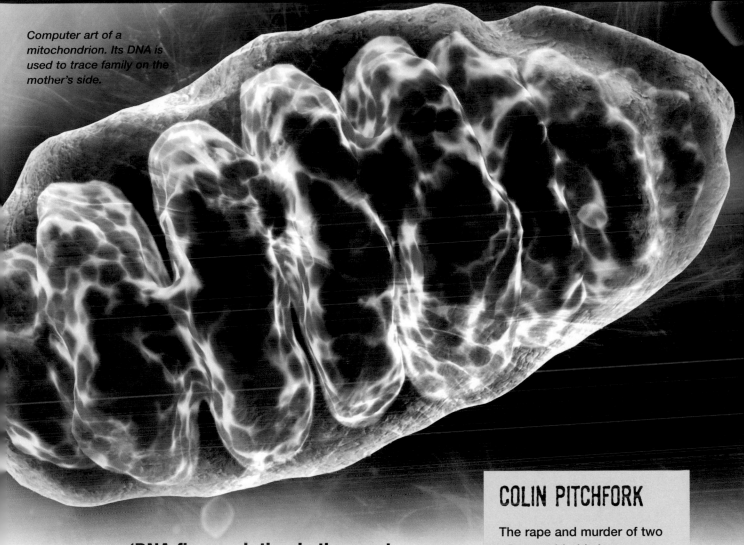

Computer art of a mitochondrion. Its DNA is used to trace family on the mother's side.

'DNA fingerprinting is the most powerful criminal investigation tool there is.'

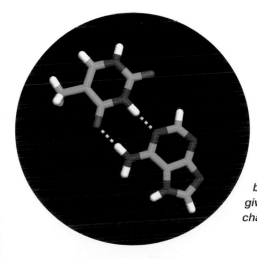

Computer artwork of an A-T (adenine-thymine) base pair. A-T is one of the two base pairs found in DNA (along with C-G (cytosine-guanine)). The positioning of these base pairs along the DNA chain gives organisms their individual characteristics.

COLIN PITCHFORK

The rape and murder of two 15-year-old girls in Narborough, Leicestershire, in in 1983 and 1986 led to the first forensic application of DNA profiling. Blood samples were taken from the male population of the area, but no match turned up. However, when a woman overheard Ian Kelly boasting he had given a sample for Colin Pitchfork, a local baker, investigators took Pitchfork's sample and it matched. He then confessed and in 1988 was sentenced to life imprisonment.

79

The History of DNA Research

DNA was discovered in 1869 by the German medical researcher, Johann Friedrich Miescher, at the University of Tübingen, working under Felix Hoppe-Seyler. Undertaking research with white blood cells, he isolated a white, slightly acidic substance he called nuclein.

Miescher worked on his discovery for the remainder of his life, believing that the proteins in chromosomes were responsible for heredity.

His discovery took place at about the time that the British scientist Charles Darwin, and the Austrian botanist and monk, Gregor Mendel, were also publishing papers on genetic theories.

THE GENOME

The complete set of DNA within a cell is called its genome. The name combines 'gene' and 'chromosome' and was coined in 1920 by the botanist Hans Winkler at the University of Hamburg. Human chromosomes have from about 50 million to 300 million base pairs. Each chromosome contains up to thousands of genes for making proteins. Each gene in the human genome makes an average of three proteins.
All humans and primates share a large amount of the genome, so our DNA is identical to that of chimpanzees.

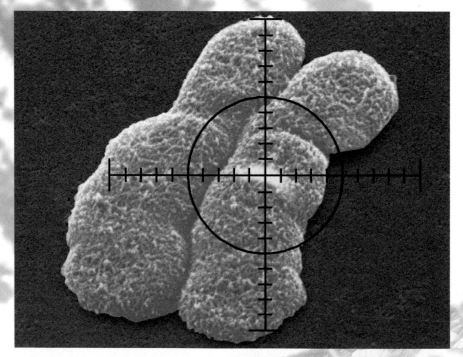

A coloured scanning electron micrograph (SEM) shows a targeted gene (yellow) on a human chromosome that contains DNA.

FRANCIS CRICK AND JAMES WATSON

The discoverers of DNA's structure came from totally different backgrounds. Francis Crick (right in photo) was born in 1916 near Northampton, and studied physics at University College, London. In 1949 he joined the Medical Research Council Unit at the famous Cavendish Laboratory in Cambridge and worked on the structure of proteins.

James Watson (left in photo) was born in 1928 in Chicago and studied zoology at the University of Chicago. He gained a PhD in zoology in 1950 from Indiana University. He became interested in the structure of DNA after attending a symposium in 1951 in Naples, Italy.

Crick and Watson became friends, and the American joined Crick in Cambridge in 1951. That year their first effort to understand the DNA structure failed but two years later they discovered the double-helical configuration. Both were awarded the Nobel prize in 1962 for their discovery.

In 1928, the British medical officer Franklin Griffith found that genetic information could be transferred from bacteria cells killed by heat to live ones. He called this 'transformation'. Subsequently, in 1944 American bacteriologist, Oswald Avery, identified the transforming agent as DNA when he destroyed DNA and found that transformation would not occur. As previously mentioned, James Watson and Francis Crick discovered the molecular structure of DNA in 1953 and Alex Jeffreys discovered genetic fingerprinting in 1984.

In 2003, the Human Genome Project to identify all of the 20,000 to 25,000 genes in human DNA was finally completed after 13 years. This project, co-ordinated by the US Department of Energy and the National Institutes of Health, was able to determine the sequences of the three billion chemical base pairs that make up human DNA.

In 2003, after 13 years, the Human Genome Project identifying all of the 20,000 to 25,000 genes in human DNA was finally completed.

A technician removes frozen cell lines from cryostorage for the Human Genome Project.

Taking DNA Samples

The normal method of collecting DNA samples is by swabbing the mouth. The swab is put into the mouth and moved across the inside of the cheek to collect cellular material.

This will usually take about 15 minutes. In many countries, trained police officers are supplied with DNA kits that contain everything needed to take a sample, including two swabs and disposable gloves to prevent contamination.

DRAGNET

Mouth swabs are also used in a 'sweep' or 'dragnet' of people living

A doctor uses a tongue depressor and a swab to take a sample from a girl's throat.

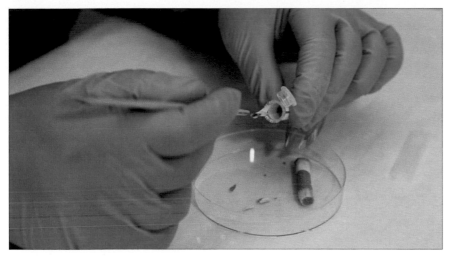
A forensic scientist takes a sample from a cigarette stub to see if traces of DNA from saliva can be found to identify the smoker.

in the area of a crime. In the United States, samples from 2300 men were taken in 1994 in Miami when six prostitutes were murdered, and in Baton Rouge, Louisiana, 1200 men were tested in 2003 during the hunt for a serial killer. The sweeps failed to find the criminals who were arrested by other means, and a 2004 survey at the University of Nebraska at Omaha found that only one in 18 sweeps identified the perpetrator.

Mouth swabs for other offences will sometimes lead to an unexpected connection with a previous crime. This happened in 2006 when Sukhdarshan Singh was arrested for drink driving and police took a mouth swab. His DNA matched the sample taken 18 years before when a woman was raped in Bridgend, Wales. Singh was jailed for four and a half years.

At a crime scene without suspects, common sources of DNA are trace samples of blood, semen, saliva, sweat, hair follicles, bone and skin. In fact, any biological sample with cells is a potential DNA source. Samples are carefully preserved for comparisons with the mouth swabs of suspects and with DNA databases.

TERESA CORMACK

Patient police in New Zealand tested DNA in a murder case three times in 14 years, certain that advances in the science would eventually lead to the killer. Six-year-old Teresa Cormack was murdered in 1987. DNA swabs were sent to Britain for testing, but they contained insufficient material. More tests in the 1990s were unsuccessful. Then, in 2001, a tiny amount of saved semen was tested with advanced DNA technology. Blood samples were taken from the local male population, and Jules Mikus proved a match. Hairs stored for 14 years were sent to the US for mitochondrial DNA testing and confirmed the match. Mikus was found guilty in 2002.

BIN LADEN'S DNA

In 2002, the American CBS network reported that the FBI had obtained samples of Osama bin Laden's DNA and were checking it against tissue and body parts on the battlefields of Afghanistan. The sample supposedly was obtained from strands of his hair. One Canadian-led mission that year into the Tora Bora region excavated some 23 graves of al-Qaeda fighters following speculative reports that bin Laden had been killed. DNA samples were taken from the corpses for identification, but the terrorist leader was not among them.

A swab is used to take cells from the inside of the cheek for a DNA sample.

Amplifying DNA

When identifying genetic fingerprints, a forensic scientist may want to make copies of small amounts of DNA, because some methods of analysis need more DNA than may be in a sample.

Polymerase chain reaction (PCR) is a technique that amplifies (multiplies) DNA, allowing scientists to create millions of copies in about two hours. The American scientist Kary Mullis conceived of it in 1983 (see box), and most DNA profiling today is based on his process.

PCR, which has informally been called 'molecular photocopying', amplifies specific regions of a DNA strand, such as a single gene, part of a gene, or a noncoding sequence. The process is extremely sensitive, so specific analyses can be made of tiny amounts of crime-scene DNA.

The process uses the polymerase enzyme for copying instead of a living organism, such as yeast. The DNA sample is mixed in a test tube with salty water, polymerase, the four bases and primers (two DNA fragments that attach the sides of a target sequence). This mixture is heated to separate the sides of the double-stranded DNA and then

KARY MULLIS

The inventor of PCR, Kary Mullis, was born in 1944 in Lenoir, North Carolina. He gained a degree in science at the Georgia Institute of Technology and a PhD in biochemistry from the University of California at Berkeley.
Mullis joined the Cetus Corporation of Emeryville, California, as a DNA chemist in 1979. While there, he conceived of the PCR idea in 1983 while cruising along a motorway. In 1993, he received the Nobel prize for discovering PCR. Today he is a researcher at the Children's Hospital and Research Institute in Oakland, California. Writing in *Scientific American*, Mullis summed up the simplicity of PCR: 'Beginning with a single molecule of the genetic material DNA, the PCR can generate 100 billion similar molecules in an afternoon. The reaction is easy to execute. It requires no more than a test tube, a few simple reagents, and a source of heat.'

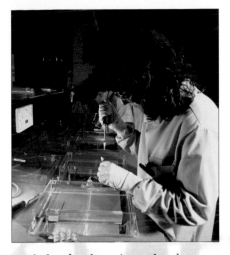

A forensic expert at ICI Cellmark Diagnostics in Oxfordshire separates fragments of DNA into bands.

Polymerase chain reaction amplifies DNA, allowing scientists to create millions of copies in about two hours.

The banding pattern of lengths of DNA sequencing is revealed under ultraviolet light.

cooled to let the primers bind to their complementary sequences on the separated strands, and to let the polymerase extend the primers into new complementary strands. The mixture is repeatedly heated and cooled to multiply the DNA exponentially.

THE GREEN RIVER KILLER

Gary Ridgway was an infamous serial killer who, from 1982 to 1998, murdered 48 women, mostly prostitutes, and dumped many in the Green River near Seattle, Washington. When police caught up with him, he gave a DNA sample, but the semen samples from his victims were too small to test. His saliva sample was stored, and the advent of PCR allowed forensic testing of the amplified DNA in 2001 that matched Ridgway's. He pleaded guilty, and confessed to more murders than anyone else in US history. He was sentenced to life without parole.

How DNA is Matched

To compare DNA samples, an investigator first uses agents such as a chloroform and phenol mixture to separate the DNA from other material in the cell nucleus.

The PCR process will normally amplify this sample. A fluorescent dye is used to tag each DNA fragment.

The double-stranded fragments are converted by chemicals into single strands and separated by length using electrophoresis, in which an electrical current is passed through a sample to move it through a gel or narrow tube, separating the fragments into a series of bands.

VNTRS

Forensic investigators check these bands for base sequences that are repeated. The two types are Variable Number Tandem Repeats (VNTRs), which can be hundreds of base pairs long, and Short Tandem Repeats (STRs), which are normally three to seven base pairs long.

PEAK PROFILE

A scanner system reads the sequence: a laser beam causes the dyed fragments to fluoresce, and these flashes are registered on a colour-sensitive detector. The results are displayed as coloured peaks on a graph. A crime scene DNA will be displayed next to a suspect's sample, and investigators check the results visually or by computer. A match is indicated if the profile of peaks is the same.

A SPEEDIER DNA ANALYSIS

About three hours is required for the replication of DNA by polymerase chain reaction (PCR) to produce a sample large enough to analyze. A new system developed at the University of Michigan, however, will cut the time needed back to only 40 minutes.

The DNA mixture must be heated to 95°C, allowed to cool to 50–60°C, and then heated to 72°C for the PCR process to work. This must be done as many as 30 to 40 times to get a sufficient sample. The new device uses convection, which keeps the DNA mixture moving in a steady, circular flow within a few minutes. This is done by placing it into a Plexiglas well between two plates held at constant temperatures: 95°C at the bottom and 50–60°F at the top.

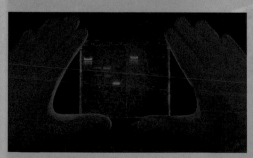

A robot arm picks up a tray of bacterial colonies which clone human DNA fragments for use in the Human Genome Project.

MISINTERPRETING DNA

Forensic experts can draw widely varying conclusions about DNA matches. When Dr Bradley Schwartz was accused of hiring a hit man to kill his former medical partner, the trial in 2006 turned on disagreements about DNA statistics.

The Department of Public Safety testified that the hit man's DNA matched samples from the crime scene, and only one in 20 million people could have such a connection. A DNA expert for the defence reduced those to one in 1658, saying the DNA at the scene had been misinterpreted. But when DNA expert Bruce Budowle of the FBI was called in, he put the number at one in 13,000. Dr Schwartz was convicted and is serving a life sentence.

A researcher uses ultraviolet light to examine an agarose gel containing DNA fragments.

Two Cases of Familial DNA

Michael Little, 53, was killed in March 2003 when someone threw a brick down onto the bonnet of his lorry as he drove on the M3 in Surrey.

In 2003 Craig Harman became the first person in the world to be convicted through familial searching.

A forensic scientist prepares an agarose electrophoresis gel used in DNA separation techniques.

Police recovered DNA from the brick and checked it against the national database. No match came up because the perpetrator, Craig Harman, had no police record.

People who are related have similar DNA, however, so using a new familial search, 25 people were located. A relative of Harman's was the closest match. Police took his DNA and it was a perfect match. Harman pleaded guilty to manslaughter, becoming the first person in the world to be convicted through familial searching.

NDNAD RESULT

Three 16-year-old girls were murdered in South Wales in 1973, and experts in the Forensic Science Service solved the case nearly 30 years later. Sandra Newton was killed in Briton Ferry and her best friends Pauline Floyd and Geraldine Hughes were murdered three months later in nearby Llandarcy. Investigators drew a blank when checking the suspect's DNA sample on the National DNA Database (NDNAD).

Forensic scientist Jonathan Whitaker, however, decided to check again for someone related to the killer, and this was the first time the NDNAD was used in this manner. This search produced a list of more than 100 men who might be related. Combined with other evidence, the DNA pointed towards a local man, Joseph Kappen, who had died. Family members agreed to give DNA samples and the strong result led to Kappen's body being exhumed in 2002. DNA tests on his remains were a match to samples from the victims.

A swab containing DNA sample evidence from a crime scene rests on top of the genetic testing results. The use of familial DNA testing has increased the number of successful results.

DESMOND APPLEBEE

The first completed case using DNA evidence in Australia was in 1989 in the Australian Capital Territory. Desmond Applebee was convicted of three charges of sexual assault after a blood test matched his DNA with that in blood and semen on briefs worn by his victim. Forensic scientists said the chance of a mismatch was one in 165 million. When this was revealed, Applebee changed his defence that he was not there to one saying the police were "not credible" and then claimed the woman had consented.

DNA DATABASE PRIVACY

The Austrian government has made privacy a hallmark of its DNA Intelligence Database, which was established in 1997 for the Ministry of the Interior in the Institute of Legal Medicine at the University of Innsbruck. When police send samples to the laboratory for testing in criminal and intelligence cases, they withhold personal information. Samples are sent in bar-coded tubes, and their personal data are kept by the Ministry. The barcode is the only link between the DNA profile and the personal information. Throughout the lab work, the sample is only known by its barcode, and the test results are posted to the Ministry through a high-security mailing system. Despite these protections, the database remains controversial.

DNA Evidence in Court

By 2006, DNA evidence had helped prosecute some 28,000 cases in US courts. It does, however, remain a mysterious science to most jury members.

Jury members depend on the forensic scientist as an expert witness to explain some of the process, but mostly they rely on the result of testing.

'Some jurors over-believe scientific evidence because they think "science cannot lie"', says the Australian forensic psychologist Jane Goodman-Delahunty, a world-renowned professor at the University of New South Wales in Sydney. 'All that DNA evidence does is establish a connection between a suspect or a defendant and the scene of the crime. That's very different to proving guilt.'

Forensic experts often work closely with the police on a case, and DNA testing helps them remain impartial in giving evidence. They cannot say DNA directly implies the guilt or innocence of a defendant, because that is left to the jurors or judges.

FALSE POSITIVES

Although the public assumes DNA evidence cannot be contested in court, clever lawyers know otherwise. Usually on the defence team and often backed by their own forensic expert, lawyers will try to prove the sample was contaminated and that a DNA result is open to other interpretations. More than one person's DNA may be on a sample and even if the DNA evidence links a suspect to the crime scene, that person may have been there when the crime was not committed.

Lawyers also know that a DNA database can contain errors giving 'false positives' that incorrectly identify an innocent person. Research shows that this happens from once every hundred times the data are checked, to once every thousand times.

CRIMTRAC

Court cases in Australia have been strengthened by the establishment in 2000 of the nation's A$50 million CrimTrac Agency, which facilitates the sharing of information among the various police departments. The following year, CrimTrac launched its National Criminal Investigation DNA Database (NCIDD) to allow the nine Australian jurisdictions to match DNA profiles. The system was also modified for disaster identification and used to identify victims after the Bali bombings in 2002 and 2005 (below).

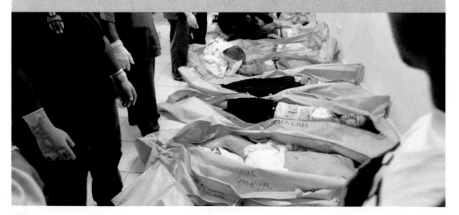

'DNA evidence establishes a connection between a suspect and the crime scene. That's very different from proving guilt.'

'THE CAT LADY'

The first use of DNA alone to convict a murder suspect in Australia was in August 1999. The veterinary surgeon 'Cat Lady' Kathleen Marshall was stabbed more than 50 times the year before. A well known palm reader, Andrew Fitzherbert, was found guilty, although he claimed he had never met the woman. However, forensic scientist Kenneth Cox told the jury that the chance of the crime-scene blood coming from anyone else was 14,000,000,000,000,000 to one. No motive or witnesses were produced in court.

A campaign to review the case is ongoing, with Fitzherbert's lawyer, Laura-Leigh Cameron-Dow, saying improvements in DNA analysis have since been made and 'DNA is not the Holy Grail. It's still a matter of interpretation.'

Scott Peterson was sentenced to death in 2005 after DNA identified bodies in San Francisco Bay as his wife and unborn son.

Maryland police are shown on television manoeuvring the vehicle of snipers John Allen Muhammad and Lee Malvo who killed 10 people in Washington, DC, in 2002.

Prisoners Freed by DNA

As well as convicting suspects, the science of DNA has also uncovered numerous miscarriages of justice, and allowed many innocent men and women to go free.

Because some innocent prisoners had been awaiting execution, the governor of Illinois, George Ryan, decreed a moratorium in his state in 2000, and then in 2003 commuted the sentences of all 156 death-row inmates to life imprisonment. 'Our capital system is haunted by the demon of error', he said. By 2007, nearly 200 inmates in the United States had been released by DNA results.

In a Canadian case in 1984, large samples of hair and fibre helped convict Guy Paul Morin in the killing of nine-year-old Christine Jessop in Queensville, Ontario. The jury convicted Morin after being told that a hair found on the victim could have come from Morin, fibres collected from her clothing and bag could have come from his home and car, and hairs discovered in Morin's car could have come from the victim. In 1995, however, DNA tests exonerated him, and a special inquiry noted in its 1400-page report that the jurors had been 'blinded by bad science'.

'Our capital system is haunted by the demon of error.'

After DNA results found innocent prisoners on death row, Illinois Governor George Ryan (facing camera) changed all death sentences to life.

AFTER INNOCENCE

The true story of prisoners exonerated by DNA evidence was the subject of the movie *After Innocence* that won the 2005 Special Jury Prize at the Sundance Film Festival. The documentary followed seven men and their emotional journeys back into society. It also featured Barry Scheck (pictured) and Peter Neufeld, founders of the Innocent Project, which has helped exonerate prisoners through DNA testing. The movie was described by *Variety* as "remarkable stories that highlight injustice, courage, and endurance."

In a court case beginning in 2007 in the United States, Steven Avery seemed likely to be the first prisoner convicted of murder by DNA who had been previously freed by DNA from another conviction. He had been behind bars for 17 years of a 35-year sentence for sexually assaulting and beating a woman in Manitowoc, Wisconsin. After DNA testing arrived, hairs at the crime scene were matched to another man in prison. Avery was exonerated in 2003 and two years later the Wisconsin legislature passed the Avery Bill to prevent wrongful convictions. On the same day, 31 October 31, Teresa Halbach went missing. Her remains were uncovered, and DNA bloodstains in her vehicle matched Avery's blood.

The Angola penitentiary is one of the world's largest with more than 5000 inmates and two death row units.

THE PRICE OF FREEDOM

In 2007 an American exonerated by a DNA test was awarded $3.9 million in Louisville, Kentucky. William Gregory, 59, had already collected $700,000 from the state to settle his claims against the state forensic examiner who had testified against him.

Gregory was convicted in 1993 of raping one woman and attempting to rape another. He spent seven years behind bars before being freed in 2000 after DNA tests on hair found at the crime scene showed he was innocent.

Lab-on-a-Chip

One of the latest advances in DNA testing is a miniaturized device known as a lab-on-a-chip. These portable micro laboratories can be used to speed up DNA tests by automatically analyzing samples.

The simple, low-cost portable instruments will make DNA analysis more widely available.

One version developed at the University of Michigan is a glass and silicon chip, which is far less expensive than conventional methods of analyzing DNA in a specialized lab, but just as sensitive. In contrast to lab equipment, it is virtually a hands-free instrument. All components are contained on a single chip that includes systems for measuring and mixing microscopic liquid samples of DNA with reagents, moving the mixtures to a temperature-controlled reaction chamber, separating the DNA molecules by size through gel electrophoresis, and determining the results with an on-board fluorescent detector.

Another lab-on-a-chip version was funded by the space agency NASA and developed at the California Institute of Technology. The device can be altered to perform rapid DNA tests, though it was primarily created to perform blood tests in space for astronauts, which had not been possible previously because of the large size of blood-analysis instruments.

Lab-on-a-chip technology is being taught in American and British universities. It will be an undergraduate subject at the new state-of-the-art forensics research centre at the University of Teesside, Middlesborough, and was a main topic of discussion when forensic experts from the UK and Europe attended a crime conference there on 8 June 2005 to mark the opening of the centre.

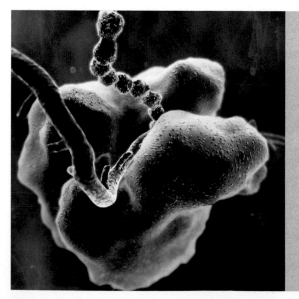

DNA BOOST

A new forensic technique piloted in 2006 by the UK's Forensic Science Service (FSS) could solve tens of thousands of 'cold cases', which have lain dormant in police files. The computer-based software-analysis system is expected to boost the FSS crime detection rates by more than 15 per cent and will continue to be used for new cases. Known as DNAboost, it enables investigators to work with a poor-quality sample of DNA, or one that lacks the necessary quantity. It also allows investigators to work with DNA with a mixed profile, which is a sample that has more than one person's DNA on it. Previously, forensic experts had been unable to split the profiles of mixed-profile DNA.

In contrast to most laboratory work, lab-on-a-chip DNA tests can be done on a single silicon chip.

DNA AND THE CRIME NOVELIST

Some 3000 specialists from around the world who deal with DNA attend training programmes each year at a private institute, which was the brainchild of bestselling crime novelist Patricia Cornwell. Having first worked in Virginia's crime lab for years, she donated $1.5 million, matched by state funds, to start the Virginia Institute of Forensic Science and Medicine in 1999 near Richmond. It is a private nonprofit institute, where about 800 people have completed continuing-education seminars since its doors opened. Annual fellowships of $23,000 are offered to some students to enable them to study for up to 50 hours a week.

A scanning electron micrograph shows part of a microfluidic microchip used for DNA analyses.

Novelist Patricia Cornwell worked for four years in the medical examiner's office in Virginia.

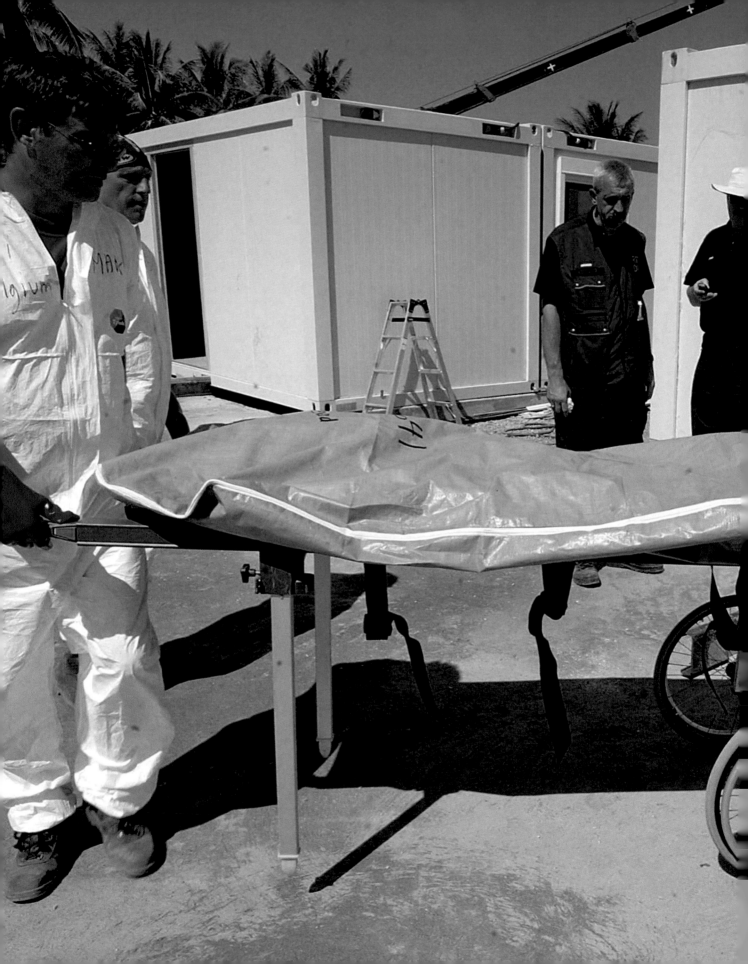

Chapter Six

Identifying a Body

A CORPSE IS OFTEN ANONYMOUS, FOUND WITHOUT ANY CREDIT CARDS, DRIVING LICENCE OR OTHER MEANS OF IMMEDIATE IDENTIFICATION. In major tragedies, such as natural disasters, air crashes or terrorist bombings, the victims will be separated from their personal and travel documents. If nobody comes forth to enquire about the missing or to identify the remains, the case becomes a forensic puzzle.

DNA has become the standard test for identification, but investigators still struggle when confronted with near total destruction. The terrorist attacks on the World Trade Center on 11 September 2001 led to the recovery of almost 20,000 body parts. The identification task came to an end in February 2005, with 1585 of the total 2749 victims being identified. The families of the remaining 1,164 victims were told that DNA technology was not yet sufficient for more results. The DNA samples had been degraded, subjected to intense heat, water and bacteria.

Identities were also lost in the Southeast Asian tsunami of 2004, which killed more than 200,000 people. Although DNA samples were taken soon after the deaths, the same DNA degradation meant only five per cent were identified this way. Instead, dental records and fingerprint examinations were relied upon. By contrast, when hurricane Katrina hit the US in 2005, the majority of the approximately 1500 victims were identified by DNA and other forensic methods, as well as by personal effects.

A forensic scientist uses calipers to measure a skull. This can be used for a facial reconstruction to help identification.

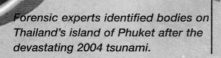

Forensic experts identified bodies on Thailand's island of Phuket after the devastating 2004 tsunami.

New York Port Authority Officer Tony Basic examines evidence on 29 April 2002 from the World Trade Center terrorist attack of 11 September 2001.

97

Identifying Crime Victims

Most homicide victims are easily identified, being killed at home or nearby by someone close to them. Other victims are known before they die, such as a child who has been abducted.

Yet it is not uncommon for authorities to be baffled by the unknown remains of a victim. The process of identification can take anywhere from days to years, and, ultimately, some bodies are never given a name.

Forensic identity searches rely on several sources, often in combination. They include DNA, dental records, fingerprints, personal effects such as jewellery and clothing, tattoos, birthmarks and scars, as well as the person's age and race. The description is soon given to the news media, normally along with an artist's sketch of the deceased. In skeletal remains, a forensic sculptor may do a facial reconstruction in clay.

REMOVING SIGNS

Visual clues are not always possible to re-create. If the remains are old, have been disturbed by animals or decomposed by the weather, it can cloud the identification process.

Criminals often attempt to remove signs of identification by using fire, quicklime or acid. In extreme cases, they may mutilate or dismember the body, cutting off the victim's fingers, hands or even the head.

In rare cases, a living victim may be unidentified. Examples involve infants and very young children, victims in a coma or suffering memory loss, and even crime victims who want to remain anonymous.

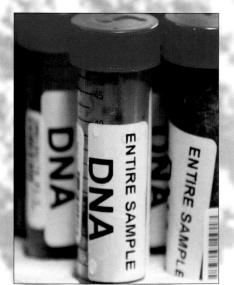

Vials with DNA samples provided by relatives of the 9/11 victims are stored in the New York City morgue.

WHEN VIEWING FAILS

Matters seem certain when relatives or friends view a body for identification purposes, but this is sometimes unreliable. The body may be burnt or disfigured. Or, the person identifying can be emotionally upset, too squeamish to take a proper view or may not have seen the victim for years. In some cases, the viewer may give a false identification to cover a crime or gain an inheritance.

Murders have even been committed in order to falsely identify the body. In a US case, Joseph Kalady, facing trial for producing fraudulent documents, killed William White in 2001. Kalady's brother, Michael, falsely identified the body as Kalady's. Investigators, however, identified White through fingerprints, and Kalady was charged with murder, dying in prison in 2003 before the trial.

IDENTIFYING WAR VICTIMS

A team of international forensic experts went to Kosovo for six months in 2002 to identify the remains of victims from the 1999 conflict in which at least 10,000 people are estimated to have been killed or gone missing. The experts included some 80 pathologists, anthropologists, mortuary technicians, liaison officers, and information technology experts from Australia, Canada, Costa Rica, Denmark, Italy, Malaysia, Poland, South Africa, Sri Lanka, and the United States.

The examinations were carried out at about 100 burial sites on more than 1,250 remains, with the team performing exhumations, autopsies, and identifications before returning the bodies to family members. The project was headed by British Professor Peter Vanezls, director general of the Center for International Forensic Assistance (CIFA) that provides forensic expertise as an instrument for truth and justice.

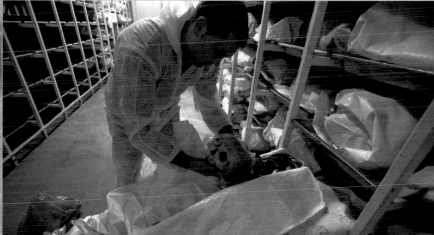

A forensic anthropologist examines remains in Bosnia-Herzegovina for the International Commission on Missing Persons.

In rare cases, even a living victim may remain unidentified.

A birthmark, such as this 'strawberry' mark, can be an invaluable aid in identifying victims.

Cases of Victim Identification

Investigators will often follow up what appears to be a successful identification with other supporting tests. This happened in the brutal murder of the former British Airways stewardess, Lucie Blackman, in 2001 in Tokyo.

The remains of the 22-year-old woman were unearthed in a cave on a beach southwest of the city. The corpse was cut into eight parts and the head encased in concrete.

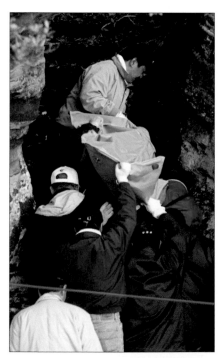

Police officers remove the remains of Lucie Blackman from a cave in Misaki City, Japan on 9 February 2001. After she was identified, the wealthy property developer Joji Obara was charged with her death.

Her dental records first identified Lucie. To confirm the identity, Tokyo police then matched her fingerprints and took DNA tests. Joji Obara, a businessman she knew who lived near the crime scene, was arrested, but was found not guilty of Lucie's murder. He was, however, sentenced to life imprisonment for other crimes.

THAMES TORSO

In one unusual case, the headless and limbless torso of a boy of about five years of age was found in the River Thames near Tower Bridge in London. Police named him Adam.

A DNA analysis was made of Adam's bones, because these would reflect his diet in geological terms. Nigeria

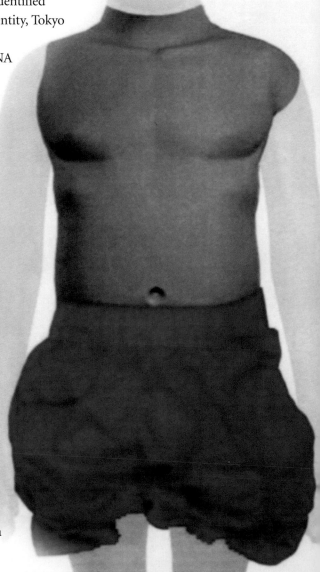

was indicated, and the forensic team spent two and a half weeks there collecting soil, rock and bone samples. They matched Adam to an area between Benin City and Ibadan in the country's southwest.

Evidence that the boy's blood had been drained and his first vertebra removed led a South African pathologist, Professor Hendrik Scholtz, to suspect a traditional African ritual slaying. Pollen in the boy's stomach showed he had been alive when he came to London, and police are seeking a criminal network involved in people trafficking.

Pollen in the dead boy's stomach showed that he had been alive when he came to London.

The Metropolitan Police released this computer image of the torso of 'Adam' found in 2001.

ADOLF HITLER

Germany's Nazi leader Adolf Hitler was hardly a victim, but the identification of his remains following his suicide in 1945 has long been a mystery. Russian troops recovered his body that had been burned by aides, but the Soviet regime kept this secret.

Finally in 1995 retired Soviet intelligence officers revealed that his dentist had identified Hitler's body. 'At the beginning he was a bit shocked, unable to speak', said General Leonid Siomonchuk, who was there. 'Then he said, "Hitler is dead".'

ANASTASIA

Bones found in 1991 in a grave in Russia were identified two years later as the remains of Tsar Nicholas II, the Tsarina, and three of their five children, all of whom were killed in 1918 by a Red Guard firing squad. Testing the DNA of Prince Philip, the Duke of

Tsar Nicholas II is shown in 1913 with his family (left to right), Olga, Marie, Tsarina Alexandra, Anastasia, Alexei and Tatiana.

Edinburgh, who is a grand nephew of the Tsarina, proved their identities. The discovery also refuted once and for all the claim of a US immigrant, Anna Anderson Manahan. For more than 30 years until her death in 1984, she claimed to be the Tsar's youngest daughter, Anastasia, asserting she had escaped the firing squad.

Fingerprints of Victims

Matching an unknown victim's fingerprints is difficult when the deceased person's prints are not on an official file. However, relatives can bring personal objects which might bear the victim's prints.

Difficulties often exist in fingerprinting the dead because of deterioration of the skin. Testifying in 2004 at a court case concerning a 1976 murder, retired FBI agent John Munis said the body had decomposed, causing the hands to shrivel and the fingers to close. A pathologist had to remove the hands and they were shipped in individual containers to the FBI laboratory, which secured prints and identification.

Technology now allows identity searches to be done from a crime scene. The Garda, the Irish Republic's police force, has a new Fingerprint Mobile Laboratory Vehicle for scanning prints at the crime scene. These are sent back by telephone lines to the Technical Bureau for instant processing.

While massive databases exist of criminal fingerprints, other sources must be explored to identify ordinary victims. Fingerprints, for instance, are taken and filed by the military and some employers; they also exist on biometric cards used for security access. Non-criminal databases are rapidly increasing for security reasons. The US already tracks foreign visitors by using electronically scanned fingerprints, and all new European passports will include two fingerprints from early 2008.

The US already tracks foreign visitors by using electronically scanned fingerprints.

THE BLACK DAHLIA

One of Hollywood's most gruesome murders came to light on 15 January 1947 when the body of a nude young woman was discovered in Los Angeles. She had been cut in half and undergone other mutilations. Detectives had no idea who she was. They took fingerprints and gave them to the Los Angeles Examiner, which enlarged and sent them to the FBI in Washington, DC. Their database then had 104 million prints on file, mostly criminals. This time they were lucky, matching them to Elizabeth Short, 22, who had been fingerprinted twice: for a job at a California army base, and for her arrest for underage drinking. Friends had nicknamed her 'Black Dahlia' for doing her black hair in a flower-like style and for wearing black garments.

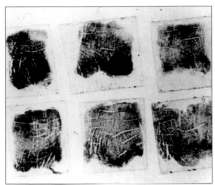

These fingerprints from the corpse of the 'Black Dahlia' identified her as Elizabeth Short.

LIVESCAN FOR THE DEAD

In 2006, the University of Leicester, working with the Leicester Constabulary and the Institute of Legal Medicine at the University of Hamburg, demonstrated the first use of an electronic hand-held device to recover fingerprints from the dead. It was developed from the larger Livescan computer device that takes prints from fingers pressed against a coated glass platform.

The Home Office introduced Livescan itself to all police forces in 2007. The state of California has not accepted inked fingerprint cards since 2005, only Livescan images.

A US official checks fingerprints of a tourist crossing from Canada to Niagara Falls, New York.

Identifying Tsunami Victims

The world's largest disaster victim identification programme occurred after the 2004 tsunami struck Southeast Asia. Interpol and 20 national police forces came together on the island of Phuket, Thailand, to examine forensic data.

From 2005 to 2006, nearly 2000 personnel from 31 nations were involved with help from labs in the UK, Sweden, China and Bosnia. By 2006, nearly 3000 of 3750 unidentified victims had been named using fingerprints, dental records and DNA samples. DNA was able to identify only 800 of the victims because the extreme heat had decomposed their corpses.

The forensic experts developed a way of recovering fingerprints from corpses. Fingers were removed and placed in boiling water to make the rigid skin pliable. Corporal Wayne Oakes of the Royal Canadian Mounted Police explained: 'It re-hydrates the digits and enables the technician to then, in most cases, get a print that can possibly result in identification.'

For comparisons, fingerprint records from the various countries came from criminal databases, national ID cards, or homes of any victim who was unidentified. 'The sort of thing we are looking for', said Interpol fingerprint specialist Mark Branchflower, 'is a glass of water that somebody had the night before they went on holiday, which they left beside their bed.'

FBI DISASTER SQUAD

The FBI Disaster Squad was formed in 1940 to recover and identify victims of disasters. Its 49 members are highly trained forensic examiners from the FBI Laboratory, and each trains for nearly two years in fingerprint science.

By 2006, they had assisted in 230 disasters involving 10,687 victims and had identified 6809 victims by fingerprints, palm prints, or footprints. (These totals do not include their work on the 9/II attacks in 2001 and the tsunami of 2004.)

One of their largest challenges was Hurricane Katrina in 2005. In the two months following, the Disaster Squad had identified 155 bodies through fingerprints, aided by the Fly Away Identification Team of the US Criminal Justice Information Services and by the Louisiana State Police. The Disaster Squad also analyzes latent fingerprints submitted by law enforcement agencies across the US, and trains federal, state and local partners how to collect latent prints.

Fingers were placed in boiling water to make the rigid skin pliable, so that prints could be taken.

Forensic officials working in Thailand scan a fingerprint of a victim of the 2004 tsunami.

INTERPOL'S FINGERPRINT GUIDE

Interpol's Disaster Victim Identification guide notes that no international standards or agreements currently exist for the identification of disaster victims, and this can create doubts between countries concerning methods used. It advises that it may be more expedient in disasters to file and compare fingerprints by sex, race and age. The fingerprint expert, it adds, should keep a consecutive list of fingerprints by date, time, and reference number, also including comments.

A coroner's team remove a body for identification in New Orleans, Louisiana in the aftermath of Hurricane Katrina in 2005.

105

Dental Identification

Dental records are extremely valuable in establishing an unknown identity. Teeth are especially hard and almost indestructible, remaining after burial in earth and water for years and even surviving fire.

The impressions of each individual's teeth are different, due to chips, fillings, misalignments, and missing teeth.

Dentists routinely make notes about the surfaces of each patient's 32 adult teeth. A comparison with dental records, which most people

Dental X-rays scanned and stored on computers speed up comparisons to identify bodies.

A comparison with dental record remains the primary means of identification when obtaining fingerprints is not possible.

have, still remains the primary means of identification when obtaining fingerprints is not possible. DNA technology, in contrast, is expensive and often obtaining results takes weeks or months. Dental records are also much cheaper to enter onto a database.

In identifying crime victims, a total and accurate dental examination should be made, including X-rays of the teeth and jaws, which can now be done at the crime scene using a portable instrument. Forensic odontologists can compare several areas with dental records, including the number of teeth, cavities and filings, bridges, restoration, spacing and special details, such as an overbite or overlap of teeth. As well, the materials and methods used in dental work can indicate the country where the treatment was administered.

DENTAL IDENTIFICATIONS IN HISTORY

The unique marks of teeth have been used throughout history: The Roman emperor Nero identified his mother Agrippina, whom he had murdered in 59 CE, by her teeth. William the Conqueror used to bite the wax seals on his letters with his crooked teeth to verify they were from him. The first formally reported case of dental identification was for John Talbot, the Earl of Shrewsbury, who fell at the battle of Castillon in France, in 1453.

Sir John Talbot died on 17 July 1453 at the Battle of Castillon during the Hundred Years' War.

The American patriot Paul Revere was able to identify his friend Dr Joseph Warren 10 months after he was buried, a victim of the 1775 Battle of Bunker Hill, in Massachusetts. This was an easy identification, because Revere had fashioned dentures for Warren. In 1865, a dental identification was made of John Wilkes Booth, the assassin of President Abraham Lincoln.

The first disaster victims to be identified by their teeth were killed in a fire in 1849 at the Vienna Opera House. Dental records were also used to establish identity after 126 rich Parisians were killed in 1897 in a charity bazaar fire.

PROBLEMS OF DENTAL IDENTIFICATIONS

Despite the hardiness of teeth and the prevalence of dental records, problems may be encountered with this type of identification. In some cases, investigators encounter partial or no dental records, or may fail to recover all teeth and their restorations. Even the improvement of dental health, thanks to the increasing use of fluoridation, works against identification because it means people generally have fewer cavities and restorations. In addition, laws also exist in some countries, such as the US, to protect medical records and therefore may slow an investigation slightly.

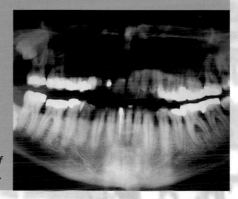

Dental fillings help identifications. The white areas in the teeth of this 45-year-old man show teeth with fillings.

Dental Identification Cases

Forensic dentists provide the key to identifying bodies that have virtually been destroyed by time or violence. An example of the former was the discovery in May 2002 of the skeletal remains of Chandra Levy in a park in Washington, DC.

A policeman closes off the area where the skeletal remains of Chandra Levy were found.

She had been dead just over a year, so the remains had to be identified through dental records provided by her family. She was a former US government intern whose affair with California Representative Gary Condit ruined his career. The murder case remains unsolved.

Terrorist bombs invariably require dental or DNA identification. The explosions on London's underground and a bus on 7 July, 2005, created special identification problems because many of the bodies were jumbled together and badly damaged. Forensic experts took weeks to identify those killed.

Extra efforts also are made when foreigners die and dental records must be obtained from their country. This happened in Naples, Italy, on 26 May 2006, when the body of a man with a kitchen knife in his abdomen was found in a storm drain below a manhole. His body was greatly decomposed, but three days later dental records had identified him as Lewis Brooks Miskell, a Canadian diplomat based in Vienna, Austria, who had disappeared in early March at the start of an Italian holiday. The killing remains a mystery.

HELENA RANTA

Finland's Helena Ranta is, at the age of 61, one of the world's most renowned forensic dentists. Working in the Department of Forensic Medicine at the University of Helsinki, she was involved in identifying Russia's murdered Tssar Nicholas II and his family, looking for victims of Saddam Hussein, identifying victims of the tsunami in Southeast Asia and testifying at the trial of the former Serbian president, Slobodan Milosevic.
During her work identifying bodies in Bosnia-Herzegovina, she had to dodge snipers' bullets, and once ordered US forces to use their tanks to protect her working group. Nothing has deterred her important occupation, including death threats to cancel a trip to the Balkans. 'I sleep well at night', she said. 'If there are threats, there are arrangements for dealing with them.'

TOOTH PRINTS FOR CHILDREN

Tooth printing for children has been adopted in several US states as a means of identification in case a child is abducted. It is part of a Child Identification Program (CHIP) that includes DNA and fingerprints. Because many children have no cavities or dental work, Dr David Tesini of Natick, Massachusetts, developed a system using thermal plastic wafers. It is warmed until pliable, a child bites on to the wafer to leave his or her tooth prints. Once the wafer hardens, the record is preserved. The state of Massachusetts, alone, has had more than 1500 dentists volunteer their time for the programme, and 37 school systems in the state participate.

Actress Jamie Lee Curtis announced a child ID programme in 2001.

Skin Marks

Some of the most distinctive marks of identification are found on the skin. Birthmarks, scars, and tattoos are easy to recognize, such as the red birthmark on the forehead of the former Russian president, Mikhail Gorbachev.

Such marks have been important indicators throughout history. King Harold's body was identified after the battle of Hastings by a tattoo over his heart, reading 'Edith and England'.

TATTOOS

Tattoos, in fact, have now become acceptable body decorations, such as those worn by celebrities like David Beckham. Their permanence and their prevalence among criminals has proved to be a blessing to police. Especially helpful are the chosen names or slogans, as used by gang members. When identifying corpses, investigators try to match the tattoos to the known work of tattoo artists. Sometimes pigments from the skin are even extracted and analyzed to trace the source. Another recent trend, piercing the ears, nose, eyebrows, and other body parts, is also a strong indicator for identification.

'SCARFACE'

Forensic investigators also look for scars acquired from operations, plastic surgery or fights. The gangster Al Capone was nicknamed 'Scarface' after his cheek was cut with a knife during a dispute in his early days. Birthmarks have fine identifying characteristics because they have irregular shapes, and skin blemishes like moles have been used to identify bodies.

NATASCHA KAMPUSCH

A pale and distressed 18-year-old girl ran to an elderly man on 23 August 2006 in Vienna, Austria, saying she had escaped after being kidnapped and held captive. Her name, she said, was Natascha Kampusch. This was verified by her family who identified her by a scar on her upper arm that went back to an operation she had as a child. The identity resolved one of Austria's most famous criminal mysteries. Hours after her escape, the man who had snatched her from a Vienna street and held her for eight years, committed suicide by throwing himself in front of a train.

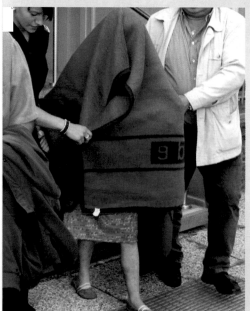

Covered by a blanket, Natascha Kampusch is escorted by police on the day she escaped.

King Harold's body was identified after the battle of Hastings by a tattoo over his heart, reading 'Edith and England'.

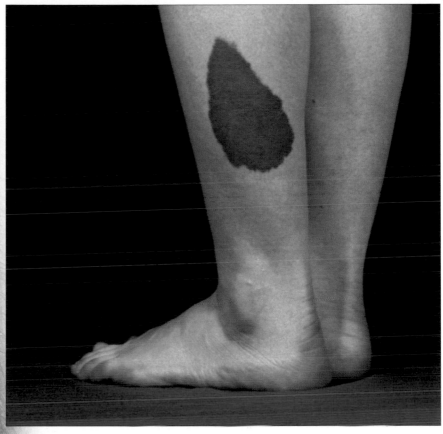

Birthmarks have led to numerous identifications, such as this large pigmented one on a young woman's calf. These will occur in different forms, with some composed of small blood vessels, including the strawberry mark, and some being like a port-wine stain.

Scars like this one on the forearm of a male patient are excellent identification marks.

THE SHARK ARM CASE

A tiger shark caught by fishermen was an attraction in Coogee, Australia, on 25 April 1935 at the nation's annual Anzac Day celebration. Fun became fear, however, when the animal suddenly thrashed about and coughed up a tattooed human arm. Searches for the rest of the body all failed. The fingerprints were found to be those of James Smith, a construction worker, and his wife identified his arm from the tattoo showing two sparring boxers.

After this identification, the renowned English forensic pathologist Sir Sydney Smith examined the arm and said it had been cut off rather than bitten off by the shark. This indicated murder, because Smith had been involved in the drugs trade. A key witness was subsequently murdered, and an inquest was abandoned due to an old law that said a body was necessary and 'a limb does not constitute a body'.

Indications Within the Body

Clues to identification are sometimes hidden inside a corpse. The victim may have had a disease, accident, or operation, and these signs are normally discovered in an X-ray or during an autopsy.

The evidence of diseases such as tuberculosis, AIDS and cancer has identified bodies. Bones damaged by disease are good indicators, with identifications made from osteoporosis, the progressive myeloma, and childhood deformities like scoliosis and rickets.

Among the easiest clues to identity are artificial implants, such as pacemakers, heart valves, defibrillators and artificial hips. These all bear engraved serial numbers, which can be traced back to a hospital where the operation took place. In 2004, in Florida, the body of a 35-year-old female investment banker was found under the house of an unlicenced cosmetic surgeon encased in cement in a suitcase. She was identified by the serial numbers on her breast implants. In another Florida case in 2007, a prosthesis metal rod in one leg identified a 73-year-old man.

This X-ray, revealing metal pins supporting a fracture of an arm, could lead to an identification.

Artificial implants, such as pacemakers and defibrillators, bear engraved serial numbers, which can be traced.

NEFERTITI

A mummy unearthed in 2003 in Luxor's Valley of the Kings, in Egypt, may be the Egyptian queen, Nefertiti. The team, led by Dr Joann Fletcher, a specialist from the University of York, took X-rays that showed a female pelvis and the disease of lumbar scoliosis. The joints were fused, showing it was an adult. Dr Fletcher said the complete X-rays should establish any diseases, injuries and even the cause of death.

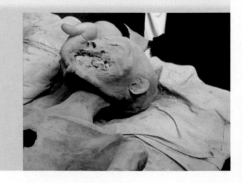

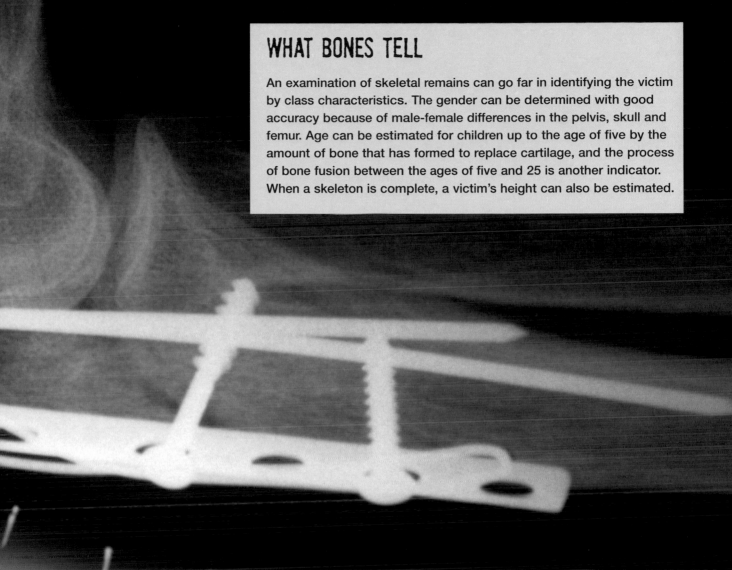

WHAT BONES TELL

An examination of skeletal remains can go far in identifying the victim by class characteristics. The gender can be determined with good accuracy because of male-female differences in the pelvis, skull and femur. Age can be estimated for children up to the age of five by the amount of bone that has formed to replace cartilage, and the process of bone fusion between the ages of five and 25 is another indicator. When a skeleton is complete, a victim's height can also be estimated.

IDENTIFICATIONS IN HISTORY

Injuries have led to identifications throughout history. When the Scottish missionary and explorer David Livingstone died in 1873, his body was embalmed in what is now Zambia, and taken on a 1600-kilometre (1000-mile) journey to the African coast. Back in England, a broken bone in his shoulder, caused by an encounter with a lion, positively identified him.

Modern instruments can also peer into the past. When the French queen, Marie Antoinette, was executed, her son Louis Charles was kept in prison until he died of tuberculosis in 1795. Several people later claimed to be Louis. The heart of the imprisoned man had been preserved, and mtDNA tests were conducted in 2000. The result was matched to a lock of Marie Antoinette's hair, proving he was her son.

Facial Reconstruction

When only a skull is recovered from a nameless crime victim, forensic sculptors may be called in to reconstruct the face in modelling clay, a highly skilled procedure.

The likeness of a living person is difficult to recreate, but the skull gives an indication of the form and contours needed. The 'American model', devised in the US, uses knowledge of the tissue depth that covers the various bony landmarks of a skull. There are from 20 to 35 tissue depths to contend with around the face, and the forensic artist has known measurements for gender, different ages and ethnic groups.

The process begins with small wooden depth pegs, often cocktail sticks, fixed to the skull or a cast at the different tissue depths. Strips of clay 'muscles' are applied, with their thickness measured to the height of the pegs. The sculptor then fills the gaps between the strips, smoothes out the clay, removes the pegs and begins modelling the nose (the most difficult because of the lack of bone), eyes, mouth, ears, chin and jowls. Prosthetic eyeballs are placed into the eye sockets to increase the realism of the look.

The artist must make several guesses, including the plumpness of the face, hairstyle, structure of the eyelids and facial expressions. As well, there may be only just a portion of recovered skull, the shape of which must be filled in.

A forensic sculptor carefully works on a model of a dead person's head. Such models can be used to construct a likeness of a person from their remains, aiding in the identification process.

COMPUTER FACIAL RECONSTRUCTION

Digital reconstruction is the latest tool in identifying crime victims. A scan is taken of the skull as it rotates on a turntable, and the computer programme creates a digital skull that can be manipulated on the screen. The technician then selects a computer tomography (CT) 3D scan of a real person estimated to be the same race and about the same age. As this scan is digitally merged with the one of the skull, it adjusts to correspond and moves its facial tissue into a shape that resembles the victim. The hair and eyes are estimated and added to provide a life-like image. Computer reconstruction has the value of giving a view from any angle, but retains the limitations of clay reconstruction.

The Unit of Forensic Art, opened in 2005 at the University of Dundee, has a groundbreaking program that allows the user to 'feel' the surface of the reconstructed face on the screen.

The skull gives an indication of the form and contours needed to recreate the likeness of the living person.

A modelling tool is used by a sculptor to recreate the muscles of a skull's face.

A human skull reassembled with wax. Forensic experts rebuild skulls to enable facial reconstructions when there are no other means of identifying the remains.

SUPERIMPOSITION

The technique of photo superimposition can be used alongside, or instead of, facial reconstruction. This is helpful when a missing person might be matched to skeletal remains. It involves photographing the skull onto transparent film, and then superimposing this image over a photo of the individual. Matches can be seen in the teeth and key bony features, such as the supraorbital ridges above the eyes. Today's computer techniques have made the process much easier to manipulate.

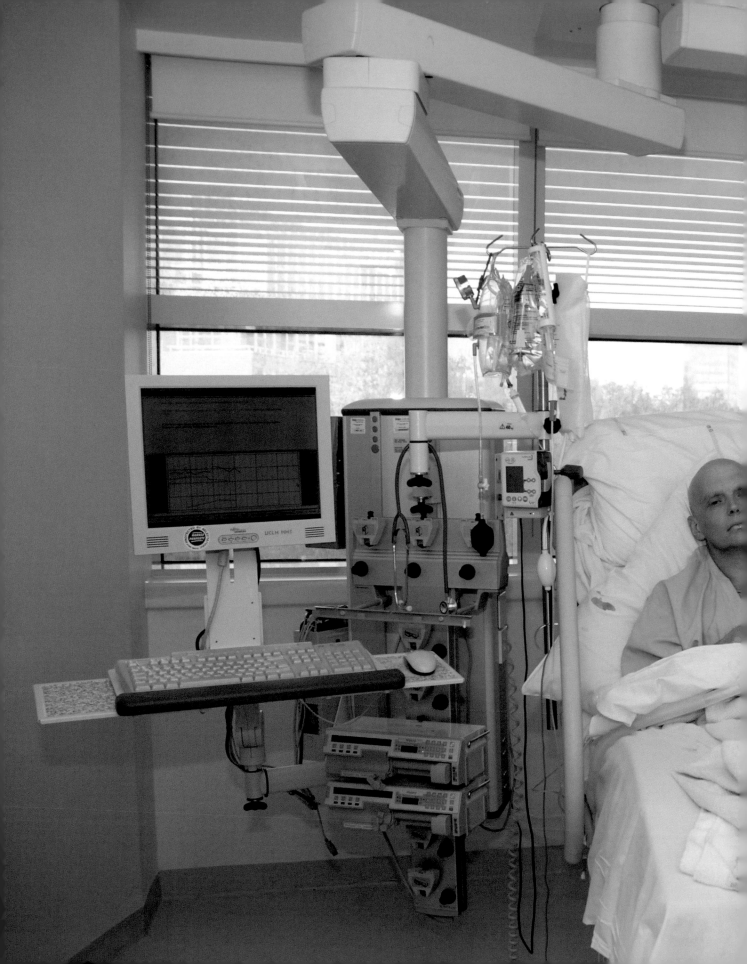

Chapter Seven

Cause of Death

Homicide, suicide, accident, natural causes. Only the first creates a crime scene and, if possible, forensic investigators must quickly decide the cause of death.

A violent assault will be obvious, but many cases will not be that simple. It is the coroner in England and Wales, however, who must officially decide the manner of death, including if a crime has been committed. This is based on the evidence of the pathologist, who will normally give an opinion on whether the scene indicates a homicide.

Officers remove 39 bodies after the mass suicide in 1997 of members of the Heaven's Gate cult near San Diego, California. They left a video describing their plan.

A forensic exam may find that a skull fracture was the cause of death, but the coroner must declare the manner of death, such as an assault with a hammer, which would give the police a homicide case. These decisions are made easier by related forensic evidence, such as a weapon, blood splatters or a forced entrance.

Has an apparent suicide been staged by a murderer? Was a fatal drug overdose an accident or administered by another? Was a fire death caused by arson? Pathologists help answer questions like these after investigating the body and scene, or they may require laboratory work like DNA or toxicology tests. Often it may take an autopsy, a postmortem examination, to reveal the truth. The latter is ordered by a coroner in England and Wales and by the procurator fiscal in Scotland.

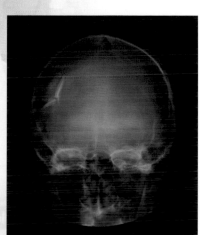

When Alexander Litvinenko was fatally poisoned by polonium in London in 2006, doctors first thought the cause might never be known.

A coloured X-ray shows a skull fracture as red in the upper left-hand side. A forensic scientist would say the cause is due to a high-energy impact from a blunt object.

Two Pathology Cases

On May 1, 1999, the Nigerian asylum-seeker Marcus Omofuma died after three Austrian policemen bound and gagged him during a flight from Austria to Sofia, Bulgaria where he was to fly to Nigeria.

At the policemen's trial, three forensic pathologists gave their opinion on the cause of death. The Bulgarian forensic pathologist, Stojcho Radanov, said the taping of Omofuma's mouth and binding of his thorax caused his death. The Viennese forensic pathologist Christian Reiter decided a heart weakness caused it. The German forensic pathologist Bernd Brinkmann said it was asphyxiation. The policeman were first suspended but argued that gagging was a normal practice, and Omofuma had been aggressive in resisting his deportation. They were each sentenced to eight months' probation for involuntary manslaughter.

THE PATHOLOGIST IN COURT

The forensic pathologist, like all scientific experts, is normally giving evidence for the prosecution on a cause of death. In the public's eye, this tends to look like science being used to secure a conviction, and the pathologist has been unfairly called 'a policeman in a white coat'.
In fact, the scientist is considered by the court system to be impartial, and this is normally accomplished. The cause of death is given, and the judge or jury must decide if the facts are true. The forensic expert uses simple descriptions for complicated matters, and he or she informs the court on its scientific limitations, so its members will not jump to conclusions.

US pathologist Dr Ira Kanfer points out injuries in a 2002 Connecticut trial.

WRONGLY CONVICTED

Pathologists have also freed prisoners who were incorrectly convicted. Patrick Nicholls was sentenced to life in 1975 for murdering 74-year-old Mrs Gladys Heath, a family friend, that same year at her home in Worthing. Nicholls claimed he had found the body at the bottom of the stairs, but two pathologists concluded that she had died of a heart attack after being suffocated, and then severely beaten about the face.

After Nicholls had served 23 years in jail, Professor John Crane, a pathologist in the Irish Republic, reviewed his case. Crane said the victim's facial injuries were trivial and probably came from a fall caused by her heart attack. Nicholls' conviction was therefore quashed in 1998. 'They have stolen a third of my life, haven't they?' Nicholls said.

Patrick Nicholls stands outside the High Court building after winning his appeal in 1998.

Pathologists have also freed prisoners who were incorrectly convicted.

THE DEATH CERTIFICATE

The cause and manner of death are recorded by a medical practitioner on the death certificate, based on standards set by the World Health Organization. The certificate can be issued immediately if the death is natural, or it may have to wait for a postmortem examination if the cause is unknown or suspicious. If a body is to be cremated, a second medical exam is needed before a death certificate can be issued.

President John F. Kennedy's death certificate was signed by his personal physician Dr George Burkley on 22 November 1963.

The Postmortem

A postmortem examination is used to establish the cause of death. It will involve more than the opening of the body. A photographer will also be present to photograph the body laid out in the morgue.

A photographer will be present to photograph the body laid out in the morgue. The first photos will record the corpse in the clothing worn when found, and each time the pathologist removes a piece, another photo will be taken.

Before the dissection, the pathologist will measure and weigh the body and record the age, sex, race and hair and eye colours. The pathologist then will check the clothes for trace evidence, check for marks on the skin, collect a sample of hair and clip or scrape the fingernails. Swabs will be taken from the mouth, rectum and sexual organs. X-rays may also be taken, because these will reveal the size and shape of knife wounds and how, for example, bullets moved through the body.

Dissecting the body normally follows a set routine. An incision is made, organs like the heart and lungs removed and weighed, the abdomen examined and samples taken from the stomach. The skull is then opened to view the brain. Finally, the organs are returned to the body, which is closed with sutures and released to the family for burial.

CHRIS PENN

When the actor Chris Penn died unexpectedly in Santa Monica, California, on 24 January 2006, an immediate postmortem examination was unable to determine how he died. There were no obvious signs of foul play or suicide. However, the 40-year-old younger brother of actor Sean Penn had a history of drug abuse.
A Los Angeles coroner ordered a blood toxicology test. When this was added to the earlier autopsy, it was found that Penn had died of an enlarged heart and the effects of mixing several medications.

Chris Penn died the day before his film, The Darwin Awards, *premiered at the Sundance Film Festival.*

This autopsy room in a hospital morgue has scales used to weigh the major organs.

12

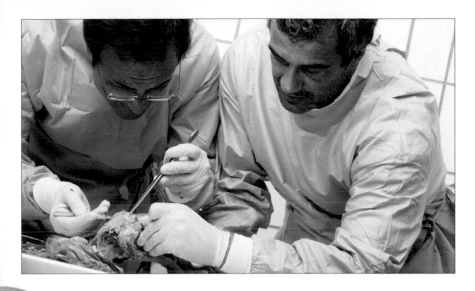

These forensic pathologists wear latex gloves to dissect the shoulder of a cadaver during an autopsy. Others present at the examination may include a police witness and an exhibits officer who examines materials on the body.

A MUSLIM AUTOPSY

Although Islam requires that a dead body be buried quickly without cutting or disturbing it, the Maldives' government approved that Muslim country's first autopsy in April 2007 after a request by the relatives of the deceased. This followed the death of Hussain Salah, a Maldivian opposition activist. His Maldivian Democratic Party accused prison authorities of beating him to death. A government spokesman said Salah had been released from prison from a narcotics charge, and his body was found floating in the sea. The government flew Salah's body to Sri Lanka for the autopsy. Dr. LBL De Alwis, the chief judicial medical officer of Sri Lanka, conducted the post-mortum examination and found that Salah drowned. He said minor injuries to the nose, face, and left leg could have been sustained in the water. "There were no major injuries to bones, soft tissue, or internal organs," he said, "and therefore death by physical violence is excluded."

Before the dissection, the pathologist will measure and weigh the body.

HT.
C.R.
H.C.
:.C.
A.C.
A[?]ENTA

Dissecting the Body

A dissection begins with an incision down the front of a cadaver, but the manner of the cutting will depend upon whether the death seems natural or suspicious.

• •

If natural, one simple incision is made from the larynx to the pubic region, and the organs will be removed for examination. If the deceased is a possible victim of crime, a cut in the shape of a T or Y is done to provide better access to the body cavity.

The ribs and clavicles are cut and the breastplate removed. Samples are taken of fluids like blood, bile and urine for analysis. All of these could reveal any drugs taken hours before the death.

A pathologist may remove the major organs together, such as the

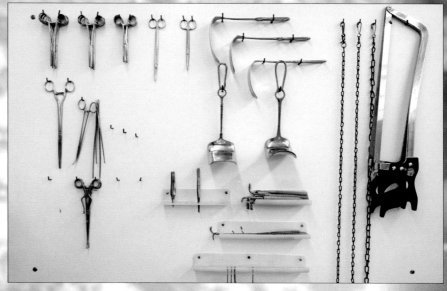

Autopsy instruments include the bone cutter and cranium chisel.

heart, lungs, trachea and oesophagus, but they are sometimes removed separately. The organs are weighed, and samples taken for microscopic examination. The contents of the stomach and intestine are inspected and samples also taken for toxicological tests.

Cutting the scalp and then sawing open the skull reveals the brain. The pathologist views the brain in place and then removes it for a closer examination. Thin slices of the brain tissue are removed to be examined microscopically.

Although the torso is normally dissected first, if there is evidence of the victim having been strangled, the pathologist will begin the autopsy with the head and neck.

TWO TYPES OF AUTOPSIES

If a death is presumed to be unknown or suspicious, a legal authority asks for a medico-legal autopsy, sometimes called a forensic autopsy. The unknown death will often have no foul play suspected. Only pathologists who are on the Home Office list can carry out this type of autopsy in England and Wales.

A clinical autopsy, also known as an academic or hospital autopsy, is performed to verify a cause of death that is usually known, such as cancer or a stroke. They are also used to judge the effectiveness of treatment, study the processes of a disease, and educate medical students and personnel. These autopsies cannot be performed without the consent of the next of kin of the deceased.

The hand of a woman is shown here during a postmortem examination. She had been dead for two days.

THE FIRST AUTOPSIES

Around 300 BCE, the Greek anatomist, Herophilus, was conducting dissections to teach human anatomy, and a century later the Greek physician Erasistratus of Ceos began using them in order to understand diseases. In the late 1400s, the Italian physician Antonio Benivieni published the first book concerning anatomical pathology, *Remarkable Hidden Causes of Disease*. In the eighteenth century, the French physician, Marie François Xavier Bichat, conducted more than 600 autopsies.

Sir William Osler, a Canadian physician, was a great promoter of the autopsy in the late nineteenth century. He wrote that investigating the causes of death in this manner to prevent and treat disease 'is one of the highest objects of the physician'.

If the deceased is a possible victim of crime, a cut in the shape of a T or Y is made to provide better access to the body cavity.

The French pathologist Marie-Francois Xavier Bichet (1771–1802) worked in a Paris hospital for the poor and founded modern histology, the study of tissues.

125

Trace Evidence

Although trace evidence is more associated with identifying a suspect, it is also of value in finding the cause of death. Both mysteries can be solved at the same time.

For example, a trace of arsenic in soup will confirm the cause of a victim's death and point to the spouse as the prime suspect. Other cases have identified the cause but not the criminal. When the former Russian spy, Alexander Litvinenko, died in London in 2006, pathologists found traces of polonium 210, a lethal radioactive substance, but police could only theorize over a Russian connection.

Traces of drugs near bodies are strong indicators of an overdose.

Autopsies also turn up traces within a body that will overturn the original conjecture of death. This occurred in a Florida case in 2005. In Wellington, a husband and father, aged in his late forties, died in his sleep apparently of a heart attack. An autopsy, however, found he had overdosed on a combination of cocaine and oxycodone.

Homicides can also be revealed by drug traces in the body. In 2006, Daniela Toledo do Prado brought her convulsive daughter, Vittoria, to

a hospital in Sâo Paulo, Brazil, saying she had drunk milk that had gone off. After the child died of heart failure the next day, doctors found a suspicious white powder on the girl's tongue. The mother said it was milk, but tests identified it as cocaine. Traces were later found in the baby's bottle, and the mother was charged with murder.

MARILYN MONROE'S AUTOPSY

Marilyn Monroe died on 4 August 1962, and her autopsy was conducted by Dr. Thomas Noguchi. Afterward, Coroner Theodore Curphey said she died from an overdose of barbiturates. Traces of the drug pentobarbital (sleeping pills) were discovered in her liver and chloral hydrate in her blood. He ruled her death a "probable suicide." Despite this, many still believe it was accidental and conspiracy theorists say it was murder.
The autopsy consisted of a Y-shaped incision. A sample of blood was taken, and the liver, kidney, stomach and contents, urine and intestine were saved for further toxicological study. Her brain was weighed at 1440 grams (50.79 ounces) and her heart was 300 grams (10.58 ounces).

This sketch was part of the Coroner's Autopsy Report on Marilyn Monroe's death. The report was featured in an exhibit about the star in the Hollywood Museum.

Craig Harvey, chief at the Los Angeles County Coroners Office, handles a body in the crypt. Some are stored for up to seven years.

HOW HAIR TRAVELS

Forensic research carried out in Australia reveals that hair found at a crime scene may not indicate a suspect, since it could have been transferred several times. Josephine Dachs investigated how hair clings to different fabrics while she worked in forensic services at the Australian Federal Police. The results were published in the journal *Forensic Science International*.

Dachs found that hair is easily passed on in a car, by contacting someone else, or even through washing clothes. For her research, she attached stray hairs to people who then went about their normal activities. A lot was in the first hour or so through movement, but several stayed put for some time.

Los Angeles County Coroner Dr Lakshmanan Sathyavagiswaran presents evidence during the 1995 O.J. Simpson murder trial.

Two Historic Cases

Was the Egyptian pharaoh Tutankhamun, who died about 1350 B.C.E., murdered? Ever since his tomb was excavated in 1922 by the British archeologist Howard Carter, scientists have tried to solve this question.

In 1968, a team from the University of Liverpool took skull radiographs of the mummy and discovered a piece of bone in the skull cavity. Professor R. G. Harrison, who led the investigation, said: 'This could mean that Tutankhamun died from a brain haemorrhage caused by a blow to his skull from a blunt instrument.'

By 2005, however, a team headed by Egyptian archaeologist Zahi Hawass took a 15-minute CT scan of the mummy that produced 1700 images. It revealed no evidence of a blow to the back of the head, only a hole apparently drilled by embalmers. A fracture on the left leg was scanned and the most likely cause of death was the result of gangrene.

NAPOLEON

Recent DNA tests have indicated that the French emperor, Napoleon Bonaparte, was murdered. He died on 5 May 1821 after being banished to the remote Atlantic island of St Helena. The original diagnosis had been death from stomach cancer.

The new scientific evidence was presented to the French senate in 2000 by a dozen French toxicologists, coroners, police

Napoleon Bonaparte (1769–1821) was defeated by Britain's Duke of Wellington at the battle of Waterloo in 1815 and exiled to St Helena.

Egyptian archaeologist Zahi Hawass examines a mummy, one of many that require identification.

forensic scientists and cancer specialists. His valet had kept a lock of the emperor's hair, and forensic tests by the FBI and other laboratories found arsenic levels hundreds of times higher than normal. They also revealed that the arsenic had been ingested over a period of four months.

ARSENIC POISONING?

The theory of death by cancer had been questioned previously, because Napoleon was fat when he died, and when his body was returned to Paris in 1840 for burial, it was perfectly preserved, a symptom of arsenic poisoning. Suspects include his British captors, led by the island's governor, Hudson Lowe, and Charles Tristan, marquis de Montholon, exiled with Napoleon, and aware the emperor had had an affair with his wife.

WHO ARE CORONERS?

Coroners in England and Wales are normally lawyers but doctors are chosen for some cases. A coroner is an independent judicial officer whose duty is to find out the medical cause of a death if it is unknown and to enquire into the cause when the death is sudden, unexpected or unnatural.

Los Angeles Deputy District Attorney Gregory A. Dohi (left) asks Jeffrey Gutstadt, medical examiner with the Los Angeles County Coroner's Office, to identify bullets at the 2003 murder trial of actor Robert Blake, who was found innocent.

UNKNOWN CAUSES

It is not always possible for a coroner or medical examiner to determine the cause of death. Most US states follow a reporting system similar to Michigan after an investigation fails to discover the cause. The examiner must write 'Based upon autopsy, toxicology, and a thorough investigation of the circumstances, a cause of death cannot be explained.' Unknown deaths are labelled as 'sudden death' when witnessed but unexplained, and 'found body' for unwitnessed and unexplained deaths.

Non-Criminal Deaths

The correct identification of a homicide is vital. If a criminal death is wrongly registered as a suicide or attributed to natural causes, the murderer is not punished and may strike again.

Conversely, if a non-criminal death is judged to be a homicide, much police time will be wasted. The latter happened in the parachute death of Stephen Hilder, with the police arresting two people and searching ten months for a murderer who did not exist.

A verdict of death by natural causes covers many situations: old age, fatal diseases and accidents that range from drug overdoses to traffic fatalities. An inquest will be held only if the death is unexpected or its cause unknown. Among the most difficult non-criminal deaths to analyze are suicides, so suspicions should always be present in a suicide investigation.

CAUSES OF DEATH

The causes of homicide deaths, such as a bullet in the head, can be straightforward, but in deaths by natural causes, it is generally more difficult to find the underlying manner of death. The cause may be a heart attack, but it could have been the result of any number of events, from jogging to robbery. Studies have found that physicians completing death certificates often put down coronary heart disease as a default cause when the specific cause cannot be determined. This is particularly true when elderly people die. Heart disease remains the most common official cause of death in the world's developed countries.

DEATH BY SELF-NEGLECT

When a lottery millionaire, Philip Alan Kitchen, aged 58, was found dead in 2002 at his home in Burnt Green, Worcestershire, an inquest turned in the unusual verdict of 'death from self-neglect', although he had died of bronchial pneumonia. The principal cause was spending long periods of time without moving.

Kitchen had won a £2 million jackpot three years earlier. The former master carpenter had a history of heavy drinking and had not eaten properly for six weeks before his death. Pathologist Paul Geddy said Kitchen had first-degree burns to his thighs and lower back that had turned to blisters due to spending several months immobile on his sofa.

Right: The British skydiver Stephen Hilder (upper left, in black) links with members of the Army Parachute Association during a dive in 2005. A week later he fell to his death. It was ruled an open verdict.

DISPUTING AN AUTOPSY

Family members almost never challenge the results of an autopsy, but this happened with the French postmortem examination of Henri Paul, who drove the car that crashed in 1997 in Paris killing Princess Diana, Dodi Al Fayed, and himself.

Mohammed Al Fayed, Dodi's father, disputed the French findings that the driver was drunk. He believes the crash was a homicide and alleged that the autopsy failed because blood samples could have been switched or taken from the wrong corpse. In 2006, French authorities responded, saying they had now verified the results by DNA tests.

A forensic pathologist analyzes a blood sample to determine if a death was from natural causes.

Suicide

Authorities often misdiagnose suicides or, being unsure, declare an open verdict. It is indeed difficult to determine if an overdose or motor fatality is a case of self-destruction.

Attempts are made by some families to conceal a suicide death, perhaps from religious reasons or because insurance policies would be jeopardized. Murderers, as well, have frequently tried to mask their crimes by faking a suicide, and a pathologist would need to look carefully to detect homicide in a drowning case if the victim bore no signs of violence because he was drugged beforehand.

SELF-INFLICTED

Despite such problems, more than 30,000 suicides are recorded each year in the US. About one-quarter of the suicides leave notes. Forensic pathologists can also be fairly certain when confronting traditional suicide methods. A death by inhaling carbon monoxide from the exhaust pipe of a car is a simple case if the body shows no sign of physical distress or a struggle. These cases are normally suicides, as are hangings, although a bruised body will arouse suspicions. Homicides represent a small percentage of poisoning deaths because of modern detection methods, so the vast majority are accidents or suicides. Self-inflicted gunshot deaths, which are the most common form of suicide in the US, can be detected by the position of the bullet hole and the bullet's angle of trajectory (see Sabow box).

The carbon monoxide in car exhaust fumes has been frequently used in suicides. Changing the shape of the exhaust pipe would make it more difficult to attach a hose.

JAMES SABOW

Family members and other physicians frequently dispute an official ruling of suicide. US Marine Colonel James Sabow was discovered dead in 1991 in his backyard at the El Toro, California, Marine Corps Air Station. A bullet fired from a shotgun had blown his head apart.

The coroner and three military investigations ruled he killed himself, but Sabow's brother, Dr David Sabow, believes he was murdered and in 2005 a San Diego gunshot-residue expert, Dr Bryan Burnett agreed. He said the blood-spatter patterns and a total absence of gunshot residue on the victim's hands showed he was murdered. As well, he noted, smears on Sabow's hand indicated it was moved twice after his death. The US press continues to debate the colonel's uncertain cause of death.

Despite many celebrity deaths being ruled non-criminal, conspiracy theories always abound.

Above: The wreckage of James Dean's Porsche belies the rumor that he was not travelling fast enough to be killed.

CELEBRITY DEATH CONSPIRACIES

Despite many celebrity deaths being ruled non-criminal, conspiracy theories always abound. Many believe that the suicide of Marilyn Monroe was a murder instigated to cover up her affairs with President John Kennedy and his brother Robert. The overdose suicide of Kurt Cobain, lead singer with Nirvana, is claimed by some to have actually been a murder with a shotgun and heroin overdose.

Theorists also contest deaths that have been ruled accidental by coroners. They say the damage found on the Porsche that took actor James Dean's life supposedly reveals that the speed the car was travelling at was not fast enough to kill him.

Fans grieve outside the building where singer Kurt Cobain died.

Italian Prosecutor Pietro Grasso shows photofits of mafia boss Bernardo Provenzano in 2005. He was captured a year later after more than four decades on the run and is now serving a life sentence.

Chapter Eight

The Criminal Trail

THE FOREMOST GOAL OF A FORENSIC INVESTIGATION IS TO IDENTIFY ONE OR MORE SUSPECTS WHO COMMITTED THE CRIME. THIS IS DONE USING PHYSICAL EVIDENCE THAT LINKS THE PERPETRATOR TO THE VICTIM AND/OR THE CRIME SCENE. This process may begin with a search for a face captured on a CCTV surveillance camera or an eyewitness description that is re-created by a forensic artist. A faceless crime, however, may rely entirely on trace evidence.

A scientist works with a computer which recognizes expressions to create a facial 'map'.

During a criminal investigation, nobody is ruled out as a suspect, even the person who reported the crime. Even such evidence as bloodstains, a suicide note or a confession that appears to be reliable must be questioned. In order to have any impact in the courtroom, the forensic expert's conclusions should be as certain as possible. A scientist can point out strong evidence leading to a suspect but cannot directly attribute guilt to anyone.

The laboratory expert has a great responsibility in drawing scientific conclusions that may incarcerate a person for life or, as in the US, lead to his or her execution. In identifying a suspect for the police and an impressionable jury, a forensic scientist should only state the facts and let the opposing lawyers argue their merits. After all, a homicide victim's hair on a suspect's coat may have been exchanged at their meeting months before the murder. Or the murder weapon owned by a suspect could have been stolen and used by another, the killer.

Closed-circuit television (CCTV) cameras, like this one mounted on a wall, act as deterrents and have helped solve many cases.

135

The Forensic Artist

In the world of modern technology, the sketchpad is not dead. Photofit composites and E-FIT computer programmes are now available to create a criminal's facial features.

After the 1995 bombing of the US Federal Building in Oklahoma City, which killed 168 people, an FBI forensic artist, Raymond Rozycki, met for two to three hours with a witness.

To create an accurate sketch, Rozycki showed the witness the FBI's facial catalogue. It contains photographs of faces broken down by the overall shape and separate characteristics, such as eyes, eyebrows, cheeks, chin, ear and hair. Each of the 25 categories has 16 different photographs. After the parts were selected and combined, Rozycki used further details from the witness to fine-tune the drawing. The witness described the man who rented the van that carried the bomb. The resulting sketch Rozycki made identified the bomber as Timothy McVeigh, and he was soon apprehended.

CCTV EVIDENCE

Artists are also asked to make sketches from surveillance-camera evidence in order to clarify and simplify the images. This happened after a suicide car bombing on

2 March 2006, near the American consulate in Karachi, Pakistan, which killed one diplomat and four other people. A day later, the Pakistani police artist drew a sketch from camera images and eyewitness accounts.

The sketch by FBI forensic artist Raymond Rozycki produced a striking resemblance to the bomber Timothy McVeigh.

Timothy McVeigh is escorted in 1995 by authorities to the courthouse in Oklahoma City.

ARTISTIC AGEING

Forensic artists also help find people who have been missing for several years. This is done by 'age progression'. The artist uses photographs and knowledge of the growth of bone structure to create a sketch of how the person might have aged, as seen in this computer imaging of Elvis Presley. Such artists work, for instance, for the UK's National Missing Persons Helpline.

One manner of estimating advanced age involves siblings. If the missing person has a brother or sister, the artist can use a photograph of the sibling and merge it with an old photo of the missing person. A computer programme will show how the face might have matured.

With the help of the eye witness, the artist was able to produce a sketch which identified the bomber as Timothy McVeigh.

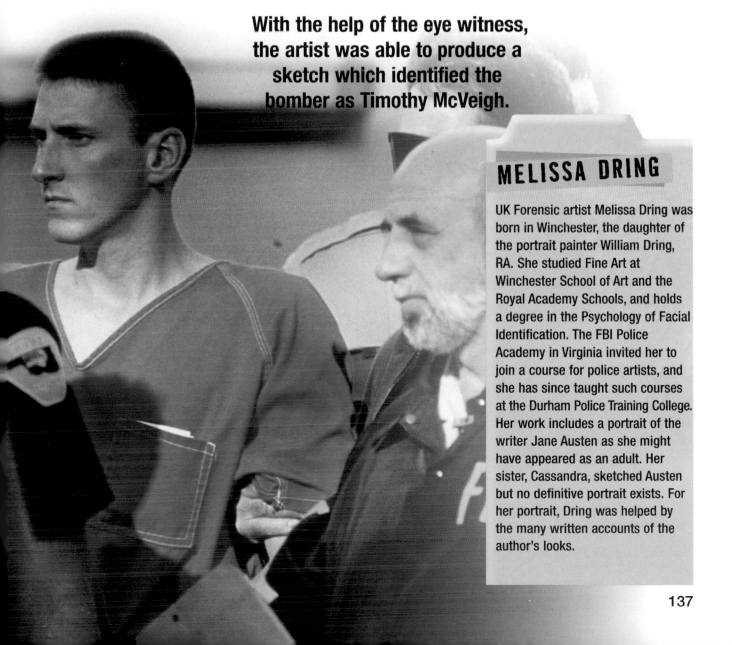

MELISSA DRING

UK Forensic artist Melissa Dring was born in Winchester, the daughter of the portrait painter William Dring, RA. She studied Fine Art at Winchester School of Art and the Royal Academy Schools, and holds a degree in the Psychology of Facial Identification. The FBI Police Academy in Virginia invited her to join a course for police artists, and she has since taught such courses at the Durham Police Training College. Her work includes a portrait of the writer Jane Austen as she might have appeared as an adult. Her sister, Cassandra, sketched Austen but no definitive portrait exists. For her portrait, Dring was helped by the many written accounts of the author's looks.

E-FIT Programmes

The reconstruction of a suspect's face was done by identikit and from 1970 mostly by photofit. Both require a witness to select a series of different facial features and fit them together like a jigsaw puzzle.

Identikit uses sketches, and photofit uses photographs. With the advent of computers, the old system, which produced rather disjoined images, was replaced by the electronic facial identification technique, commonly known as E-FIT, a name coined by Janina Kaminska at the Home Office in 1984.

An E-FIT software programme, which stores hundreds of facial features, is used by such law enforcement agencies as Scotland Yard, the FBI, and the Royal Canadian Mounted Police. This computerized photofit system is also a feature of the BBC's Crimewatch television programme.

In 2005, advanced E-FITs were unveiled in London at a conference on crime-fighting technology. The software now uses a genetic algorithm to mutate a screen image as the witness gives the description. This cuts down the old selection of parts from hours to minutes.

One system, EigenFit, has been developed at the University of Kent, and another, EvoFit, at the University of Stirling. Both packages produce nine random faces based on the gender, race and hairstyle of the suspect. The witness chooses the closest likeness, and the face evolves according to additional details fed in to the system. A more realistic face is created by the programme's attention to variations in a face's shape, shading, and the relationship between the features.

Detective Chief Inspector Stuart Mace talks with the press after releasing E-FIT images of the suspect who shot a 19-year-old woman in Walthamstow, London, on New Year's Day 2002 to steal her mobile telephone. The victim was left with a gash on her forehead and recovered.

STUYVESANT TOWN RAPIST

Detective Stephen Mancusi, the senior forensic artist with the New York Police Department, has had many successes. However, the most unusual one involved the 'Stuyvesant Town Rapist', who had raped four women in that residential area of Manhattan.

The last victim recalled the rapist's features and worked with Mancusi on a composite sketch. It was quickly printed on posters and distributed around the city. A Bronx assistant district attorney spotted one and immediately recognized her half-brother, Anthony Mane. He was arrested, convicted and sentenced to up to 40 years.

Above: A crime victim (left) works with a police artist to create a computerized image of the criminal.

A man's head is overlaid with a contour map to produce a computerized facial image. The grid compares specific points.

IRA BOMBERS

When Teresa Redmon began working as a forensic artist for the Kentucky State Police in 1994, she created her composite sketches of criminals and missing persons by drawing them by hand. More recently, the police have invested in software technology, and Redmon chose E-FIT because it was the one that focused solely on law enforcement and, she notes, contained the world's largest database of hairstyles, facial features, and other attributes. From the first 14 E-FIT composite faces she created, the police made 10 arrests, and the overall successful rate now is 80 percent. Today, as she travels in Kentucky working with state and local police, she carries along her laptop computer loaded with E-FIT and other face composite systems.

Surveillance Cameras

They may give fuzzy, jerky images, but closed-circuit television (CCTV) cameras have proved invaluable in identifying criminals and tracing the last movements of victims.

Closed-circuit television (CCTV) cameras, as the one pictured left, beam their images back to monitors in a security control room.

SWISS VANDAL

Surveillance cameras in Thailand caught a drunk Swiss man spraying black paint on several portraits of the Thai king Bhumibol Adulyadej and this led in March 2007 to a sentence of ten years in prison. Oliver Jufer, 57, at first blamed a German who had left for the Philippines, but decided to confess after the cameras recorded his vandalism. He could have received 75 years, but the judge reduced the sentence because he had confessed. Jufer has lived in Thailand for a decade, and the 79-year-old monarch had studied in Switzerland. The king had previously said he would pardon anyone jailed for insulting him.

140

Technical advances now allow the captured faces of suspects to be compared with mug shots by using imaginary points, or 'landmarks', on the faces.

Cameras have also been successful in locating vulnerable missing persons and for preventive surveillance, such as locating football hooligans in a crowd.

WATCHING THE POLICE

There are an estimated 25 million CCTV cameras in the world. In 2007, Britain led all countries in having up to 4.2 million, with a city person's image captured about 300 times a day. Some worry this is an invasion of privacy, but the Association of Chief Police Officers (ACPO) said many safeguards are in place to stop abuses by officers. 'The police use of surveillance', said ACPO's Graham Gerrard, 'is probably the most regulated of any group in society.'

In some areas of Britain, CCTV has reduced crime by 95 per cent. In the Wakefield District of West Yorkshire during the first quarter of 2006, a total of 401 arrests were due to the 68 cameras in the center of the city of Wakefield and a further 80 across the district.

SURVEILLANCE SLIPS

The value of CCTV is especially appreciated when cameras fail.

This occurred during the London bombings of 7 July 2005, when the camera was not working on the bus that was attacked. Police have stressed that tapes must be changed daily and tested, and that the time and date displays need to be correct.

A CCTV camera observes passengers on a London bus. These cameras, used as deterrents and for evidence of crimes, were installed on all London buses in 2007.

SHOPLIFTING

Private surveillance cameras are making it much easier to catch shoplifters. One of the famous catches was American actress Winona Ryder who was filmed in 2001 in the Beverly Hills Saks Fifth Avenue store as she stole more than 20 items worth $5,560. A Saks security guard, who operated the cameras from a basement control room, played the videotape during Ryder's trial in 2002. It showed her entering a dressing room in the store's luxury boutique carrying a red bag, then leaving with the bag looking much larger. She also bought items during her hour-and-a-half visit. The cameras helped convict Ryder, who was given a three-year probation, 480 hours of community service, $2,700 in fines, and ordered to pay Saks for the stolen items.

CCTV Cases

Many arrests come from surveillance cameras in private businesses. This is what caught Paul Agutter, known as the 'Safeway Poisoner'. A biochemistry lecturer at Edinburgh's Napier University, he tried to poison his wife's gin and tonic drinks in 1995 with atropine in order to marry his lover.

To throw the blame elsewhere, he placed bottles of tonic injected with the poison on supermarket shelves. CCTV footage revealed him putting the tonic on a shelf in Safeway's Edinburgh branch. He was convicted and received a 12-year sentence. Released in 2002 after seven years, he became employed as a part-time lecturer on philosophy and medical ethics at the University of Manchester.

Police can also manoeuvre surveillance cameras to target high-risk situations. A junior off-duty police officer, Noel Duke, saw a girl walking home alone at 3:15 a.m. in Doncaster. He notified colleagues who trained CCTV cameras on the area and captured Dieter Graw grabbing the girl and trying to carry her off into the bushes. Graw released her when she screamed and struggled. Police were on the scene seconds later, and he was arrested and sent to prison for four years.

Footage from CCTV proves to be solid evidence in court. When a gunman went on a shooting spree in north London, injuring two people, cameras filmed him. John Laidlaw, 24, was caught on camera as he rampaged through London's Finsbury Park underground station brandishing a gun as onlookers cowered in fear. The footage was shown to jurors at his trial in 2007, and he was found guilty and sentenced to life with a minimum of 15 years in prison.

Above: A CCTV camera stands out among a city's lights. Britain has the most cameras per head of population, and the US is quickly increasing its numbers.

Left: CCTV is frequently used in conjunction with mirrors to provide a 360-degree view for security officials.

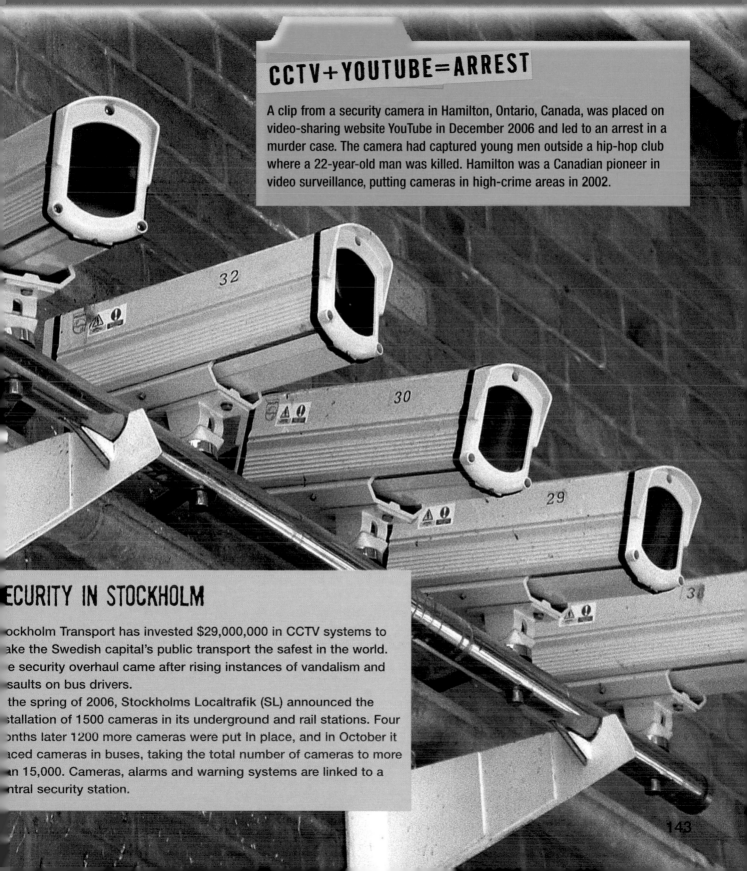

CCTV + YOUTUBE = ARREST

A clip from a security camera in Hamilton, Ontario, Canada, was placed on video-sharing website YouTube in December 2006 and led to an arrest in a murder case. The camera had captured young men outside a hip-hop club where a 22-year-old man was killed. Hamilton was a Canadian pioneer in video surveillance, putting cameras in high-crime areas in 2002.

ECURITY IN STOCKHOLM

ockholm Transport has invested $29,000,000 in CCTV systems to ake the Swedish capital's public transport the safest in the world. e security overhaul came after rising instances of vandalism and saults on bus drivers.

the spring of 2006, Stockholms Localtrafik (SL) announced the stallation of 1500 cameras in its underground and rail stations. Four onths later 1200 more cameras were put in place, and in October it aced cameras in buses, taking the total number of cameras to more an 15,000. Cameras, alarms and warning systems are linked to a ntral security station.

Connecting Victim and Suspect

When a crime is not directly witnessed, linking a suspect to the victim must solve it. In some rare cases this is not even enough, because an innocent person may be found holding the murder weapon as he stands over the body.

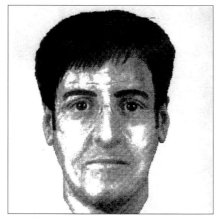

Police released this E-FIT image in 1999 of the suspected murderer of the BBC presenter Jill Dando.

Still, connecting the perpetrator to the crime in some way will normally lead to a conviction. The link is most often DNA, fingerprints or trace evidence. A guilty verdict is virtually assured by forensic proof showing that items such as hair, fibres or blood have been exchanged between a victim and suspect.

Most murderers are close to the victim, such as spouses and lovers. Others have no previous relationship, as is the case in many kidnappings. And a lack of a relationship is what makes contract killings so difficult to solve. The instigator of the murder has an established alibi and is not the real murderer. They are often caught, however, when either the hired hit man or a go-between contacts the police with information.

Forensic awareness has helped some parents recover their children. A mother in Philadelphia, Pennsylvania, USA, regained custody of her daughter in 2004 after a six-year kidnapping. Seeing the child at a birthday party, she took a hair sample and sent it to a DNA lab that verified the identification and led to the kidnapper's arrest.

Most murderers are already close to the victim, such as spouses and lovers.

THE WEAPON CONNECTION

Possibly the most blatant evidence of guilt is the murder weapon handled by a suspect. Ballistic tests, as an example, linked the rifle used to kill 10 people in the Washington, DC, area in 2002 to John Allen Muhammad and Lee Malvo, helping convict them. Muhammad was sentenced to death and Malvo received several life sentences. Perpetrators make great efforts to dispose of incriminating knives and guns, and some are never located. This was the case when Sam Sheppard, the US doctor who inspired the television series and movie, *The Fugitive* , was convicted of his wife's murder in 1954. Nevertheless, the connection seemed strong enough when the coroner described the missing weapon as a surgical instrument.

JILL DANDO

One of London's most infamous murders occurred on 26 April 1999, when BBC television presenter Jill Dando was callously shot in broad daylight on her doorstep in what first resembled a contract killing. Police seemed baffled as the search stretched on for two years. However, on 25 May 2000, they arrested Barry George, a known sex offender who lived half a mile away from her home. George did not know Dando, but forensic scientists matched a strand of fibre found at the crime scene with his trousers. A single speck of residue from the murder gun was also found in Dando's hair and matched residue discovered in George's coat pocket. He was convicted and sentenced to life.

A policeman stands guard outside Jill Dando's home where she was shot on the doorstep.

Domestic Violence

Forensic experts have less evidence to work with in cases of domestic violence. The violence often happens behind closed doors, and the alleged victim is often the only witness.

Since spouses are normally in constant contact, trace evidence is hardly needed to place the perpetrator at the crime scene or to make a link with the victim.

It is of value, however, in establishing the violence of murder. When suitcases containing the body parts of a man washed up in 2004 in Chesapeake Bay, in Virginia, police arrested his wife after specks of human tissue were found on her shoes.

As in other cases, forensic evidence is virtually needed for a conviction. Its lack in the murder trial of Hollywood actor Robert Blake in 2005 even overcame testimony of a stuntman who said Blake had asked him to 'snuff' his wife, Bonny Lee Bakley. She was found shot through the window of their car as Blake went into a restaurant, he said, to collect his gun. Forensic examiners could find no weapon, no gunshot residue on the actor and no blood on his clothing, so Blake went free.

SELF-DEFENCE

The lack of self-defence evidence is also crucial. Self-defence is a frequent plea by women who claim their husbands have been abusing them. Jane Andrews, the former dresser for Sarah Ferguson, the ex-wife of Prince Andrew, used it in 2001. The evidence, however, failed to back up Andrews' claim that her

FAMILY CONTACT

Because family members often find the body and have contact with it, evidence is contaminated and a case can become complicated. Sion Jenkins was accused of murdering his foster daughter Billie-Jo in 1997 in Hastings after she was beaten to death on the patio with an iron tent peg. A case was built on 150 blood spots on his clothing, but the defence argued that these were caused by air being released from the girl's lungs as he moved her. His former wife also accused him of violence towards her.

Although he was convicted of murder in 1998, appeals finally brought about Jenkins' release in 2006 when the jury failed to reach a verdict in his third trial.

Self-defence is a frequent plea by women in murder trials who claim their husbands have been abusing them.

murdered boyfriend, Thomas Cressman, had stabbed himself on a kitchen knife she was holding for protection. It was found that she had first struck him with a cricket bat. She received a life sentence.

KITCHEN KNIFE

The self-defence plea also failed for Susan Polk after she stabbed her millionaire psychotherapist husband to death in Orinda, California, in 2002 and then declared she had suffered years of abuse. She said she grabbed a kitchen knife from her husband as he attacked her, but the autopsy revealed she had no defensive wounds, and she was sentenced to life, with the recommendation that she serve at least 16 years.

Jane Andrews arrives handcuffed at the High Court in London on 24 September 2003 .

Expert Witnesses

When forensic scientists give evidence in court, they are known as expert witnesses. Because of their specialized knowledge, they can give both facts, such as test results, and also their opinions, which may be an estimation of the number of people eliminated by a certain DNA result.

Juries are often swayed by the clarity and confidence demonstrated by the expert witness.

FORENSIC MISTAKES?

American researchers have found that forensic test errors and false or misleading testimony by forensic scientists was the leading cause of wrong convictions in 88 cases in which the DNA exonerated the convicted person. The study was done by Jonathan Koehler, professor of behavioural decision-making at the University of Texas, and Michael Saks, a law professor at Arizona State University. Koehler told the magazine, *National Geographic*, in August 2005 that 63 per cent of the wrongful convictions were due to forensic science testing errors and 27 per cent came from wrong testimony by expert witnesses. He believes that false testimony is the result of the close relationship between the police, prosecutors and forensic scientists.

In the US trial of sniper suspect Lee Malvo in 2003, a psychiatric expert witness argued unsuccessfully that he was legally insane.

An expert witness is different from a professional witness, such as a police officer or security guard, who is also allowed by the court to present facts and opinions connected to their duties. The third type, a witness of fact, comes from the general public and has information about the events or people involved in a crime. A witness of fact cannot express opinions in court.

IMPARTIAL

Both the prosecution and defence may call upon forensic scientists to give testimony that will support their case, and many trials have forensic experts who present opposing facts and interpretations. Despite this, an expert witness is expected to be impartial and assist the court in dispensing justice.

CROSS-EXAMINATION

Forensic scientists on the stand will give their names, qualifications and experience, before being examined by the side that called for their testimony. The expert will answer questions based on test reports he or she drew up. The opposing side's cross-examination will try to discredit any facts or interpretations detrimental to their case. Juries are often swayed by the clarity and confidence demonstrated by the expert during this cross-examination.

Some 80 witnesses arrive in the courtroom in Auxerre, France, in 2004 for the trial of Emile Louis, a suspected serial killer.

TALKING TO A JURY

Dr Henry C. Lee, an American who is one of the world's most famous forensic scientists, has investigated more than 6000 cases and testified at many trials. Interviewed by Courtroom Television's *Crime Library*, he gave this advice on presenting scientific evidence to a jury:

'You cannot use long words. The jury is intelligent. I approach them in a

logical way to present scientific facts – only the facts. I don't get into speculation. Let the jury make its own decision. I use simple life examples. Instead of naming a chemical test, I just say "chemical test". I don't try to impress them. If a bullet wound is found in the upper body, I just say, "upper body" instead of "superior" or "anterior".'

Dr Henry C. Lee shows ink smears to the jury in the 1995 O.J. Simpson trial to explain smear patterns of blood.

Organizers work at setting up a network at the sixth HOPE (Hackers on Planet Earth) Convention in 2006 in New York City.

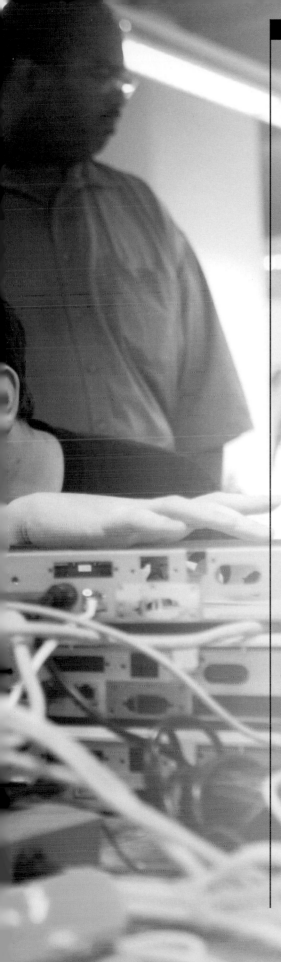

Chapter Nine

Crimes Without Violence

Murder and other violence against individuals stand out as the most abhorrent crimes, but lives can be ruined by an array of illegal activities. Such white-collar crimes as office theft, embezzlement, bribery, fraud, forgery and counterfeiting, are normally devised to steal money or property.

A soldier cleans oil from rocks after the oil tanker Prestige *sank off the Spanish coast in 2002.*

Workplace fraud in the US has been estimated at more than $652 billion annually, with 30 per cent of business failures directly related to employee theft. Many cases are difficult to prosecute because the criminals use sophisticated systems to cover their tracks.

Around the world, police and forensic scientists are constantly refocusing their efforts to deal with evolving high-tech crimes such as identity theft. New forensic computer teams combat hacking, Internet fraud and the transfer of illegal money.

Crimes against the environment are also devastating. Pollution, wildfire arson, poaching and the trade in endangered species are a few of the activities pursued by authorities and processed through forensic labs.

British passports, like those from other nations, have been counterfeited and stolen, with 200,000 UK stolen ones listed on the Interpol database. They are normally sold to illegal immigrants.

Commercial Crimes

The US criminologist Edwin Sutherland coined the term 'white-collar crime' in 1939. He defined it as 'crime committed by a person of respectability and high social status in the course of his occupation'.

Commercial crimes do land high-profile executives in prison. In the UK, four executives with the Guinness drinks company were jailed in 1990 for attempts to manipulate the stock market. A year later media tycoon Robert Maxwell's death saved him from a similar fate for embezzling staff pensions. Homemaking guru Martha Stewart was imprisoned in 2004 for insider trading, and by 2005 executives from the bankrupt US energy corporation Enron were in jail for securities fraud. In 2007, two officials of Russia's bankrupt oil company, Yukos, were imprisoned for embezzling $13 billion.

Most crimes committed within businesses are, of course, on a smaller scale, but the average loss in the US is $190,000. Embezzlement is among the most common and relatively easy to detect. Forensic investigators often trap embezzlers through forged signatures on checks and other recorded movements of money. In a Scottish case in 2006, Jackie Aitchenson was caught using Internet banking to embezzle £26,000 from a medical centre in Perthshire.

Opposite: Martha Stewart, America's homemaking advocate, departs Federal Court in New York City. She was convicted in 2004 of lying about a stock sale and received five months' imprisonment.

POSTAL FRAUD

Fraud is delivered straight into the home in the form of scams designed to obtain money, and these can frequently be traced back to the sender. They often appear in the form of a commercial misrepresentation, such as get-rich-quick promises and work-at-home opportunities. Other illegal mailings include fraudulent charities and religious organizations soliciting donations. In some fraud cases, merchandise that has been ordered and paid for is diverted on its way to the rightful owner. The latter, as well, has become a common type of Internet fraud.

Fake invoices are also a common scheme. In 2007, in Canada, the Toronto Police Service warned the public about letters being sent out claiming the recipient owed money in back taxes. The letters said payments by cheque could be made out to Stephen Smith at the Consumer Service Bureau. The police reminded the public that the government never asks for cheques payable to an individual.

Former Enron Chief Executive Jeff Skilling (center) arrives at a courtroom in Houston, Texas in 2006. He was found guilty of corporate fraud and received 24 years in prison.

Homemaking guru Martha Stewart was imprisoned in 2004 for insider trading.

CLUES TO FRAUD

Forensic scientists play a key role in investigating business fraud. They often detect it by examining questioned documents and identifying handwriting and signatures. According to Britain's Forensic Science Service, a document examiner can reveal altered documents, fake identities and false bank accounts by using chemical tests, specialized lighting and the enhancement of hidden entries. The sequence of documents can also disclose a history of events in an illegal business transaction.

Forensic tests, including DNA profiles, can link suspects to documents, computers and other office equipment. Valuable information can also be recovered from office security cameras, office computers, PDA palmtop computers and mobile phones, including mobile-phone site analyses.

This file is at the computer forensics lab in Menlo Park, California, where fraud and other crimes are investigated.

Cases of Fraudulent Documents

Commercial fraud leaves a trail of paper that forensic investigators carefully trawl, looking for, among other clues, false documents and counterfeit signatures. As the following cases indicate, fraud is an international problem.

EVIDENCE OF FRAUD

According to the UK Association of Police Officers, if suspicions of commercial fraud are raised, there are three main ways of securing evidence:

- Papers and other documents should be kept as the fraudster left them. However they should be placed in clear bags or envelopes so they can be examined without obliterating forensic evidence.

- When a computer has been used in a fraud, it should not be used until a forensic scientist examines it. If that is not possible, the suspect files should be backed up.

- A record should be kept of any other facts and events, such as conversations that aroused suspicions.

John Rigas, the former CEO of Adelphia Communications, talks to the media outside the courthouse in New York City in 2005. He and his son Timothy were convicted of stealing from the company, with Rigas receiving 15 years in federal prison and his son 20 years.

The UK's Serious Fraud Office worked with Cheshire police and the FBI to uncover a bogus high-yield investment scheme devised by Cheshire businessman Peter Barry Maude. Some 195 victims each sent a minimum investment of £12,500 to an account on the Isle of Man. But, instead, the money was used to pay for Maude's house and to make expensive purchases. He was sentenced in 2001 to six years in prison.

JOHN RIGAS

American examiners went through nearly 1000 documents that were presented to the jury during the 2004 trial of John Rigas and his son, Timothy, accused of a monumental fraud against Adelphia, the nation's fifth-largest television company. This included siphoning off $100 million for personal extravagances and hiding $2.3 billion in debt. False documents helped send the two to prison, with Timothy sentenced to 20 years and his father to 15 years.

Forgery and false documents were also uncovered by forensic experts in Israel, sending the former Knesset member, Ofer Hugi, to jail in 2006. In order to receive increased government funding, he had fabricated lists of students and teachers for a technical college that did not even exist.

In Japan in 2007, Takafumi Horie, once head of the Internet firm, Livedoor, was sentenced to two and a half years in prison after document investigators found he had falsified accounts to show a profit instead of the actual losses.

A crime officer removes a computer for investigation so forensic experts can access its hard drive for data stored there.

CANADIAN SCREENING

Although Canada has a long humanitarian tradition of helping refugees, it makes sure anyone entering the country undergoes document checks along with other security screening. Documents are looked at by Citizenship and Immigration Canada (CIC) working with the Canada Border Services Agency (CBSA), the Royal Canadian Mounted Police, and the Canadian Security Intelligence Service. Responding to complaints that refugees have been admitted with false papers, the CIC said there are 'systems in place and expert personnel trained to detect fraudulent identification' and that refugees' documents are checked a second time before they become permanent residents.

A Canadian immigration official checks the passport of a Slovak citizen entering the country.

Computer Crimes

The digital age has created the new field of computer crime, known as cyber crime. This immediately gave rise to computer forensic science, one of the fastest-growing disciplines within law enforcement.

The new forensic experts specialize in digital data used for an array of criminal activities, including hacking, identity theft, fraud, embezzlement, terrorism, software piracy, computer viruses and child pornography.

DELETED FILES?

The ease of accessing computer files contributes to crime – but also to investigating it. Investigators can read 'deleted' files recovered from a hard disk. They also can find deleted e-mails, hidden files and

TERRORISTS AND THE INTERNET

The Internet has become a major weapon for Islamic terrorist organizations like al Qaeda. They use e-mails and coded messages to create a community of believers, send news of upcoming plans and spread fear through images of beheadings and bombings. For their part, government agencies maintain constant efforts to take down these web sites, although terrorists are often one step ahead, moving to new ones. Still, police forensic experts have had impressive successes. In 2004, they picked up leads on a web site that showed the execution of an American victim, Paul Johnson, and traced the clues to Abdel Azziz al-Muqrin, the former top operative of al Qaeda in Saudi Arabia, who was then killed.

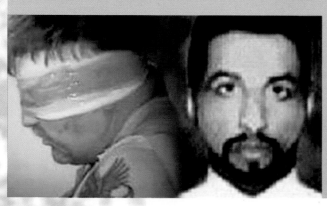

Paul Johnson (left) was a US helicopter engineer in Saudi Arabia. His beheading by a group led by Abdel Azziz al-Muqrin (right) was shown on an Islamic website.

folders, Internet activity and stolen data. Such services are available from the UK's Forensic Science Service, whose eForensic Solutions portfolio includes mobile-phone examinations. In the US, the FBI has a Computer Analysis and Response Team that co-ordinates its efforts with the Department of Defense Computer Forensic Laboratory. When forensic experts dismantle and examine computers that have been seized, they must photograph and note each part before investigating data on the hard disk. This documentation is needed to prove that the evidence was not contaminated.

UNTRACEABLE

One area in which investigators have been hindered by the switch from typewriters to computers is in tracing the source of a false document. Whereas each typewriter's letters had distinctive characteristics that could be read like its fingerprints, most computers use the same word-processing software, which is indistinguishable.

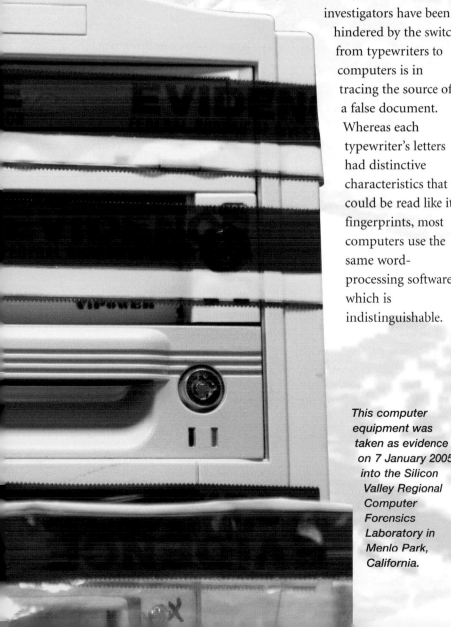

This computer equipment was taken as evidence on 7 January 2005 into the Silicon Valley Regional Computer Forensics Laboratory in Menlo Park, California.

SPYWARE EVIDENCE

Investigating the murder of wealthy American banker Robert Kissel in Hong Kong in 2003, a forensic computer specialist was aided by spyware Kissel had secretly installed on his wife's laptop. Nancy Kissel, also an American, was charged with serving her husband a milkshake laced with sedatives and then beating him to death.

Police officer Cheung Chun-kit found e-mails to the woman's lover and evidence she had searched the Internet for 'Sleeping Pills', 'Overdose Medication Causing Heart Attack', and 'Drug Overdose'. This evidence was combined with the discovery of her fingerprints on boxes of bloodstained clothes and bedding. She confessed, claiming in her defence that Kissel physically abused her, but in 2005 she was sentenced to life.

Nancy Kissel is surrounded by photographers as she leaves the High Court in Hong Kong on 3 August 2005.

Hacking

Hackers electronically break into computers to access information or sabotage the system. These attacks can compromise data, cost companies millions, and endanger national security.

It is estimated that hacking costs more than £10 billion (about $19.6 billion) in the UK, and about $40 billion (£20 billion) a year in the US. In 2006, 87 per cent of large UK companies had security incidents, with the cost of the average incident being £12,000.

Hackers either exploit vulnerabilities in the software or hardware already on computers, or

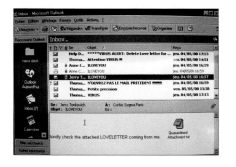

The UK Ministry of Defence announced that its computer network had been hacked into five times in 2006.

they install software that gives them access. Once they gain access to businesses, they download customer databases and credit card information. Many then notify the company in a veiled extortion threat by offering to patch the system against other attacks. The Ministry of Defence in the UK announced in

Left: 'I Love You' was an e-mail whose attachment had a virus that spread computer havoc across Europe, North America and Asia in 2000.

February 2007 that its computer networks had been hacked into at least nine times since 2002, with five successful attacks taking place in 2006. Since some hackers are clever enough to leave no trace, computer security experts believe the real figure is probably higher. One estimate says China accounts for 30 per cent of programmes designed to infiltrate networks covertly. For its part, the US government in 1997 established the National Information Protection Center at FBI headquarters to detect hacking attempts as soon as they occur.

Hacking contests were held at the Hack-In-The-Box Security Conference in 2004 in Kuala Lumpur, Malaysia.

HACKING IN RUSSIA

The Russian government has dealt with large hacking cases by criminals and, it claims, spies. In 1994, Russian hackers broke into the computers of Citibank and stole more than $10 million from customers' accounts. The bank eventually recovered all but $400,000. In one of the worst 'spying' cases, Russian authorities in 2000 arrested a Lithuanian who allegedly spied for the CIA and Lithuanian state security by hacking into Russian security service computers.

GARY McKINNON

It has been described as the 'biggest military computer hack of all time'. Gary McKinnon, a Scottish former hairdresser, was accused of hacking into 300 computers at a US naval station in New Jersey, and 97 more US military and NASA computers between 2001 and 2002. And he did it all from his bedroom in north London.

McKinnon was arrested under the Computer Misuse Act. The Home Office granted a US request to extradite him for trial, but in 2007 he continued his legal battle in the High Court against the order. He could face 50 years in prison if convicted in the US of sabotaging the defence systems.

Calling himself a 'bumbling computer nerd', McKinnon denied his intention was to disrupt security. The US charged, however, that he caused the naval bases network of more than 300 computers to become inoperable.

The US Government says Gary McKinnon caused £350,000 damage to its computers by trying to access classified information.

Identity Fraud

Identity fraud costs the UK economy £1.7 billion ($3.35 billion) each year according to an estimate in 2006, about A$1.3 billion in Australia, and an estimated $55 billion in the USA, the main victim.

INSTANT CREDIT, INSTANT IDENTITY THEFT

Bob Sullivan is one of America's leading journalists covering identity theft, having written the book, *Your Evil Twin: Behind the Identity Theft Epidemic* (2004), and more than 100 articles since 1996.

A prime reason for US identity fraud, he says, is instant credit. 'US retailers waste no time throwing credit at anyone browsing high-ticket items in their stores', he notes. 'Imposters can get their hands on valuable plastic with as little as a Social Security number and a name.' And Sullivan knows the result: 'Just as consumers can drive off a car lot in an hour with a brand new $30,000 car, so can their imposters.'

Stealing personal information normally comes from the theft of a person's letters, credit cards or chequebooks. Even documents thrown out with the rubbish, such as bills, receipts and bank statements, can be used to steal someone's identity. A person who steals another's identity can use it to open bank accounts, withdraw funds from existing accounts and apply for credit cards, loans, state benefits and documents such as passports and driving licences. At worst, false

identities are used in the commission of crimes, including terrorism.

PHISHING

E-mails are used to trick people into giving out bank personal

Holograms on a Chinese ID card help prevent counterfeiting. The colour changes with the viewing angle, so normal copying fails.

identification numbers, computer passwords, and security numbers. Criminals use a technique known as 'phishing' in which they pretend to be financial institutions or companies and send spam or pop-up messages requesting personal information.

More electronic identity theft comes from devices hidden in cash machines and card swipe machines. These skim details from the magnetic strip, while miniature cameras embedded in cash machines can record PIN numbers.

FBI Cyber Division Assistant Director Jana Monroe unveils in 2004 in Los Angeles, California, an anti-piracy seal and warning text to be placed on digital and software intellectual property.

The FBI usually has more than 1,600 active cases of identity theft being investigated at any one time. Its Cyber Division looks at such theft occurring over the Internet or through computer hacking. Forensic analysts review suspicious activity to identify and target those criminal organizations engaged in identity theft. They use a search engine called Choicepoint, which can provide the criminal's social security number and the names of potential family relatives and partners, along with addresses.

Nearly 30,000 phishing attacks were reported in January 2007 to the Anti-Phishing Working Group.

IDENTIFYING THE IDENTITY THIEF

Forensic scientists, especially forensic accountants, have ways of tracking identity thieves:

- If the thief uses a stolen credit card in a shop that has surveillance cameras, his or her image may have been captured and can be retrieved by checking the time of purchase on the invoice.

- If the perpetrator receives fraudulent checks, credit cards or merchandise in the mail, the postal authorities may help identify them.

- When a credit card is applied for under a false name, discrepancies can sometimes be seen in other information provided, such as employment history or addresses.

Identity Theft Cases

A British pensioner was held in a South African police cell for nearly three weeks in 2003 because his identity had been stolen and used to commit a variety of crimes.

Derek Bond, 72, had been on holiday with his wife when the FBI asked the South African authorities to arrest him, since he was one of America's most wanted men. They thought he was a fugitive named Derek Sykes, a telemarketing fraudster. However, investigators soon discovered that the real Sykes, an American, had stolen Bond's identity in 1989 and was carrying a British passport in Bond's name. The FBI subsequently arrested Sykes in Las Vegas and issued an apology to Bond.

CREDIT FRAUD

In what was the largest US identity-theft case ever investigated and prosecuted, Philip Cummings stole personal consumer information from 30,000 victims across the US and Canada between 2000 to 2002, causing more than $11 million in losses. Cummings was an employee at a Long Island company that provided customers with access to the three major commercial credit bureaux. He downloaded consumer credit histories and sold them to people, some of whom used the information to loot thousands of personal savings accounts and run up fake charges on credit cards.

Investigators from the FBI and US Postal Inspection Service tracked the documents to Cummings. He confessed and was sentenced to 14 years in federal prison.

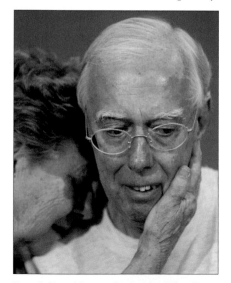

Derek Bond is comforted by his wife, Audrey, as he addresses the media after being released from a Durban jail on 26 February 2003.

HOW TO TELL IF YOUR IDENTITY HAS BEEN STOLEN

Several signs will normally occur if someone has stolen your identity. A few of the most obvious are:

- You are denied credit although your financial position is good.
- A collection agency or creditor contacts you about unknown debts.
- Invoices and statements do not arrive, since they have been forwarded to a new address.
- Your bank or card company contacts you about suspicious transactions.
- Purchases or withdrawals not made by you appear on statements.

AVOIDING IDENTITY THEFT

Identity theft in Australia is estimated to be above $1.1 billion a year and the true figure is thought to be much higher because of undetected identity fraud. To combat this, the Australian National Crime Prevention Program launched an information programme to help people prevent and respond to identity theft. Some tips include:

- Order a copy of your credit report regularly
- Don't carry personal information unless you have to
- Destroy personal information before discarding it
- Avoid giving out personal information over the phone, by mail or on the Internet
- Remove your name from mailing lists

Identity thieves like polling cards because they bear no photo or signature.

Above: A Mexican passport seen under ultraviolet light reveals the white security symbol at right that is printed with fluorescent ink.

Left: This Barclays Bank cashpoint has been fitted with an anti-skimming device. Criminals place their own devices into cash machines in order to steal customers' PIN numbers and credit card details.

For customer protection this machine has been fitted with a device to prevent card fraud.

Tampering with this device will result in the machine going out of service.

BARCLAYS

Environmental Crimes: Pollution

Crimes against the natural environment have seldom been prosecuted successfully in the past, but the emerging discipline of environmental forensics is making it easier to legally link such crimes to the perpetrators.

Finding the chemical 'fingerprints' and tracing them back to the sources do this job in cases of pollution. Such work often requires the co-operation of chemists, biologists and toxicologists.

Illegal waste lies at the proposed site for a 2012 Olympic Stadium in London. 'Fly tipping' is both a danger and a blot on the landscape.

According to Professor Bob Kalin at Queen's University Belfast, environmental forensics concentrates on identifying how and when contamination took place, its extent and impact and whether any attempts were made to illegally cover up the incident.

THERMAL SCANNING

With the technology available today, air, water, and soil pollution can quickly be discovered and analyzed. The UK Environment Agency, for instance, uses a thermal scanner on an aircraft to monitor water pollution as well as hotspots in landfill sites. Such technology and forensic techniques have been used to track down the illegal dumping of waste, which is often masterminded by criminals.

Forensic detection has helped bring about convictions around the world. Some have involved individuals, such as John Tapscott, a persistent illegal dumper of waste in Plymouth. In 2007 he conned

FIGHTING POLLUTION WITH SOIL

The Centre for Australian Forensic Soil Science (CAFSS) is the first formal international network of forensic scientists who combine research, training, and services in soil forensics to fight environmental pollution, as well as crime. Its forensic work with soil has assisted environmental agencies and police forces with environmental disasters in Australia and overseas. Recent cases involved soil removed from a site containing aboriginal artefacts, ferns stolen from a conservation park, and the identity of a polluting cement plant.

Chemists, biologists and toxicologists cooperate to find trace the sources of pollution.

customers into believing he was a legitimate waste operator. He charged up to £200 to illegally dump lorry loads of rubbish at a beauty spot in Devon. The Environment Agency and local authorities tracked him down and he was subsequently sentenced to 16 months in prison.

Corporations pay a dearer price. A US petroleum refinery located in Memphis, Tennessee, was fined $2.2 million in 2007 for violating the Clean Air Act. Investigators from the US Environmental Protection Agency found that the Williams Refining Company violated regulations about benzene emissions, a chemical that Congress has labelled a hazardous air pollutant.

A researcher in protective clothing analyzes the local environment with a magnifying glass, the result of an industrial chemical spill.

BROWNFIELD POLLUTION

Brownfield sites are urban areas that have a potential for new building developments. Major projects include the recent replacement of a former goal-gas plant in Amsterdam, the Netherlands, with a cultural centre and park, and the site for the 2012 Olympic Games in London.

Many sites, however, are polluted by chemical contamination of the soil, and under a European Union Environmental Liability Directive, which came into force in 2007 the polluters have to be identified so they can pay for the cost of restoration. Environmental forensics will be used, making the legal proceedings quicker and less expensive.

Environmental Crimes: Endangered Species

International agreements exist to outlaw the trade in endangered species and their body parts. Many Asians believe in cures requiring animal parts, which bring high prices for medicinal uses, like rhino horn pills and tiger bone juice.

Endangered species also find their way onto restaurant menus, often under cleverly deceptive names.

Forensic tests such as DNA and serology can readily identify animal parts. Otherwise, authorities would have to catch suspects in the act of killing the animals or in possession of the carcass. Sometimes the killer turns out to be another animal. Bones, teeth, claws, tusks, hair, hides, furs, feathers, stomach contents, as well as poisons, arrows and bullets, are all items of evidence that may be examined forensically.

Because of the value of their tusks for ivory, elephants have always been a prime target for poachers. Despite an international ban on ivory in 1990, it is estimated that 216 tonnes were smuggled out of Africa in 2006, representing the death of about 24,000 elephants.

IVORY FINGERPRINTS

Forensic scientists are now obtaining DNA 'fingerprints' from stolen tusks that have been seized, and can trace them back to where they were poached. Samuel Wasser, at the Center for Conservation Biology at the University of Washington, supervises the extraction of DNA samples from ivory pulverized into a fine powder. The result is matched with DNA from wild elephants to ascertain the location they originated from.

When a large seizure of ivory was made in the port of Singapore in 2005, the crates came from Zambia, but officials there swore poaching was extremely rare. Wasser's DNA tests, however, traced it back to Zambia, a finding that forced the head of the Zambian wildlife department to resign.

Authorities recover piles of tusks of African elephants killed illegally. The ivory is sold for jewellery and supposed medicinal properties.

A WILDLIFE CRIME LABORATORY

The US is the only country in the world with an official wildlife crime laboratory. The US National Fish and Wildlife Forensics Laboratory opened in 1989 in Ashland, Oregon, costing £2.3 million. Among its divisions is a genetics unit that conducts DNA and protein analyses to identify unknown species, a pathology unit to verify illegal killings, a criminalistics unit using microscopic and chemical techniques to compare items of evidence and a morphology unit to trace wildlife parts back to the family, genus or species source.

A Chinese pharmacy display shows packets of tiger bone and dried seahorse alongside those of plant medicines. These 'remedies' can be produced in the form of powders, pills, tonics and oils.

DNA tests on whale meat in Japanese restaurants traced it to endangered stock.

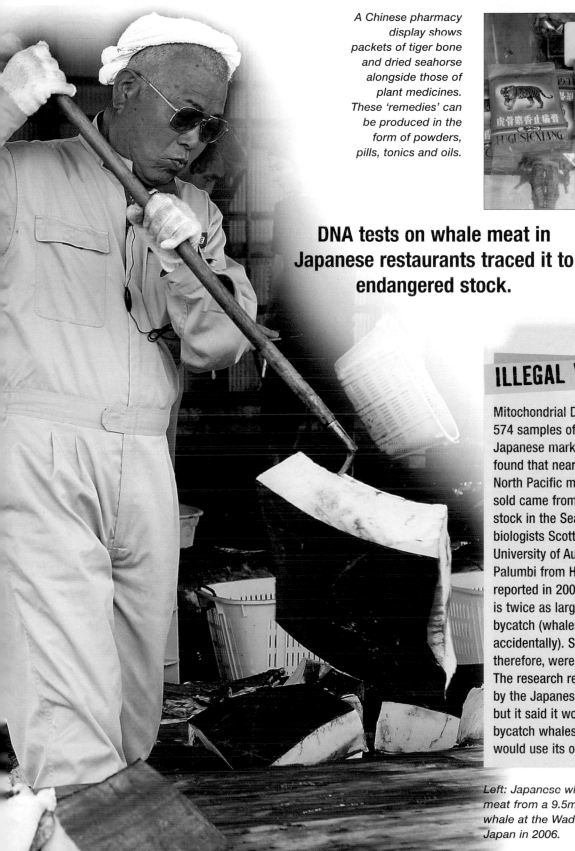

ILLEGAL WHALE MEAT

Mitochondrial DNA tests run on 574 samples of whale meat in Japanese markets and restaurants found that nearly one-third of North Pacific minke whales being sold came from the endangered stock in the Sea of Japan. Marine biologists Scott Baker from the University of Auckland and Steve Palumbi from Harvard University reported in 2000 that this number is twice as large as expected from bycatch (whales killed accidentally). Some minkes, therefore, were possibly poached. The research results were disputed by the Japanese Fisheries Agency, but it said it would monitor the bycatch whales more carefully, and would use its own DNA testing.

Left: Japanese whalers cut blocks of meat from a 9.5m (31ft) Baird's beaked whale at the Wada port in Chiba, Japan in 2006.

169

Arson

Arson is considered to be a white-collar crime when the perpetrator sets a fire for financial gain, usually to collect insurance or to destroy company records. Financial arson is a serious crime that could accidentally kill.

The malicious setting of fires in the UK now averages 2,100 incidents each week.

THE MIND OF AN ARSONIST

Australian psychologist Rebecca Doley has studied serial arsonists for more than 10 years, interviewing more than 140 offenders. She says they receive more enjoyment from the aftermath than from the fire itself. Staying to watch the chaos they have caused gives the arsonists a sense of power. The fear of being caught does not act as a deterrent, she noted. 'They understand what they are doing and the consequences of their actions, yet they choose to do it anyway.'

The malicious setting of fires in the UK now averages 2100 incidents each week, including arson attacks on cars, and the last decade has seen 2.4 million recorded arson fires. The annual cost is estimated to be some £3 billion. In recent years, the US has annually recorded more than 63,000 arson offences with an average damage of £180,000 to industrial and manufacturing buildings. About 4,000 people are killed and 20,000 injured by arson attacks each year in the US.

Although most evidence would seem to be destroyed by fire, several clues can point investigators toward arson. Finding the 'seat' of a fire, or its point of origin, can reveal how it started and spread. Accidental fires spread upwards, creating a 'V' shape pointing down to its origin. Fire started deliberately may have several 'Vs' where an arsonist began separate fires. These may travel unnaturally across a floor, which indicates accelerants like petrol, or paint thinners were used. An accelerant that does not burn will leave an odour and liquid accelerants create pool marks on the floor.

Arson investigators search burnt debris in a similar way to forensic examiners working through a crime scene. They identify and collect evidence, preserving it carefully for laboratory tests and court proceedings. They wear protective clothing, and their tools include

Firefighters search carefully through the debris of a burnt house. Evidence that is collected from the scene can help distinguish arson from an accident.

digital and video cameras, notebooks and pens, knives, screwdrivers, hammers, crowbars, evidence tags and tape, and evidence containers.

A family often loses everything they own in a malicious arson attack.

ABORIGINAL FIRESETTING

It may seem like arson to some, but the practise of setting fires by Australian Aboriginals is not classified as such by the Australian government. These natives, who arrived in Australia some 50,000 years ago, were using fire for land management long before European settlers arrived. The importance of these fires is evident by the different names the Aboriginals give to various types. Aboriginal peoples continue to light fires even when new agricultural practices mean that they are no longer needed or desirable. In some cases, the fires can cause property damage or livestock losses. The Australian government considers this firesetting not malicious in nature, since the bush is not set alight to destroy or damage property. It is therefore not classified as arson, excluding some Aboriginal people who might be guilty of traditional arson.

Wildfire Arson

Unlike fires intentionally set in buildings for various motives, wildfires tend to be random and the arsonist has no special investment or strong link to the targeted area.

For these reasons, few perpetrators are convicted. While this is not an attack on another person, the unpredictability of wildfires can easily cause the deaths of firefighters and residents.

The immense area covered by many of the fires hampers investigators, but they can still discover the point of origin by following the burn patterns. Forest fires, like house fires, spread outward in the shape of a 'V'. Investigators can retrace the direction of the fire by studying the sides of trees and even the way burnt grass is bent. Wind direction at the time of the fire is also taken into account.

ARSON BY FIREFIGHTERS

In rare cases, a firefighter or forest worker may set a devastating fire. The worst wildfire in Colorado's history occurred in 2002 in Pike National Forest. A forest service employee, Terry Barton, burnt a letter from her estranged husband, and the blaze suddenly spread. It burned 55,485 hectares (137,000 acres), destroying 133 homes, and caused nearly $40 million in damage. She claimed she had smelled a campfire, but fire inspectors testified she could not have done so from the distance she described.

Tamara Meredith, a forest service worker in Oregon, set 28 fires in the Umpqua National Forest in 1998 to earn overtime pay for fighting them. An electronic tracking device placed on her government-owned truck to trace her whereabouts caught her. Agents flying overhead monitored her progress, and saw Meredith stopping in an open area in the forest to light a wildfire. She served three years in prison and three years on parole.

Terry Barton is sketched at her bail hearing in June 2002 with federal judge Michael Wantanabe.

SEAT OF A FIRE

Once the seat of a fire is located, authorities are able to search for footprints, tyre tracks, matches and accelerants. Even then, it may be difficult to prove the fire was not an accident. Other innocent causes also have to be eliminated, such as lightning or a downed power line.

Witnesses are sometimes available, but their view is normally from a distance. In California's San Bernardino Mountains in 2003, three witnesses saw occupants in a white van toss burning items onto the brush, starting a fire that consumed 36,969 hectares (91,281 acres), destroyed 993 homes and killed six people. The arsonists were never found.

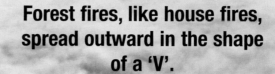

Forest fires, like house fires, spread outward in the shape of a 'V'.

Above: Smoke clouds rise from wild fires in the San Bernardino Mountains in California in late October 2003. Strong Santa Ana winds fanned the flames, helping to maintain and spread the dangerous fires.

Left: Trees burn during a forest fire at Weston, Colorado. Since trees are fuel for a fire, firefighters frequently down them ahead of an approaching fire.

PUBLIC REWARDS

In an effort to apprehend wildfire arsonists, the state of Florida offers rewards for tips from the public. The Florida Forestry Arson Alert Association, created by the state legislature, asks anyone with information about an arsonist to contact the Florida Division of Forestry. Rewards of $100 to $5,000 are paid if the information given leads to an arrest.

These counterfeit Euro banknotes abounded after the switch from familiar national currencies.

Chapter Ten

Forgeries and Fakes

APPROXIMATELY ONE-TENTH OF ALL WORLD TRADE IS MADE UP OF FAKED PRODUCTS, AND MANY OF THESE ITEMS FUND ORGANIZED CRIME AND TERRORISM. EVEN THE MOST ACCOMPLISHED FORGERS, HOWEVER, LEAVE BEHIND CLUES THAT ASSIST FORENSIC SCIENTISTS IN THEIR INVESTIGATIONS.

Document experts examine the paper, ink and printing style to identify items like counterfeit money and forged documents. The unaided eye and instruments like a magnifying glass, stereomicroscope or infrared microscope can do this careful examination, which includes comparing handwriting and signatures. Multi-spectral video microscopes can also be used to reveal if documents have been altered.

Art forgeries may be brilliant enough to hoodwink gallery experts, but they will never pass a laboratory examination. Forensic tests can reveal the age of the paper or canvas, along with modern pigments, which are identified by X-ray diffraction. Infrared scanning detects overpainting and retouching.

Despite technology, forgeries continue to be successfully sold, based on the personal opinion of experts. This has happened with such various items as Faberge eggs, fossils and the diaries of Hitler.

The Hitler Diaries gained worldwide publicity before and after they were proven fakes.

Researchers use a computerized handwriting recognition system to compare the writing on two pieces of correspondence.

Counterfeit Money

Currency counterfeiting for financial gain and to destabilize economies is an ancient crime. The US dollar, the currency most used for global transactions, is copied the most.

Computers makes it possible for unskilled operators to produce excellent colour reproductions.

HOW TO DETECT COUNTERFEIT MONEY

Here are some general tips on how to examine money to identify counterfeit notes. On genuine currency:

- Serial numbers are evenly spaced and have a distinctive style.
- Fine lines on the borders are clear and unbroken.
- Some lines and other printing is embedded. Counterfeit notes have printing on top of the paper.

Used worldwide, the dollar is the main victim of counterfeiters.

Left: An operator uses the RAPACE system to help detect counterfeit Euros. The system allows the operator and enquirer to communicate by telephone.

Below: Special fluorescent ink and strips glow bright blue and red under ultraviolet light to show this is a genuine Euro banknote.

In 2006, some 50,000 euro notes were counterfeited each month. Forty-four per cent of the counterfeit copies were 20-euro notes and a further 36 per cent were 50-euro notes. The Forgery of Money unit of Europol, the European Police force, maintains a database on counterfeiters and another monitors the technical aspects of reproducing currency.

The problem has multiplied with the advent of easily available high-resolution printers and copiers. Computer-generated counterfeiting makes it possible for unskilled operators to produce excellent colour reproductions. Forensic examination, however, can detect the printed image resting on top of the paper's surface and, under a low-grade magnification of about 20x, small particles of toner can often be seen outside the image area.

National currencies, as well, have special protective marks such a micro printing and built-in ultraviolet features. A silver foil strip is embedded inside UK paper currency, US currency has tiny red and blue fibres embedded throughout, Canadian notes have a holographic strip and Australia now produces only polymer notes with a plastic substrate.

RUSSIAN COUNTERFEITERS LIKE THE EURO

Counterfeiters in Russia are switching from the dollar to the euro, it was announced in March 2007 by Alexander Prokopchuk, deputy head of Interpol's National Central Bureau at the Russian Interior Ministry. He said that from 2005 to 2006 the number of confiscated counterfeit banknotes rose from 979 to 1,138. The new banknote total was worth €106,440. Prokopchuk also noted that the number of counterfeit ruble notes had risen 60.6 percent in a year, with 118,000 notes worth more than 104 million rubles confiscated in 2006. This is despite the introduction in 2004 by the Russian Central Bank of notes 'which would be impossible to fabricate at least during the coming seven years.' The new rubles contain a watered silk stripe filled with thin parallel lines. If it is turned, the one-colour stripe will become multicoloured with yellow, pink, and blue stripes. The new notes follow a recommendation by Interpol that all countries introduce new modified notes every five or seven years, since criminal gangs learn to make high-quality counterfeit notes in that period of time.

A Worldwide Counterfeit Case

The White House and US officials warned in 2006 that North Korea has sponsored the near-perfect counterfeiting of $100 bills that could erode the global standing of US currency.

The US Secret Service has seized some $50 million worldwide, and believes that much more is in circulation.

The notes, called Super Dollars, were first detected in the Philippines in 1989, and have spread to more than 130 countries. More than 170 arrests have been made, including several North Korean diplomats found carrying hundreds of thousands of the counterfeit dollars. In October 2006, US officials arrested and indicted Sean Garland, a leader of the Official Irish Republican Army, on conspiring with North Korea to circulate millions of fake dollars.

'A little bit of counterfeit currency of very high quality can go a very long way', said the US deputy assistant treasury secretary Daniel Glaser, who added it can cause people to 'lose their faith in the dollar, which is extremely important to the United State to maintain.'

As part of this case, three men in the UK were jailed in 2002 for taking part in the largest counterfeiting of dollars ever uncovered by British detectives. The total distribution of the fake dollars worldwide was then estimated at $27 million.

COUNTERFEIT DETECTION MACHINES

Modern technology is allowing counterfeit detectors to keep pace with the technology that enables counterfeiters to produce more and more realistic fake notes. In Japan, banks, retailers, post offices and government departments use a small device that can scan a note in 0.7 seconds using a series of light-circuit, magnetic, laser and ultraviolet sensors.
Manufactured by Matsumura Technology, the EXC-5700 and EXC-6700 check 76 points on a note. According to the company, it can yield an accuracy of 99.999 per cent, and can detect fake dollars, euros, yen and other currencies.
However, the detector requires constant updates to foil the counterfeiters. 'As soon as they figure out we've found a flaw in their counterfeits, they fix it and print more money", said Yoshihide Matsumura, a counterfeit-currency expert and president of Matsumura. 'That's why we believe detection equipment should be updated frequently.'

An examiner uses a magnifying glass to detect if a US dollar is counterfeit. The US paper currency has coloured fibres enbedded in each banknote, so the counterfeited version will be revealed under a close examination. New security marks are constantly added.

The investigation began when the National Crime Squad obtained a fake $100 note in 1999 in Birmingham. After an 18-month joint operation of the UK National Crime Squad and US Secret Service, David Levin of Worcestershire was sentenced to nine years, Terence Silcock of Gloucestershire to six and Mark Adderley of Staffordshire to four. The men were involved in a European-wide scheme that included Sean Garland of the Official IRA, mentioned earlier, as well as the Russian mafia and a former KGB agent. The fake dollars arrived in the UK via the Irish Republic. The counterfeits were of such high quality that the British banks were deceived, and the money was laundered for real currency in banks in London and Birmingham. It was then sent back to Moscow.

Counterfeit detection involves the painstaking work of checking tiny details on many currencies.

Below: A technician identifies counterfeit banknotes – US dollars in this case – by shining a light on them from a shallow angle. The counterfeit money will appear different because it uses different dyes and paper.

The counterfeits were of such high quality that even the British banks were deceived.

Document Forgeries

It is easy to produce an accurate-looking copy of any document, but forgers tend to target those involving identity, such as passports, and papers regarding money, like wills.

Experts detect altered documents by using microscopes as well as oblique light, which can expose areas deleted with an eraser or correction fluid.

Examining the types of paper, ink and glues used can discover the similarity of documents and their dating. Documents that have been printed or copied by modern machines can be analyzed for telltale marks, such as those made by a laser printer's drum or a photocopier's glass.

HANDWRITING

Handwriting styles can be duplicated, but forensic-document examiners can see through skillful forgeries. They look at the shape of individual letters, paying special attention to their size and the way they are slanted and connected. They also check for inconsistencies of spelling, preferred characters, such as the use of '&' instead of 'and', grammar, punctuation and content. It was the latter that caught the American terrorist Unabomber in 1996 when his brother compared the content and word phrases in his published manifesto to writings he had left at home.

Even signatures and sample words can be exposed as fakes. When the two-year-old son of aviator Charles Lindbergh was kidnapped and murdered, a comparison of letters in the ransom note with the signature of Bruno Hauptmann confirmed that he was the perpetrator.

Other clues to forged writing include pen lifts at odd places where the forger was checking his writing, and any retouching of the script. If tracing has been done, a heavy indentation may be visible, or the bottom original may leave evidence on the paper put over it.

FISH

The US Secret Service and Germany's Bundeskriminalamt use FISH (the Forensic Information System for Handwriting). This system, based on work carried out by German law enforcement in the 1980s, has now catalogued the handwriting of more than 100,000 individuals and found no two people with the same combinations of handwriting characteristics. FISH scans a block of text and plots the handwriting as arithmetic and geometric values.

James Sellers shows the similarity of Bruno Hauptmann's signature with individual letters on the ransom note. Sellers testified at Hauptmann's trial.

Left: Time magazine was among the world media that covered the exposure of the Hitler Diaries as fakes. Amazingly, the volumes were first judged to be legitimate by three document experts.

Right: A sample page from the Hitler Diaries. They were made on modern paper using modern ink, but some historians were still fooled.

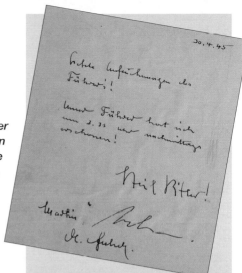

HITLER DIARIES

The German magazine *Stern* paid nine million marks in 1981 to purchase diaries, supposedly written by Adolf Hitler. Three independent document examiners compared the diaries' handwriting with Hitler's, and came to the conclusion that they matched.

However, the publishers asked the Federal Institute of Forensic Investigation in Berlin to examine them. The paper and inks proved they were fraudulent, because the bindings, and a substance used to whiten the paper, had not been invented until after Hitler's death. Tests showed the ink in one section was not even a year old when examined. The forger, Konrad Kujau, and his middleman, *Stern* reporter, Gerd Heidemann, were each sentenced to four and a half years in prison.

Terrorist Documents

Terrorists have had surprising ease in acquiring official documents allowing them to travel and conduct business around the globe. Interpol has a list of five million passports that have been stolen and a database of 13 million lost or stolen passport serial numbers.

Although the US government does not release lost and stolen passport totals for security reasons, it did announce in 2004 that for the first time it had given details of 330,000 lost and stolen passports to Interpol for its database.

FALSE APPLICATIONS

The speed required to issue large numbers of passports allows false applications to slip through the systems. In March 2007, the British government announced that its Identity and Passport Service had given passports to two terrorists among the 6.6 million issued in the UK from October 2005 to September 2006. However, only half of the 16,500 fraudulent applications were detected and destroyed during this period.

SOUTH AFRICAN CONNECTION

Government workers can also sell genuine passports illegally to terrorists. This was the way South African passports fell into the hands of al-Qaeda militants and other terrorists who use them to travel through Europe without visas. According to a report in 2004, criminal syndicates in South Africa's Home Affairs office have been

NEW PASSPORT RULES

In 2007, new US passports contained biometric data. This new electronic passport, or e-Passport, integrates the latest concepts in electronic protection and readability. Also that year, new scanners were in place to read the 10-fingerprint visas that are now required.

From 23 January 2007, US citizens had to have a passport to travel by air between the US and Canada, Mexico, Central and South America, the Caribbean and Bermuda. By 1 January 2008, this would also apply to those traveling by land or sea.

Research indicated that fewer Canadians planned to travel to the US if forced to apply for passports. There were also worries that the new requirements would reduce US visitors to Canada.

The UK has also moved into biometric identification, as on this card.

selling them for years, and British police discovered 'boxes and boxes' of the documents in a house in London.

The ubiquitous American driving licence, used as a key source of identification in the US, has also proven easy to acquire. In 2005, therefore, Congress passed an act requiring all states to deny a driving licence to those who cannot prove they are legally in the country. Several of the 9/11 suicide hijackers had obtained Virginia licences (needed to board an airplane) by establishing residency in that state. Other of those terrorists had a stolen Saudi Arabian passport, a fake Canadian passport, a stolen Social Security card and even possessed licences to transport hazardous materials.

Above: A French customs officer shows fake European Union ID documents, including passports and residence permits, at a press conference in 2006 in Ajaccio, southern Corsica. Many of these falsified documents had been seized in Corsica and southern France as they were about to be sold.

INTERPOL'S VIEW

'It's been proven in every single terrorist incident that a fraudulent passport has been used', according to Ron Noble, an American who heads Interpol.

'After September 11, if a citizen were to learn that a terrorist attack occurred by someone having entered their country with a stolen passport that was registered with Interpol but their country wasn't regularly checking it, I say governments would fall.'

Left: US immigration inspector Fred Ho shows a counterfeit passport enlarged by a microscopic camera at San Francisco International Airport in 2002. A system known as DataShare is being used at more than 300 US ports of entry to check photographs and information of visa holders.

Art Forgeries

The production of fake art has long been a lucrative business. Superficially, forged art 'masterpieces' are difficult to discern, even by some gallery, museum and auction experts.

Many cases can only be solved by forensic analyses that look at the age of a painting and compare it with other genuine pieces by the same artist.

Cracking the surface paint with varnish or rolling the canvas often ages a fake painting. A stereomicroscope can detect this more recent effort, and X-rays will reveal if the cracking reaches each paint level. Ultraviolet radiation can determine the age of a varnish and also reveal any sketching, retouching, and painted-over areas.

X-RAYS

The type of pigments used can also help dating, because the years they were introduced are known. The modern chrome yellow pigment, for example, can be identified by a scanning electron microscope (SEM), because the modern version has been coated for the past 30 years to protect it from pollution that once turned it black.

Ceramic artworks are difficult to copy, and experts use thermo-luminescence to date them, since it measures the radiation the clay has absorbed since it was fired.

Copies of metal figures are easy to cast, but an SEM can differentiate metals used today from older ones. X-ray fluorescence will date metal pieces because they emit an X-ray spectrum of the alloy used to make it.

Right: A forgery of a painting by Lucas Cranach the Elder is exposed by ultraviolet light which causes it to fluoresce. The dark areas were retouched.

Above: A technician at the Doerner Institute in Munich, Germany operates the infrared scanner that found the forged painting supposedly by Lucas Cranach the Elder.

184

LASERS AND CERAMICS

A forensic scientist in Perth, Australia, is using lasers to trace pottery back to its kiln site to expose ceramic forgeries. Emma Bartle from the Center for Forensic Science at the University of Western Australia developed the scientific method to authenticate porcelain.

Bartle said forged Chinese Ming and Japanese Imari porcelain is a multimillion-dollar industry in Southeast Asia. 'These modern fakes are so detailed and sophisticated', she noted, 'that gone are the days whereby trained experts can authenticate pieces using visual examination alone.'

The lasers analyze the porcelain's chemical composition to trace its origins back to production in China or Japan. 'Each site has a different combination of trace elements, such as strontium and lanthanum, which is unique', she said.

Ultraviolet radiation can determine the age of a varnish and reveal retouching.

COMPUTER ANALYSIS

Professor Hany Farid and his colleagues at Dartmouth College in Hanover, New Hampshire, have developed a computer tool for analyzing digital images to detect art forgeries. Announced in 2004, the technique classifies paintings and drawings by a digital analysis of an artist's style. High-resolution digital scans break down an image into 'wavelets'. These are simple elements and can be analyzed by a complex mathematical model to check for consistencies between works of art or within a single one.

When applied to 13 drawings, the technique automatically grouped the eight real works of the sixteenth-century Flemish artist Pieter Bruegel the Elder, separating them from five modern copies.

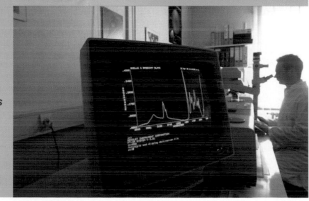

A popular method for detecting art forgeries is by using a spectrophotometer that can reveal the type of resin in the paint.

Successful Art Forgers

One of the most famous art forgers was an art restorer named Hans van Meegeren (1889–1947). Instead of copying existing masterpieces, however, he created entirely new paintings.

Van Meegeren created new paintings and attributed them to famous artists, such as six fake paintings by Vermeer, which he said he had discovered. They supposedly earned up to $30 million, with one going to the Nazi leader Hermann Goering.

AGEING PROCESS

Van Meegeren turned to copying the masters because his works were not wanted and he disliked the art establishment. He invented a process to age paint film by dissolving phenol formaldehyde resin in benzene or turpentine and baking it. This produced the look of a work of art of the seventeenth century. After a decade of this, he confessed to the forgeries. Forensic tests were made on his paintings, and traces of cobalt blue were found, a pigment not produced until the nineteenth century. He was charged with fraud, but died before serving his one-year sentence.

REVENGE

Tom Keating (1917–1984) was a London Cockney. Like van Meegeren, he was an art restorer who decided to create forgeries because his own paintings were unsuccessful and he wanted to upset wealthy art dealers. In the early

ELMYR DE HORY

One of the world's most talented art forgers was the Hungarian-born Elmyr de Hory (1906–1976). He studied art in Munich and Paris before being imprisoned by the Nazis in a concentration camp. He escaped from a prison hospital and bribed his way to Paris where he began to copy famous paintings, selling Picasso fakes to art galleries by claiming they came from his family's estate.
De Hory settled in Miami, Florida in the 1950s, where his painting began to fetch extremely high prices at art galleries. After suffering depression and an attempted suicide, however, he returned to Paris in 1959 and then the Spanish island of Ibiza in 1962. Already a celebrity, he told his story to the American writer Clifford Irving who published his biography, *Fake! The Story of Elmyr de Hory the Greatest Art Forger of Our Time.* De Hory took an overdose of sleeping pills in 1976 after learning that the Spanish government intended to turn him over to French authorities.

Art forger Elmyr de Hory poses with one of his fakes, which he claimed he could 'knock off' in ten minutes.

He turned to copying the masters because his works were not wanted and he disliked the art establishment.

1970s, he estimated that 2000 of his forgeries were in circulation but refused to name them. They include copies of famous works by Rembrandt, Renoir, Degas and Gainsborough.

All this came to an end in 1970 when auctioneers discovered 13 suspicious watercolours by 'Samuel Palmer' for sale. Keating confessed and was eventually arrested in 1977. Two years later his trial was ended because of his poor health. He later presented a television series for

Channel 4 on the techniques of the old masters. The year of his death, 1984, Christie's auctioned 204 of his works, and Keating's paintings now fetch up to £12,000 and more.

Right: The artist Hans van Meegeren works on a painting of Christ titled 'Teaching in the Temple.' Van Meegeren only confessed to the forgeries after he was arrested for collaborating with the Nazis. Tests by the laboratory of Belgian museums then confirmed the forgeries.

Above: To guard against charges of fraud, Tom Keating placed clues in his paintings, such as flaws in the artwork, for investigators to find. He also used modern easily identifiable materials.

Fake Products

Throughout the world, the manufacture and sale of fake products has become an immense industry estimated to represent up to seven per cent of world trade.

Above: Nestle CEO Peter Brabeck-Latmathe at the 2007 meeting of the Business Action to Stop Counterfeiting and Piracy in Geneva, Switzerland.

Right: Michel Danet, secretary general of the World Customs Organization, displays fake goods in 2004 in Brussels at the global congress on combating counterfeiting.

Main Picture: A policeman adds fake and pirate software disks to the large pile to be destroyed at a factory in Xian in Shaanxi Province, China, in 2005. Police destroyed more than 100,000 confiscated disks during the operation.

The FBI estimates that this illegal trade costs Americans about $250 billion a year, and other research found some 750,000 US jobs have been lost to fake products.

Michel Danet, the secretary general of the World Customs Organization, warns that the production of fake products is a serious criminal offence and should be considered as an act of economic sabotage.

COUNTERFEIT

It can be extremely difficult to distinguish between genuine and counterfeit products. As well, almost any item has been illegally copied, from doorknobs and shoe polish to food, drugs, watches, cigarettes, clothing, electronic equipment, perfume and even airplane engines. Worldwide research in 80 countries in 2005 by the Business Action to Stop Counterfeiting and Piracy (BASCAP), part of the International Chamber of Commerce located in Paris, found that 40 per cent of counterfeited brands involve software giants, clothes designers, pharmaceutical companies, printer manufacturers and luxury goods retailers.

SUPPORTING CRIME

'In some counterfeit goods, the quality is so good that it really takes a forensic expert to tell if it's fake or not', says Michelle Moore, a spokeswoman for the International Anti-Counterfeiting Coalition (IACC). She adds, 'And even though these places may look like innocent mom-and-pop shops, they're often connected to organized-crime rings.'

The IACC, located in Washington, DC, points out that counterfeiters do not pay taxes or fair wages and often use forced child labour. The profits have also been linked to organized crime, drug trafficking and terrorist activity. 'When you purchase a fake', it warned, 'you become part of the cycle of counterfeiting and your money directly supports these things you would never want to support.'

CUSTOMS

Every country is facing a nightmare battle. In 2007, India had 44 fake versions of Vicks VapoRub. In Malta during the first two months of 2007, customs officials intercepted over half a million counterfeit products. In Virginia, police raided 11 Newport News stores, and found that 90 per cent of the goods were fakes.

The quality of some counterfeit goods is so high that it really takes a forensic expert to tell if it's fake or not.

RECOGNIZING FAKES

Each type of product (diamonds, pearls, designer bags, etc) has been counterfeited in a different way, so it is impossible to list specific advice on detecting a fake. Consumers can follow a few general rules to educate themselves, and Ed Kelly, an intellectual property rights attorney in Thailand, says shoppers should keep the 'Three Ps' in mind:

- **Package:** Look at the quality of the product and its packaging. Watch for things like poor stitching or incorrectly spelled brand names or logos.
- **Price:** If the price is too good to be true, it probably is.
- **Place:** Brand name products are sold in shops or through the official company website, not on the streets or open-air markets.

Sources of Fake Goods

The US government estimates that international companies lose more than $60 billion a year to counterfeiting and piracy, which floods markets with low-cost fake products, mostly made in China.

Even in China, losses from counterfeiting are estimated at about one-fifth of the total sales for top brands.

As with drug crime, customer demand fuels the counterfeit industry. A fake $13,000 Swiss watch is being sold on New York streets for $10, while Louis Vuitton bags, normally about $2,000, are offered for $50 on the street and $800 on the Internet.

SEIZURES

Fake goods have become so prevalent that in one recent 10-day period, EU officials seized two million counterfeit products which had been made in China. More than 70 per cent of all fake goods seized in the EU and 81 per cent seized in the US come from that country.

US customs figures showed that Chinese fakes had increased from 2005 to 2006 by 62 per cent with apparel jumping 709 per cent and footwear by 669 per cent. These seizures are more than from all other countries combined.

Other sources of fake luxury goods include India, Malaysia and Indonesia, with much of the merchandise reaching Europe through traders in intermediate countries including Afghanistan, Guinea and the UAE.

FORENSICS AND FAKE DRUGS

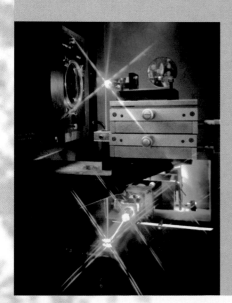

A new way of detecting fake drugs without opening the package was announced in 2007 by Dr Pavel Matousek and Dr Charlotte Eliasson of the Rutherford Appleton Laboratory in Oxfordshire.

Spectroscopy can provide an accurate fingerprint of a molecule. The scattered light from a molecule illuminated by a laser is collected by a lens and sent through a monochromator to a detector for analysis. But packaging material and the drug's coatings and inactive ingredients may add too much 'noise' to read a drug accurately.

Spatially offset Raman spectroscopy, however, avoids this problem. It can probe deep layers of material and separate out the interfering signals to authenticate the actual content of the drug. Successful tests have been done on blister packs and plastic bottles.

Left: The laser is an excellent Raman source, because it provides a narrow, highly monochromatic beam of radiation which can then be focused accurately into a small sample.

The Chinese government has promised to crack down on counterfeit goods and respect intellectual property rights, and has closed down the popular Xiangyang market in Beijing, once China's largest market for fake goods.

Left: A German custom official displays samples of fake Viagra tablets during a press conference in 2003. Officers confiscated 40,000 fake tablets in a package off a cargo plane.

Below: People shop on 11 June 2006 at the fake handbag stalls in the famous Silk Alley Market in Beijing, China. Fake bags and other goods can still be seen after Silk Alley and other major Beijing markets signed an agreement the previous week with famous brands, agreeing not to sell fake versions.

FAKE DRUGS

Consumers around the world are at increasing risk from fake drugs, according to a 2003 report by the World Health Organization (WHO), which estimates that up to 25 per cent of drugs consumed in developing countries are counterfeit. Many have no medicinal value at all, and some have been found to contain just wheat flour. Fake drugs, often originating in the Far East, are of particular concern in countries such as Cambodia, China, Laos, Myanmar, Thailand and Vietnam, where they undermine WHO health programmes.

Music Piracy

'Piracy', which involves the unauthorized duplication of commercial recordings, costs the music industry about $4.2 billion worldwide.

Music piracy drives up the cost to consumers of the legitimate product, reduces the royalties and fees earned by creative artists and harms retail businesses and the record companies.

The Recording Industry Association of America (RIAA) lists the four types of piracy as:

Pirate records: which refers to sound only without the packaging that includes the title, art, label, etc.

Unauthorized recordings: of sound and the unauthorized duplication of original packaging, trademark, label and artwork.

Bootleg recordings: also known as underground recordings, which are the unauthorized recordings of live concerts or musical broadcasts on radio or television.

Online piracy: which is the unauthorized uploading of copyrighted sound recording made available to the public as downloads from an Internet site.

The Internet has created a special danger for piracy with free file-sharing sites initiated by the Napster online music service. In 2005 the US Supreme Court issued a landmark ruling against online music file-sharing, and industry spokesmen say the practice has now been contained but not eliminated. Helping this was the RIAA, which sued more than 18,000 individuals for sharing songs online, with 4500 people settling for about £2,000 per case.

NAPSTER

University student Sean Parker and his uncle, Shawn Fanning, began the US music file-sharing service on the Internet in 1999. Opening an office in San Mateo, California, the company offered an enormous selection of music to trade and download free without royalties going to the copyright holder. Some songs appeared on Napster before they were even released.

By 2001, Napster had 26.4 million users, but several lawsuits had been filed. Napster closed its network in 2001 and attempted to convert to a fee-paying service. The following year, however, the company went bankrupt. Since then, several similar file-sharing sites have opened without a centralized network to make copyright suits more difficult.

Above: A New York University student downloads music from the Napster site in 2001. The recording industry won a victory when the US Supreme Court banned online music file-sharing.

Right: The world has been flooded by illegal music and videos that bring their producers generous profits. Their products, however, are often of poor quality and can lead to criminal cases being brought.

HOW TO SPOT PIRATED MUSIC

Some of the following signs indicate an unauthorized recording:

- The packaging has no bar code.
- The price is much cheaper than an original recording.
- There is no name and address of the manufacturer on the label or it is wrong.
- The recording is on Recordable Compact Disks (CD-Rs), which are greenish or bluish on the underside.
- The writing on the disks or inserts is often misspelt.
- Insert cards are often printed on low-quality paper and badly trimmed.
- The item is sold in such nontraditional places as a local market or car boot sale.

Left: Large amounts of illegal pirated music continues to be sold at informal markets throughout the world, such as this British car boot sale.

Two Music And Film Piracy Cases

The British Phonographic Industry (BPI), which protects music copyright in the UK, made raids in 2005 on a family-run movie rental store in Horden, County Durham. The counterfeiters' operation had netted £1.4 million.

Hundreds of people were involved selling counterfeit CDs and DVDs at pubs, markets and industrial sites in Northumbria, North Yorkshire, Cleveland, and across northeastern Britain. Because of this extensive

Piracy involves fake versions of almost any product sold, from luxury watches to shoe polish. Business groups have increased their efforts against this economic scourge.

network, BPI brought a rare private prosecution, only their third in three years. Guilty verdicts were handed down to Andrew Wood who was the ringleader and shop owner, James Cowan, and his wife Ann Cowan, all from Peterlee. Sentencing was to be in 2007.

EBAY FRAUD

An American, who with three associates made £61,500 from selling DVDs on the Internet from China, was deported in 2005 to the US to continue his jail sentence. Randolph Hobson Guthrie III, 38, is the son of a wealthy Manhattan plastic surgeon. He went to Shanghai in 1995 and built up a lucrative business, selling James Bond DVDs for £1.50 on eBay and a Russian Internet site.

After a solicitor for MGM spied one of Guthrie's eBay advertisements, the studio notified the Motion Picture Association of American (MPAA), which led to the first joint Sino-US investigation for

Members of the Motion Picture Association of America appear before a US Senate committee investigating music and video piracy.

DVD piracy. Local police found some 210,000 pirated DVDs at three warehouses Guthrie owned. The court case revealed the gang had sold 133,000 of them worth more than £200,000 to more than 20 countries, including the US, UK, Australia and Canada.

Guthrie was arrested in 2004 in Shanghai and sentenced to two and a half years in jail with a fine of £30,000. His three accomplices were all given jail terms of up to 15 months and fines between £620 and £2000. Guthrie was released to officers of the US Department of Homeland Security in 2005.

CHINA'S FREE INTERNET MUSIC

Research reveals that as much as 85 percent of all music in China is pirated. In March 2007 eleven companies sued Yahoo's China division for some 5.5 million yuan ($710,690) accusing it of violating copyright. China claimed it supports the campaign against piracy, but noted that Internet site owners are not liable for the actions of their users, which was decided in a previous suit against Baidu.com, China's biggest Internet search engine, based in Beijing. Baidu, in fact, had agreed in 2005 to remove links to websites offering pirated music. It had links to more than 50,000 files. They removed 3,000 music files alone that involved a single Chinese song. Baidu said that 22 percent of traffic on its Web site came from users of its search facility for music files.

Left: Chinese trade enforcement officers raid a display stand in 2004 at the annual China International Clothing and Accessories Fair in Beijing. Fake Pierre Cardin leather jackets were found.

The traces of a polygraph, or lie detector, may indicate false statements, but this is disputed.

Chapter Eleven

The Criminal Mind

The forensic scientist has an array of instruments and procedures at their disposal to help them discover how a crime was committed and the identity of the perpetrator. Delving into the mental state of a criminal, however, is considerably more difficult and often impossible. Indeed, the mind of a vicious murderer is like 'a riddle wrapped in a conundrum inside an enigma', to borrow Winston Churchill's phrase.

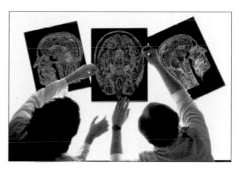

Doctors study results of magnetic resonance imaging (MRI), or brain scans. This technology is expected to be developed to analyze the criminal mind.

But criminals, like ordinary people, are creatures of habit. Investigators use such behaviour to narrow the field of suspects. Psychological profiling will build up a description of the most likely suspect until the guilty one is exposed. When he or she is apprehended, tests can be done to understand the suspect's state of mind. This will have a great bearing on the legal aspects of the case.

The instruments involved will not be familiar in the forensic lab. The polygraph, or lie detector, is a traditional, yet often discredited, tool for reading inner thoughts. Technology has now devised more reliable methods, using the electroencephalograph (ECG), magnetic resonance imaging (MRI) and computed tomography (CT) to probe the criminal mind.

Serial killer Rosemary West faces a police camera in 1995 after being sentenced with her husband, Fred West, to life in prison.

Psychological Profiling

Perpetrators of crimes, especially those driven by compulsions, will normally commit a series of crimes in a similar manner – a phenomenon which can be exploited by the forensic psychologist.

Psychological profiling, also known as criminal or offender profiling, is done in two different ways. In one, the assumption is made that a criminal, such as a serial killer, will behave as other similar criminals have in the past. It may thus be decided that a pedophile may use teenage Internet chatrooms to contact a victim and arrange a meeting.

The other way of profiling is to study the habits, or *modus operandi* (method of operating) of one criminal who repeatedly commits a crime instead of generalizing he or she is like others. A rapist may be extremely organized, such as making appointments with real estate dealers at unoccupied houses, or may have a 'signature' habit like mutilating the victim. A profiler who combines the two methods should have a better understanding of the characteristics of an offender.

Carine Hutsebaut is a psychotherapist at the International Centre for Molested and Abducted Children in Brussels, Belgium. She specializes in paedophile psychology.

Investigators also profile victims, in a process known as 'victimology'. Gaining an understanding of why they are selected at a particular place or time can lead investigators to the criminal. If several prostitutes are killed, the murderer may be a customer or even a fanatical moralist.

Profiling grew out of studies made by the FBI. The bureau's Behavioral Analysis Unit has put together reports profiling types of criminals, such as child abductors and school shooters.

Police detectives question a man after the murder of Maartje Tamboezer near a railway station in Surrey. The 1986 case saw Britain's first use of psychological offender profiling that led to John Duffy's conviction.

SIGNATURES

A criminal's signature is derived from his psychological needs and fantasies. Whereas such *modus operandi* as wearing a disguise or a particular way of lying in wait for a victim is a method of committing a crime, a signature is a criminal's personal, superfluous addition or 'calling card', which has nothing to do with pulling off a crime. Examples of signatures include torture, arranging the corpse in a certain way and taking souvenirs.

> **Gaining an understanding of why a victim was selected at a particular place or time can lead investigators to the criminal.**

RACIAL PROFILING

One danger of police profiling is discriminatory racial profiling. Muslims have complained in Britain about being stopped in airports for special checks. More common are routine stop-and-search procedures that, for example, can happen to Hispanics in the southwestern US more often than to white people. Black people in Canada even have a name for these checks, called 'DWB' for 'driving while black'.

Some, such as Haras Rafiq, spokesman for the Sufi Muslim Council in Britain, accept the reality of profiling. 'I regularly get checked, double-checked and sometimes triple checked', he noted in 2007. 'I get asked the same questions again and again. I understand the reason why they have to do this, and passengers need to be mindful and understand this as well.'

A 'Redeem the Dream' march on Washington, DC, in 2000 focused on racial profiling and police brutality.

The Polygraph

The polygraph, or lie detector, has had an unusual effect on criminal justice. Some suspects have refused to take it, thereby raising suspicions, while others have taken the chance and been proven liars.

There is no doubt that an unemotional murderer might cheat it, and a totally innocent person could panic on crucial questions and send readings awry.

This is why the instrument is seldom used as evidence in the courtroom. Yet the FBI gives about 8000 tests each year, reacting to the arrest in 2001 of Robert Hanssen who never underwent one in 25 years at the bureau, and was found to be a Russian spy. The CIA also administers tests to help stop employees from leaking information, and other US agencies now use them more than ever.

The UK government in 2007 announced trials that would give polygraph tests to paedophiles released back into communities, a program that is already established in the US.

STRESS LEVELS

A polygraph measures a person's stress level through a progression of questions. Electrodes on the suspect's fingers can detect the lower electrical resistance in the skin because of increased perspiration. A sphygmomanometer cuff around the arm also measures an increased pulse, and two pneumographs strapped around the chest measure heavy breathing caused by anxiety. The data is fed into a computer that produces a graph, a digital replacement for the old needle that used to scribble lines over a scrolling paper. The examiner starts by asking innocent questions to create a baseline of truthfulness for the purposes of comparison.

WHO INVENTED THE POLYGRAPH?

William Moulton Marston has often been credited with the invention of a simple polygraph in 1917, which measured blood pressure. His doctoral thesis at Harvard University in 1921 was 'Systolic blood pressure symptoms of deception and constituent mental states'. This was ironic because Marston also created the comic character Wonder Woman who roped evildoers with her golden lariat, which made them tell the truth.
It was John A. Larson, the first US policeman with a PhD., who devised the polygraph known today. He added measurements for heart rate, respiration and skin conductivity. This was also in 1921, while he was a student at the University of California, and he first tested it on female students.

A US murder suspect takes a lie detector test on 17 November 1926 when it was known as a 'truth detector test'. Like a polygraph, this early verson of the sphygmomanometer measured changes in blood pressure.

Right: A woman undergoes a polygraph test as part of her application to work at the FBI headquarters in Quantico, Virginia, USA. All new recruits must take a lie-detector test.

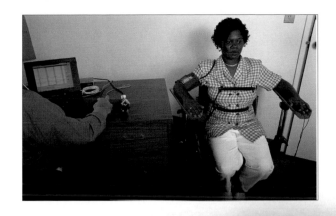

Below: Pulse meters are attached to a man's fingers for a polygraph test. The meters measure his heart rate, and under the subject's hands are the traces produced by the polygraph. These results are combined with measurements of blood pressure and respiration rate.

TWO US VIEWS

'The physiological responses measured by the polygraph are not uniquely related to deception. That is, the responses measured by the polygraph do not all reflect a single underlying process: a variety of psychological and physiological processes, including some that can be consciously controlled, can affect polygraph measures and tests.' *National Research Council, 2003*

'What is not subject to debate and appears to be beyond dispute is that the polygraph does not detect lies.' *US Congressional Research Service, 2007*

14   5   6.   7

STOELTING CO.   CHICAGO, IL, U.S.A.   CAT. NO. 25935   MADE IN U.S.A.

Polygraph Cases

The American middleweight boxer Rubin 'Hurricane' Carter, a suspect in a triple murder in 1966 in Paterson, New Jersey, took a polygraph test just hours after the murder and failed.

olice polygraph examiner John J. McGuire. had asked a series of questions twice, and Carter had failed both times. Carter and John Artis were convicted in 1967 of firing shots at the Lafayette Bar and Grill, which killed the bartender, and a male and female customer. Both men received life sentences, but were granted a new trial in 1976 because deals between the prosecution and witnesses were never disclosed to the defense.

Then the prosecution made an offer, saying they could take another lie detector test. If they passed, the charges would be dropped and they could go free. If they failed, the test would not be used against them in court.

Rubin 'Hurricane' Carter (right) and his co-defendant John Artis face newsmen outside the Passaic County Courthouse in Paterson, New Jersey in 1967 after their murder trial went to the jury. Both were convicted.

Both were re-tried because deals between the prosecution and witnesses had not been disclosed to the defence.

Before he took polygraph tests about Saddam Hussein having weapons of mass destruction, Ahmad Chalabi travelled the world seeking support for opposing the dictator.

EDWARD GELB

Edward Gelb, a renowned American polygraph examiner, has administered more than 30,000 tests, and has been in the investigative field since 1956. His famous clients include O.J. Simpson, who was accused in 1994 of killing his wife and her friend. Simpson failed the test but was not convicted. Gelb also tested John and Patsy Ramsey who were under suspicion in the 1996 murder of their daughter, JonBenet. They passed and were never indicted.

Here are crucial questions Gelb asked the Ramseys, who successfully answered 'No' to all of them:

'Did you inflict any of the injuries that caused the death of JonBenet?'

'Are you concealing the identity of the person who killed JonBenet?'

'Did you write the ransom note that was found in your house?'

John and Patsy Ramsey talk with reporters in 2001 after John was assaulted by a thief attempting to rob their home in Atlanta.

Amazingly, both men chose to decline the offer made to them.

Carter and Artis were released from prison in 1985. Carter, who still claims he passed the initial polygraph test, now lives in Toronto, Canada.

MISTAKES

A polygraph test that had worldwide repercussions involved the Iraqi leader Ahmad Chalabi who told US intelligence agents that Saddam Hussein had weapons of mass destruction.

Chalabi headed the Iraqi National Congress (INC), an exile group in London. He said Hussein had mobile biological weapons laboratories, and he passed a lie detector test that seemed to back up his information. In 2002, however, he failed another polygraph test, but intelligence analysts missed a warning that his information now was unreliable.

It has since been found that the INC had coached Chalabi to pass the first test. Though he lost friends in Washington, he is now a member of the Iraqi Governing Council, and in

2007 said his erroneous claims had achieved the aim of toppling Hussein. 'We are heroes in error', he said. 'What was said before is not important.'

Electroencephalograph

If the polygraph has its doubters, the electroencephalograph (EEG) has few. It has been used since the 1930s to track electrical waves coursing through our brains.

Computer-based 'Brain Fingerprinting', invented in the US by Dr Lawrence A. Farwell, uses the Memory and Encoding Related Multifaceted Electroencephalographic Response (MERMER). This is a brain reaction that kicks in when a person recognizes something of personal significance.

An electrical signal, known as P300, surges from the brain about 300 milliseconds after it confronts a significant image, such as a victim's face. This does not depend on the emotions of the suspect, only information stored in the brain. There is no testing to see if the suspect is telling the truth. The test can only indicate if he or she has certain information stored in their brain.

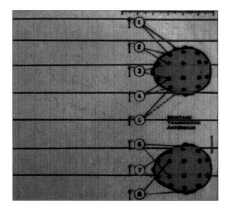

A coloured electroencephalograph (EEG) indicates a brain death. The eight brainwaves are flat because there are no electrical impulses being produced by the brain.

BRAIN FINGERPRINTING

In a Brain Fingerprinting test, a suspect wears a headband with electronic sensors that measure the EEG from several locations on the scalp. He or she is shown images, words, and phrases on a computer screen, some innocent and some connected to a crime. Brain Fingerprinting thus matches evidence at the crime scene with evidence in the brain.

The innocent images are used to establish the baseline response. The brain wave alters when an image is recognized, and guilty suspects cannot suppress their reaction as they can with a polygraph. A computer is then used to analyze the reaction.

Innocent suspects have no MERMER when, for example, they are shown a crime scene they do not know.

In tests run on FBI and CIA agents, Brain Fingerprinting proved one hundred per cent accurate. In the FBI test, 17 agents were separated from four non-agents by displaying images that only the FBI agents would recognize.

A MERMER CONVICTION

Brain Fingerprinting was instrumental in obtaining a confession and guilty plea from serial killer James Grinder in 1999 in Missouri. Dr Farwell gave the test to Grinder, showing him images connected to an unsolved murder, and the suspect's brain reaction confirmed a match. Grinder pled guilty to the rape and murder of Julie Helton and was given a life sentence without parole. He has since also confessed to killing three other women.

DR LAWRENCE A. FARWELL

The inventor of Brain Fingerprinting technology, Lawrence A. Farwell, is a former research associate at Harvard University. He is now the chairman and chief scientist of the Brain Fingerprinting Laboratories in Seattle, Washington. He also invented the Farwell Brain Communicator. This allows a paralyzed person to communicate directly to a computer and speech synthesizer using electrical brain activity.

Dr Farwell also has undertaken research that demonstrates the direct effect of human consciousness on matter at the quantum-mechanical level. As a result of his work, he wrote the book, *How Consciousness Commands Matter: The New Scientific Revolution and the Evidence that Anything Is Possible (2001).*

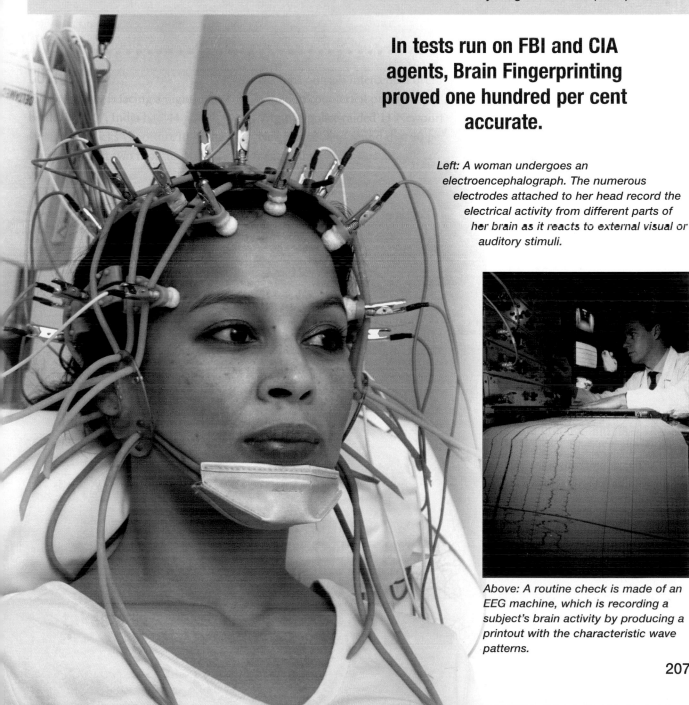

In tests run on FBI and CIA agents, Brain Fingerprinting proved one hundred per cent accurate.

Left: A woman undergoes an electroencephalograph. The numerous electrodes attached to her head record the electrical activity from different parts of her brain as it reacts to external visual or auditory stimuli.

Above: A routine check is made of an EEG machine, which is recording a subject's brain activity by producing a printout with the characteristic wave patterns.

207

Psychological Stress Evaluator

It seems logical that the stress in one's voice can indicate a lie or at least anxiety when questioned about a crime. This idea of using a 'voiceprint' as a lie detector has intrigued investigators for years and led to the invention of a psychological stress evaluator (PSE).

T his works on the assumption that a suspect's voice will reach a higher pitch when telling a lie. The voice emits inaudible vibrations called micro-tremors. Stress, which may exist when lies are told, causes the vocal muscles to tighten and the micro-tremors to decrease, producing flattened lines on a computer screen.

Voice stress analysis began in the 1970s when three retired US Army intelligence officers developed a system. All that is needed is a microphone and tape recorder, and a machine, which picks up differences

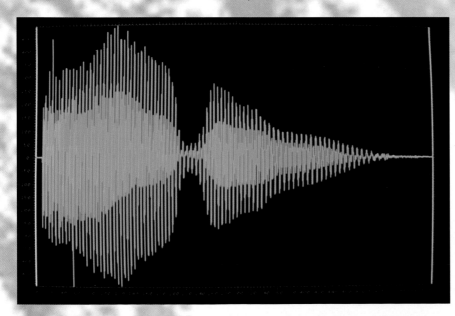

'A computer graphics image of the amplitude waveform of the word 'baby' is produced on a speech synthesizer. Amplitude means loudness, and a measurement of this could indicate stress.

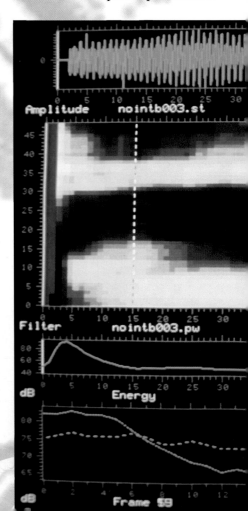

not heard by the human ear, analyzes the sound of a voice. The result is printed out onto a 'voiceprint' graph.

'MODERN-DAY OUIJA BOARD'?

Unfortunately, most scientists do not believe the system can detect lies, with one calling it a 'modern-day Ouija board'. Frank Horvath, a professor of criminology at Michigan State University who has studied lie detectors for more than 30 years, says the PSE detection rate is at 'chance levels, the same as guessing. There's no merit to it, whatsoever.' And Ian Christopherson, a lawyer in Las Vegas, adds, 'There may be something there that's measurable, but there's nothing there that correlates with the truth.'

Hundreds of US police departments, however, have recently bought one version, the Computer Voice Stress Analyzer (CVSA), in which a computer programme checks for minute vocal shifts. The National Institute for Truth Verification of West Palm Beach, Florida manufactures the machine. The company, founded in 1986, has sold the product to more than 1200 police departments and has trained nearly 5000 CVSA operators.

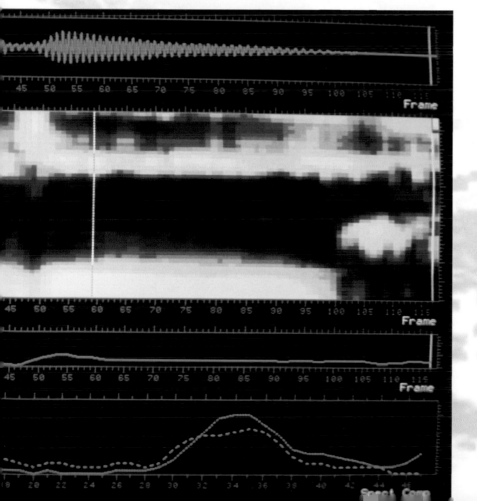

A screen image captures waveform representations of the voiceprint for the word 'baby'. From top to bottom are indications of amplitude, filtered presentation, energy level and a spectral representation.

Criminal Insanity

'Not guilty by reason of insanity' is a shaky defence that covers various mental states. The law believes a criminal cannot be held responsible for his or her actions if that person has no perception of reality.

Other definitions include whether or not the person could tell right from wrong, whether they could control their behaviour, and if they intended to act the way they did.

Forensic psychiatrists and psychologists know that it is not easy to explain the mind of the criminal within these terms. Many with mental health problems do know right from wrong, have a grasp on reality, are not subject to irresistible urges and can anticipate the results of their actions.

When ordinary neighbours commit insane crimes, they are often living in their own realities. A loving mother smothers her children to save them from the wicked world, or a reliable co-worker turns out to be a schizoid serial killer.

If a disturbed or mentally ill person commits a crime but lives in our reality, courts will often find them criminally responsible. In America, this may land them on death row. Several prisoners described as 'mentally retarded' have been executed, but the US Supreme Court ruled in 2002 that executing retarded prisoners violated the Constitution's protection against 'cruel and unusual punishments'.

Psychiatrists have pointed out other differences in the minds of violent offenders. Some have a distinctive lack of empathy for their victims, some are unable to control their behaviour, and others have predisposing factors like a history of a violent father.

SON OF SAM

David Berkowitz, nicknamed 'Son of Sam', was a serial killer who terrorized New York City in the 1970s. He wrote a strange letter to the police saying he was the 'Son of Sam' and 'Papa Sam keeps me locked in the attic too.' He was eventually caught in 1977 after receiving a parking ticket close to the scene of his latest murder. A search of his car revealed the gun. Berkowitz said that howling dogs in the neighbourhood were possessed by ancient demons that ordered him to go out and kill. This suggested a plea of insanity, but he confessed to killing six people and in 1978 received six life sentences.

David Berkowitz arrives at the Brooklyn Criminal Courts Building after his arrest on 10 August 10 1977 outside his Yonkers home.

Right: US Attorney Wendell Odom delivers his closing arguments in the second murder trial of his client Andrea Yates, in which she was found not guilty of murder by reason of insanity.

SATAN WITHIN

Andrea Yates drowned her five children one by one in the bath in 2001 in the area of Houston, Texas. At her second trial in 2006, she was found not guilty by reason of insanity after the jury was told she suffered from severe postpartum psychosis, and in a delusional state believed Satan was inside her. She said she was trying to save her children from hell. An earlier sentence of guilt was overturned, and Yates was sentenced to a mental hospital.

Yates and her lawyers George Parnham (left) and Wendell Odom react to the new verdict in 2006.

If a disturbed or mentally ill person commits a crime but lives in our reality, courts will often find them criminally responsible.

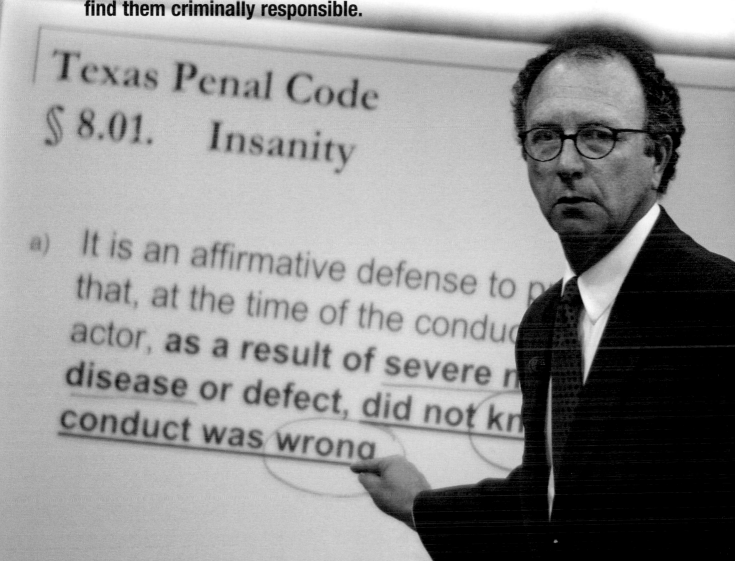

Texas Penal Code
§ 8.01.   Insanity

a)   It is an affirmative defense to p
that, at the time of the conduc
actor, **as a result of severe** r
disease or defect, did not kn
conduct was wrong

Serial Killer Cases

When David Birnie hanged himself in Australia's Casaurina Prison, south of Perth, on 7 October 2005, the story of Western Australia's worst serial killer also ended.

Birnie, 55, was serving a life sentence for abducting, raping, torturing, and murdering four women in 1986, aided by his common-law wife Catherine Birnie.

OGRE OF THE ARDENNES

Michel Fourniret's easy ability to move between Belgium and France to kill at least nine young women and girls was the reason the European Community in 2004 began to promote the increased sharing of criminal records between countries. Police believe he was responsible for many more deaths in other European countries. Dubbed the 'Ogre of the Ardennes' for the forest where he was a warden and where many of his victims died, Fourniret confessed to the murders after his wife, Monique Olivier, made accusations against him. Fourniret made his confession in 2004 from a Belgium prison cell where he was serving time for trying to abduct a 13-year-old Congolese girl.

She had left her husband and six children in 1985 to move in with Birnie and take his name. She is still serving a life sentence in Bandyup Women's Prison, eligible for parole

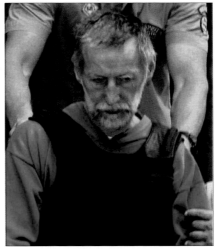

Michel Fourniret is pictured here leaving police headquarters in Dinant, France, after confessing to the murder of nine young women.

in 2007 as was he, but authorities say her release is highly unlikely.

Their five-week killing spree in October and November of 1986 involved luring or abducting the women to their home in Willagee, a suburb of Perth, then raping them before stabbing, strangling, and

clubbing them to death. This came to an end when a fifth rape victim, aged 16, escaped and alerted the police.

Birnie made a surprising confession as he was being interrogated by Detective Sergeant Vince Kaitch, who said jokingly, 'It's getting dark. Best we take the shovel and dig them up.' The serial killer shrugged and replied, 'Okay. There are four of them.'

MOORS MURDERS

If possible, Britain was even more shocked by the five children murdered by Ian Brady and Myra Hindley from 1963 to 1965. The 'Moors murders' included the children being tortured, and in some cases recorded on tape and photographed, then buried on the moors near Oldham. The killers were turned in by Hindley's brother-in-law David Smith, and the bodies discovered before their sensational trial in 1966, in which the judge described Brady as 'wicked beyond belief'. He received three concurrent life sentences, while Hindley received two concurrent ones and died in prison in 2002.

'There is free will and you never get away from that. This is a weakness but it can be overcome.'

Myra Hindley (above) appealed her life sentence but died two weeks before the House of Lords decision. Ian Brady (left) wrote to British Home Secretary Jack Straw in 1997 asking that Hindley never be released. Brady himself has never appealed.

DARK INFLUENCES

When Luke Mitchell, 17, murdered his girlfriend Jodi Jones, 14, in 2003, slitting her throat and mutilating the body, Detective Superintendent Craig Dobbie, head of the Edinburgh CID, visited the FBI's Behavior Science Unit to understand the killer's learned behavioural traits. Investigators slowly pieced together Mitchell's interests. These included obsessions with the occult, satanic worship, and the controversial Goth rock star, Marilyn Manson, a fixation with death and an unhealthy interest in knives.

The Lothian and Borders Police released this order form filled out by Luke Mitchell for a 'Skunking knife' in December 2003.

The History of Profiling

Criminal profiling was virtually created in England by Dr Thomas Bond, a police surgeon, when he was assigned to do the autopsy on Mary Kelly, who would turn out to be Jack the Ripper's seventh, and final, victim.

He profiled the killer as being daring, physically strong, mentally unstable, but a quiet loner. Jack was never caught, but England was impressed with this new art of offender profiling.

CLOTHES OF A KILLER

Psychiatrists took over from surgeons to usher in modern profiling in the middle of the twentieth century. When nearly 40 bombings occurred in the 1940s and 1950s in New York City, Dr James Brussel, a Freudian psychiatrist, provided the police with a profile that predicted, oddly, that the man wore a double-breasted suit and lived with an unmarried sister or aunt in the states of Connecticut, New Hampshire or Maine.

When the police in 1957 finally caught up with the perpetrator, George Metesky, he did fit most of the profile, including his age, ethnicity, and religion, wearing a double-breasted suit, and living with two unmarried sisters in Connecticut.

BEHAVIOURAL ANALYSIS

Criminal profiling became organized when the FBI took an interest. Its Behavioral Science Unit opened in 1972 and it was soon specializing in areas like serial murder and child

PROFILING IN RUSSIA

Russia's serial killer, Andrei Chikatilo, raped, brutalized, and killed at least 53 women and children from 1978 to 1990. Impressed by the FBI's work in profiling, the chief investigator Viktor Burakov asked Dr Alexandr Bukhanovsky, a psychiatrist, to draw up a profile of the serial killer. It said he was probably an

ordinary, solitary, nonthreatening sexual deviant, who suffered from sexual inadequacy.

Chikatilo was caught through other police work but refused to confess. Dr Bukhanovsky returned and saw that the criminal matched the points he had emphasized. When he read his original report to Chikatilo, describing his mental illness and its causes, the killer was so affected by the mirror image that he broke down and confessed.

Psychiatrist Alexandr Bukhanovsky sits at home to look through the case files on Andrei Chikatilo, one of the worst serial killers of modern times.

abuse. Then, after the terrorist attacks of 11 September 2001, the organization was divided into three Behavioral Analysis units: counter-terrorism and threat assessment, crimes against adults, and crimes against children. The FBI has recently replaced the 'criminal profiling' term with 'criminal investigative analysis'.

Left: A profile by psychiatrist Dr James Brussel led to the arrest of George Metesky (wearing glasses), who set off bombs in New York City from 1940 to 1956.

Left: Andrei Chikatilo, called the 'Rostov Ripper', was a shy man who had a wife and two children. The psychiatrist's accurate profile said he was a paranoic sadist about the age of 45 to 50.

FORENSIC PSYCHOLINGUISTICS

If a suspect has been in verbal or written contact with the victim or investigators, profilers can learn much from the language used. Some major clues are:

- **Geographic origin:** Regional dialects are hard to lose.
- **Ethnic group:** This is often apparent through choice of words and the word order.
- **Age:** Teenagers and different age groups tend to use different words and terminology.
- **Gender:** Women have been found to use a more tentative language, such as "It seems to me that…"
- **Education level:** The use of correct grammar and more difficult words are keys to a better education.

The Mind of a Terrorist

Profiling terrorists, to many people, concerns ethnic and religious targeting. There is no doubt a criminal profiler would include this in a description of a sought terrorist, despite its racial element.

Four years after the 11 September attacks on New York City in 2001, Mayor Michael Bloomberg said that terrorists come 'in all sizes and shapes and forms', and it was not fair for police to profile terrorism suspects because they have a Middle Eastern appearance. 'I think if we've learned anything', he said, 'it is you can't predict what a terrorist looks like.'

RACIAL PROFILING

In the other camp, supporting 'racial profiling' is Roger Clegg, a contributing editor to the US conservative magazine, *National*

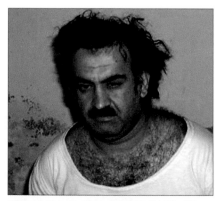

The al-Qaeda terrorist Khalid Sheikh Mohammed allegedly confessed to his role in the 9/11 attacks and 29 other terror plots.

Review. He takes the hypothetical situation of identifying members of a terrorist ring and then finding the rest. The profile of the captured group was Middle Eastern descent, Muslim, trained pilots, young or middle-aged males booked on transcontinental flights. Clegg notes: 'Any problem with assuming that there is a good chance that the remaining members of the ring are likely to meet this profile, too?'

PERSONALITY

This is only one facet of identifying a terrorist, for forensic experts put much effort into investigating the mind of such a perpetrator. The Australian psychologist Robert Heath of the University of South Australia notes that terrorists are both born and made, having a psychological predisposition to violence, and scoring high as being a psychotic, neurotic sociopath.

Professor Susan Greenfield, a leading brain scientist and director of the Institute for the Future of the Mind, says neuroscience can be a weapon against terrorism. She notes that terrorism is basically a set of

tactics founded on a belief system, and that the brain is essentially hardwired the first 18 years of life in how we perceive and respond to our world.

As well as being director of the Institute for the Future of the Mind, Baroness Susan Greenfield is the director of the Royal Institution of Great Britain and and the Fullerian Professor of Physiology at Oxford University.

THE PSYCHOLOGY OF FEAR

Psychologists analyzing the tactics of terrorist agree that their battle is being waged with the psychological weapon of fear. This seemed to be the tactic when Khalid Sheikh Mohammed confessed in March 2007 from the US prison in Guantanamo, Cuba, that he had planned 31 terrorist attacks, including those of 9/11. He might have exaggerated the number to spread 'the message of fear', according to Jerrold M. Post, director of the Political Psychology Program at George Washington University.

The same tactic was seen in January 2007 after Britain foiled a terrorist plot in Birmingham to abduct, torture, and murder a British Muslim soldier on film. Noted Professor David Wilson, a specialist in the mind of criminals and terrorists: 'They would have been saying, "nowhere is safe, not even your home".' He added, 'Terrorists are seeking to destroy the sense of safety and security normally associated with coming home.'

Above: Two men, later identified as terrorists Mohammed Atta (right) and Abdulaziz Alomari, are captured on CCTV going through security at Portland airport on the morning of 11 September 2001. The pair would later hijack American Airlines Flight 11, which Atta would pilot into one of the towers of the World Trade Center in New York City.

Fingerprint records from the French police archive are matched with new images from the digital database.

Chapter Twelve

History of Forensic Detection

orensic examinations of a sort have been recorded since ancient times, when a Roman pathologist, Antistius, performed an autopsy on the corpse of the slain Julius Caesar. But the first true book of forensic science did not appear until 1247, in China.

Amateur work was seen in America in the eighteenth century, with Paul Revere identifying the body of General Warren by his false tooth. Arthur Conan Doyle's fictional Sherlock Holmes popularized detection through observation in the latter nineteenth century. At that same time the Frenchman Alexandre Lacassagne was doing impressive forensic work in his laboratory at the University of Lyon.

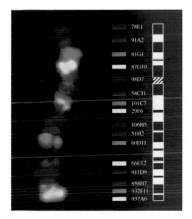

A chromosomal rainbow is created in this fluorescent light microgram and diagram of human chromosome 10.

In 1902, in England, fingerprints were accepted as evidence for the first time. By 1932, the FBI had established its Technical Crime Laboratory, and in 1967 started its National Crime Information Center.

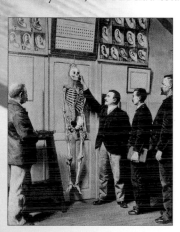

French criminologist Alphonse Bertillon at the Paris police headquarters shows his Bertillon System of identifying criminals by using anthropometric measurements.

Forensics in the Ancient World

Early civilizations had an awareness of the value of fingerprints for identification. The ancient Babylonians impressed their fingers into clay tables when conducting business.

By 200 BCE, Chinese rulers were using thumbprints for identification on important documents sent to government officials who knew the distinctive imprint. In the seventh century, the Arab merchant Soleiman described how a debtor's fingerprints were placed on a bill and given to the lender as legal proof of the debt.

The Greek mathematician Archimedes (c.287–212 BCE) perhaps recorded the first forensic evidence, when he exposed a fake product by testing its displacement in water. By measuring its buoyancy, he was able to prove that a crown, which people had claimed was made of gold, was in fact a fake.

EVIDENCE IN EGYPTIAN COURTS

The ancient Egyptians placed great importance on the use of evidence in their courts, using specialists to examine documents. One case was recorded in which examiners decided to falsify the documents of a property dispute. The petitioner, Moses, brought in witnesses to testify that his father had cultivated the land and paid taxes. Ultimately though, Egyptian courts believed that witness testimony was more important than documents. Judges would also visit a crime scene to collect evidence, taking along the accused to the scene where he or she would be asked questions about the alleged crime.

It was also a Greek, the physician Erasistratus (c. 250 BCE), and founder of a school of anatomy at Alexandria, who developed the first known lie detection test. He discovered that his patients' pulse rates increased when they told him falsehoods.

JULIUS CAESAR'S MURDER

The ancient Romans further developed the Greek knowledge of anatomy and applied it to crime. Antistius, the Roman pathologist, made a careful examination of Julius Caesar's body after his assassination in 44 BCE. He reported that Caesar had been stabbed 23 times but only one wound, found on his chest, had been fatal.

By 100 CE, Romans were introducing crime-scene evidence in court. One famed orator, Quintilian, was able to demonstrate that bloody palm prints had been left to incriminate a blind man for his mother's murder.

Two types of written documents are exhibited at the Khotan Museum in China. One is a confidential document with a sealed cover that is made of clay. The other document is on a piece of wood.

In the seventh century, the Arab merchant Soleiman described how a debtor's fingerprints were placed on a bill and given to the lender as legal proof of the debt.

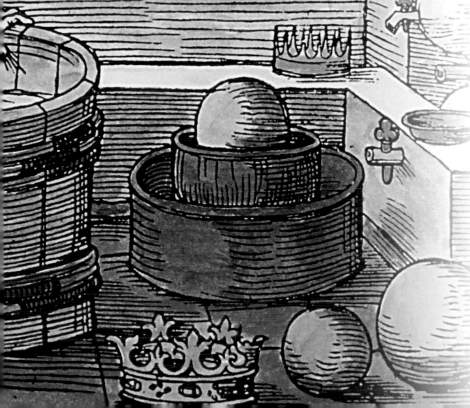

EARLY POSTMORTEMS

The Greek anatomist Erasistratus of Chios, who taught in Alexandria, conducted some of the first recorded postmortem examinations, although these were done to explain the human body, not to solve crimes. He dissected and examined the human brain, and was near to discovering blood circulation. However, he had it circulating in the wrong direction. He believed the veins carried the blood, the arteries the 'vital' spirit, and the nerve the 'animal' spirit.

Left: This artwork shows the Greek scientist Archimedes in his bath where he supposedly discovered that a body in a fluid displaces fluid equal to its own volume.

Forensics in the Middle Ages

The first recorded account of an investigator using insects to find a perpetrator occurred in thirteenth-century China. The victim had been slashed to death in a rural village, but no one confessed.

The investigator, Sun T'zu, asked all of the villagers to bring their harvesting sickles and lay them on the ground. He knew that flies have the ability to sense odours not detectable by humans. Soon the insects, attracted by tiny traces of blood and tissue remaining from the murder, began to settle on one sickle. Sun T'zu accused the man who owned the sickle, who confessed immediately.

This account was included in the first written report of medicinal knowledge being used to solve criminal cases, entitled Xi Yuan Ji Lu ('Collected Cases of Injustice Rectified'). Song Ci (1186–1249), a presiding judge in Chinese high courts, wrote the book in 1247. It also describes how to distinguish between drowning and strangulation. The work became a coroner's textbook.

OPIUM AND WINE

In Italy, surgeons were beginning to use their skills to assist in legal cases in Bologna. Hugh of Lucca, surgeon to the Crusaders, founded the school of surgery at the University of Bologna. He introduced the idea of using wine to clean wounds, and became a medico-legal expert for the city in 1249. His son and pupil, Theodoric of Lucca, also taught at Bologna. Theodoric introduced the use of sponges soaked in opium as an anaesthetic.

By 1302, Bartolomeo de Varignon had performed a medico-legal autopsy to verify a suspected murder of a nobleman named Azzolino.

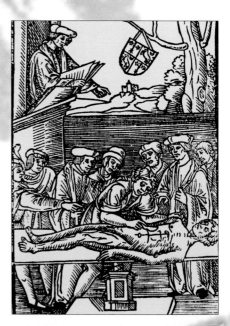

This historical print depicts a demonstrator performing a dissection of a corpse for students enrolled at a medical school during the fifteenth century.

THE FIRST MEDICAL EXPERTS

Although medical evidence had sometimes been introduced in the courts of antiquity, the thirteenth century saw its general acceptance in the legal matters of northern Italy. New laws allowed for the appointment of medical experts to advise the courts, and rules were even listed for someone to qualify as an expert medical witness. During these years, police surgeons were also becoming recognized as new professionals and were appointed to law-enforcement bodies.

MEDIEVAL DISSECTIONS

Autopsies were seldom done in the Middle Ages because of the Roman Catholic Church's belief in the resurrection of the whole body. Many popes condemned dissection and threatened to excommunicate or even burn at the stake anybody who 'molested the dead'.

When dissections were done in the famous medical schools at Bologna, Padua, and Montpellier, they were performed as rapidly as possible, and in the winter. Few human dissections occurred – Padua recorded one male and one female each year – so surgeons often dissected pigs.

The purpose of Medieval dissections was normally not to investigate why a person died or to advance medical treatment, but rather to do research on how the body functions, especially its organs. This was to verify or disprove information about anatomy from earlier philosophers and scientists, such as Aristotle.

Left: A dissector works on a suspended cadaver. This image appears in a manuscript by Guy de Vigevano of Chantilly, dated 1345.

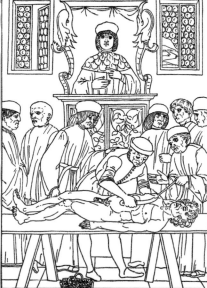

Right: A fifteenth-century woodcut shows an anatomical lecture at the famous University of Padua, Italy, showing the professor standing in his professorial chair (background) and presumably lecturing to the group of students below.

Early Forensic Breakthroughs

A renowned French surgeon, Ambroise Pare, published a court report on legal medicine in 1575, but Italy was again in the forefront of forensics in the sixteenth century.

PAOLO ZACCHIA

Italian physician Paolo Zacchia (1584–1659) first defined forensic medicine in his nine-volume work, *Quaestiones medico-legales* (Medico-legal questions). In it, he covered such topics as malpractice, and legal and medical ethics. Strongly advocating more authority for physicians, his method in legal cases was to follow a crime's sequence of events in order to establish its medical chronology. Zacchia was the personal physician to the popes Innocent X and Alexander VII and legal advisor to the Rota Romana, the second-highest ecclesiastical court of the Roman Catholic Church, so his views were influential. His comprehensive medico-legal textbook remained in print into the late eighteenth century.

In 1598, the physician Fortunatus Fidelis began to use 'the application of medical knowledge to legal questions', and another Italian doctor, Paolo Zacchia, gave legal medicine its name between 1621 and 1651 when he published *Quaestiones medico-legales* (Medico-legal questions).

In England, in 1658, Sir Thomas Browne, a physician often considered an early forensic archaeologist, discovered the formation of adipocere, a waxy substance, which forms in decaying corpses. Today, forensic scientists analyze adipocere to estimate time of death. That same year in Italy, at the University of Bologna, a professor of anatomy, Marcello Malpighi, carefully described the

Christiaan Huygens (1629–1696), Dutch physicist and astronomer, invented the two-lens eyepiece for microscopes in about 1684. Here he is shown colliding balls to derive the laws of elastic collisions.

ridges, spirals and loops in fingerprints, but did not consider their unique nature and possible application in identification.

MICROSCOPES

Microscopes, so vital to forensics, were now being developed. The first practical one was devised in 1590 by the Dutch spectacle-maker Zacharias Janssen and his father, Hans Janssen. In Germany in 1628, Christoph Scheiner, a professor of mathematics and Hebrew, refined the compound microscope, a prototype for modern microscopes. Innovation returned to Holland when the amateur scientist Anton van Leeuwenhoek invented the first precision microscope in 1670, using a single lens to achieve a magnification up to 270x. The physicist Christiaan Huygens devised a two-lens eyepiece about 1684.

Ambroise Pare (1504–1590), the French surgeon, wrote influential reports concerning legal medicine. He was a barber-surgeon in the army and is considered to be the father of modern surgery. He greatly improved the treatment of sword and gunshot wounds.

Adipocere, a waxy substance which forms on corpses, was discovered in 1658 and is still examined today to estimate time of death.

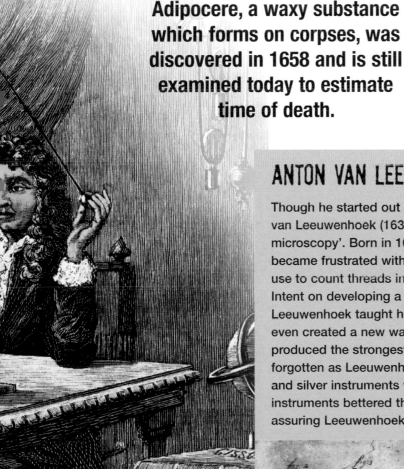

ANTON VAN LEEUWENHOEK

Though he started out counting threads in a dry goods shop, Anton van Leeuwenhoek (1632–1723) is today often called the 'father of microscopy'. Born in 1632 in Delft, Holland, as an apprentice he became frustrated with the weak magnifying glass he was forced to use to count threads in cloth.

Intent on developing a more powerful instrument for his work, Leeuwenhoek taught himself how to grind and polish lenses and even created a new way of increasing the curvature of the glass. This produced the strongest magnification of his day. The threads were forgotten as Leeuwenhoek concentrated on producing beautiful gold and silver instruments with a single lens of very short focus. These instruments bettered the performance of all the existing microscopes, assuring Leeuwenhoek of his place in history.

This drawing of human sperm by Anton van Leeuwenhoek was in a letter he sent to the Royal Society in London.

Global Forensics

The national forensic science laboratories and systems established in the twentieth century are now working together as efficient international networks of forensic scientists.

FBI agents instruct a group of Eastern European police officers in 2000 at the International Law Enforcement Academy in Hungary.

Authorities are able to access various types of criminal evidence in the powerful databases of the FBI in the US, the FSS in the UK, and Interpol in Europe.

Individual countries are also joining forces more often to help identify victims of natural disasters and to apprehend criminals who move across borders. Since it was founded in 1995, the International Law Enforcement Academy (LEA) in Budapest, Hungary, has taught forensic techniques to more than 2000 professionals from 27 nations,

INTERNATIONAL COURTS

Forensic scientists work closely with the two major world courts, both based in the Hague in the Netherlands: the International Court of Justice, which is the principal judicial body of the United Nations, and the International Criminal Court, an independent agency. The latter compiles and maintains a list of expert witnesses that includes those in forensic medicine and ballistics.

The forensic identification of victims of war atrocities has provided evidence for cases by both courts, such as the indictment and highly publicized trial of Serbian President Slobodan Milosevic for war crimes. Extensive evidence was presented, but the case ended when he died in his prison cell on 11 March 2006.

from Albania to Uzbekistan. Terrorism has been a catalyst in speeding up cooperation around the globe.

SHARING INFORMATION

Forensic scientists share the latest technical advances through many international organizations. The European Network of Forensic Science Institutes, begun in 1995, holds regular meetings for its membership of forensic laboratories. The American Society of Crime Laboratory Directors maintains an International Liaison so lab directors can collaborate across the global forensic community.

Many specialist associations also exist, such as the International Association of Bloodstain Pattern Analysts, with headquarters in Tucson, Arizona, and the International Association for Identification, based in Mendota Heights, Minnesota, with some 6700 members and 60 divisions worldwide.

Educational institutions are doing their part. In 2006, for example, the University of Florida Global Forensic Science programme in the US signed an agreement to exchange academic and research information with the Centre for Forensic Science at the Canberra Institute of Technology in Australia.

Below: The impressive International Court of Justice building is in the Hague, in the Netherlands. The court, also known informally as the World Court, was established in 1945 and began work the next year. Its 15 judges serve for nine-year terms.

ORGANIZED CRIME AND POLLUTION

Interpol has undertaken an international project to see whether pollution crimes are linked to organized crime. In the first phase, surveys were taken with five participating countries, the UK, US, Canada, Sweden and the Netherlands. The results released in 2006 confirmed a connection, based on data from 1995 to 2005.

For example, 36 case studies involved organized crime in the illegal import and export of waste, illegal hazardous waste disposal, and illegal movement of ozone-depleting substances. Some cases linked terrorism and pollution crimes, such as the illegal waste disposal by terrorist groups in Northern Ireland.

Above: A child in a Third World country walks beside a wall of bags containing electronic waste illegally transported from developed nations.

Establishing Forensic Standards

Forensic medicine, also known as 'legal medicine' and 'medical jurisprudence', was a recognized field by the early nineteenth century, but had developed no specialties. The two about to emerge were forensic pathology and toxicology.

This historical illustration is from the title page of the 1892 book Finger Prints *by the renowned British anthropologist Sir Francis Galton (1822–1911). The prints shown are his own. Galton was largely responsible for the introduction of fingerprinting as a means of identifying individuals in criminal investigations.*

Physicians were routinely performing autopsies, but information and training was scarce, so most practitioners developed their own postmortem procedures.

The growth of forensic work in the late 1800s in Britain was due in part to the new organization and bureaucracy of criminal investigation, with the expansion of the court system and police. Photography was first used in the 1860s to document crime scenes.

Europeans also made advances in standardizing evidence collection.

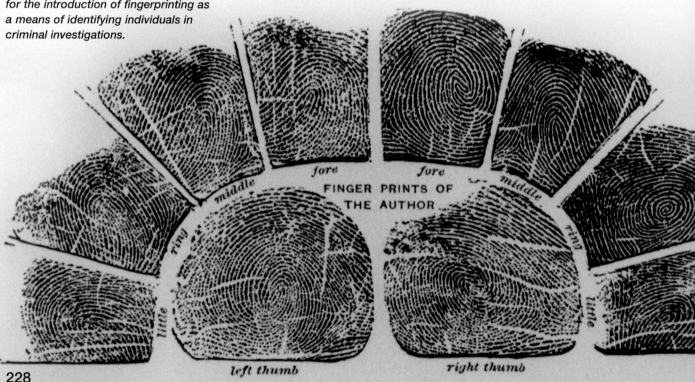

FINGER PRINTS OF THE AUTHOR

fore fore
middle middle
ring ring
little little

left thumb right thumb

Dr Henry Faulds's Guide to Finger-print Identification *(1905) included this artwork. Faulds (1843–1930), a Scottish missionary and scientist, was an early developer of fingerprint analysis. Convinced that the patterns of ridges on fingertips were unique, he set about trying to develop a system of analysis by describing several identifying features.*

In 1879, the German pathologist Rudolph Virchow became the first scientist to test hair as evidence, yet warned that it had limitations in court testimony. In 1891, Hans Gross, an Austrian professor of criminal law at the University of Graz, wrote *Criminal Investigation*, the first definitive volume on physical evidence used to solve crimes.

FINGERPRINTING

Equally important, fingernail technology was being introduced into police and court procedures. Sir William James Herschel, a British chief administrative officer in Bengal, India, began to use fingerprinting to identify prisoners in 1877, and two years later

Dr Henry Faulds, a Scottish missionary working in a Tokyo hospital, used fingerprints to identify a thief who stole the hospital's alcohol. He wrote about the forensic use of fingerprints in 1880 in the scientific journal *Nature* but failed to interest Scotland Yard in this type of identification because they could not establish the individual uniqueness of fingerprints. The British anthropologist Francis Galton proved this, however, when he announced his results in 1892 in his textbook, *Finger Prints*.

JUAN VUCETICH

The Argentine policeman Juan Vucetich was the first person to develop a fingerprint classification system and the first to convict a murderer by fingerprints.
He developed the first criminal fingerprint identification system in 1891, and a year later, he investigated the case of Francisca Rojas who had murdered her two sons and cut her own throat, saying they were attacked by an intruder. At the crime scene, however, Vucetich found a bloody fingerprint that matched hers and led to her conviction.
The Argentine police adopted his method of classification, and it was soon used in police departments worldwide.

Juan Vucetich (1858–1925) wanted to fingerprint the whole population of Argentina. He had emigrated from Croatia to Argentina as a young man.

FINGERPRINTS IN FICTION

The acceptance of fingerprint evidence by the public (including juries) was accelerated by popular fiction in the late nineteenth century. In 1883 in his book *Life on the Mississippi*, Mark Twain had a murderer identified this way. He used this idea again in his serialized novel *Pudd'nhead Wilson* in 1893 and 1894.
The British author Arthur Conan Doyle used his stories of the brilliant fictional detective, Sherlock Holmes, to stress the importance of fingerprints and other trace evidence, with the first volume published in 1887.

The Twentieth Century

The turn of the century ushered in the total acceptance of fingerprint identification. Scotland Yard adopted the system in 1901, and the following year the New York Civil Service Commission initiated the first systematic use of fingerprints.

The New York State Prison System first used this for criminal identification in 1903. In France, the forensic scientist Edmond Locard presented his theory that 'every contact leaves a trace' in 1904. At the Sorbonne in Paris, Victor Balthazard, professor of forensic medicine, and Marcelle Lambert published the first comprehensive study on identifying hair, *Le poil de l'homme et des animaux* (Human and Animal Hair) in 1910, and three years later Victor Balthazard published the first article on identifying bullet markings.

The power and resolution of microscopes were now evolving rapidly. In 1925, the Americans Philip Gravelle and Calvin Goddard invented the comparison microscope used to compare trace evidence side by side, and in 1931, Ernst Ruska co-invented the powerful electron microscope, which can view objects as small as the diameter of an atom.

SIR EDWARD RICHARD HENRY

While serving in 1891 as the Inspector-General of Police of Bengal, India, Edward Richard Henry became convinced that fingerprints could be used for identification if they were divided into groups. He devised a classification system of 1024 primary groups and instituted it in Bengal in 1897. That same year, the Indian government adopted his system.

It proved so successful, a British committee in 1900 recommended that it replace the Bertillon anthropometric system then used. The

next year, Henry was transferred to England. There he set up Scotland Yard's Central Fingerprint Bureau, Britain's first, and published *Classification and Uses of Fingerprints*. In 1903, he was appointed the Commissioner of the Metropolitan Police.

Sir Edward Richard Henry (1850–1931) was born in London. His Henry Classification System is still used in many nations, including Britain and the US.

THE COMPARISON MICROSCOPE

The comparison microscope is a staple of the crime laboratory. It consists of two compound light microscopes with a magnification of 40x to 400x. The optical bridge, a series of lenses and mirrors, projects images of two different specimens into a single eyepiece so a known sample, such as a suspect's hair, can be compared to a sample from the crime scene. It is often used to compare fibres, tool marks and ballistic evidence.

Two years after the instrument's invention in 1925 in the US by Philip Gravelle and Calvin Goddard, a comparison miscroscope matched bullet casings to uphold the convictions of the anarchists Nicola Sacco and Bartolomeo Vanzetti.

Calvin Goddard, inspecting a gun barrel, was also a pioneer in forensic ballistics and helped the FBI apply science to detective work.

CRIME LABS

Perhaps the most valuable contribution of the twentieth century was the evolution of crime laboratories. This began in France on a small scale in 1910 with Edmund Locard's laboratory in Paris. The first US crime lab was created in 1923 in the Los Angeles Police Department, and the high-tech FBI crime lab was created two years later. In 1935, London's Metropolitan Police forensic laboratory was opened.

Below: Discoverers of the DNA double helix James Watson (left) and Francis Crick (next to him) and Ernst Ruska (fourth from left), co-inventor of the electron microscope, join other scientists in San Francisco, California to receive the 1960 Albert Lasket Awards for medical research and public health advances.

The Advent Of Crime Labs

Edmund Locard's small technical laboratory, first established in 1910 in the attic of the Paris police station, used the best scientific techniques of its day, including microscopes and photography.

Before it created a fingerprint computer database, the FBI's forensic scientists had to compare samples in a time-consuming way.

Another police laboratory, America's first, was put together in 1923 in the Los Angeles Police Department by August Vollmer, who had also begun the School of Criminology at the University of California, Berkeley. The first private forensic laboratory was established in 1929 at Northwestern University in Evanston, Illinois, as the offspring of an investigation into the city's infamous St Valentine's Day Massacre.

In 1932, the United States Bureau of Investigation established its

THE BONE DETECTIVES

When the FBI began setting up its first crime lab in Washington, DC, in 1932, its agents were delighted to find a collection of 'bone detectives' just across the street in the red Gothic towers of the nation's Smithsonian Institution. These anthropologists were already working with the world's largest collection of human skeletons, and were more than happy to lend their expertise to the new laboratory, helping the FBI with such tasks as distinguishing between human and animal bones. The partnership also helped develop the field of forensic anthropology.

Technical Crime Laboratory in Washington, DC, conducting some 1000 forensic examinations the first year, and then moved a year later to larger premises under the new name of the Division of Investigation. The final name change occurred in 1935 as the Federal Bureau of Investigation (FBI), and its laboratory was given its own division within the bureau in 1942.

In 1935, London's Metropolitan Police Forensic Science Laboratory was opened. It retained its name in 1996 when it merged with the Forensic Science Service.

Right: The FBI began to emphasize science when it established a crime laboratory in 1932 in the Southern Railway Building in Washington, DC.

A LABORATORY CREATED BY GANGSTERS

They did not build it, but Chicago's gangsters were responsible for the creation of the first private US forensic laboratory. It began with Dr Calvin Goddard, the co-inventor of the comparison microscope, who investigated the bloody St Valentine's Day Massacre in a warehouse on 14 February 1929 when Al Capone's gang dressed as policemen to trap and murder seven members of the rival gang of George 'Bugs' Moran.

The crime scene yielded shell casings from some 200 bullets fired from submachine guns, and Goddard put them under his new microscope and found they did not match those from submarine guns issued to the police. After this was revealed, police raided the home of a Capone gang member and found two guns that Goddard used to successfully match the shells.

Goddard's impressive work with firearm identification attracted the interest of two businessmen on the coroner's inquest jury. They subsequently provided the funds for the private laboratory that opened in 1929 as the Laboratory Corporation. One year later it was renamed as the Scientific Crime Detection Laboratory.

Right: Moran's gang was lured to the garage by a promise of cheap whisky. After murdering them, the Capone men fled in a stolen police car, having missed killing Moran, who arrived late.

Left: The Smithsonian Institution has given the FBI generous assistance through the years. Known as 'the nation's attic,' the Smithsonian was established by the US Congress in 1846 and undertakes considerable scientific research.

Recent Forensic Advances

DNA fingerprinting has been hailed by forensic scientists as the greatest forensic advance since fingerprinting. To some its impact ranks with the invention of the Gutenberg printing press.

As discussed in Chapter 5, constant refinements in DNA testing are assuring faster and more accurate testing. Among the important new innovations are mitochondrial DNA (mtDNA) tracing ancestry through mothers, familial DNA searches to find family members, polymerase chain reaction (PCR) to multiply DNA samples, DNAboost to improve poor samples, and ever more sophisticated instruments, such as the miniaturized lab-on-a-chip device.

HUMAN GENOME PROJECT

The future of DNA forensic investigation seems limitless and will be accelerated by such giant strides as the 2003 completion of the Human Genome Project, which identified all of the genes in human DNA. 'Forensic DNA analysis is not a single technique', Dr. Lee said. 'It is a swarm of techniques based on the vast expanse of the human genome.'

Technical advances in other areas of the forensic sciences have been impressive, such as a 3D computer reconstruction of a crime scene, including a house and garden. New innovations continue in the field of fingerprinting. Once it depended on a brush to dust for prints, but now it uses any of 250 different chemicals and instrument techniques. Two advances include:

A new generation of portable lasers that speed trace evidence recovery at crime scenes. This third-generation laser system is an optically pumped semiconductor (OPS) laser that can find trace evidence under the most adverse conditions, including old fingerprints and those on porous materials like paper and stone. The traditional lower-power ion laser could miss such evidence.

Nanoparticles only one-billionth of a meter in length are being used by scientists at the University of Sunderland to produce a wipe-proof fingerprinting technique that provides a much clearer image than fluorescent powder now being used. Each nanoparticle has a sticky surface that attaches tightly to oily residue left by a fingertip. They are also dyed to assist scene-of-the-crime officers identify prints.

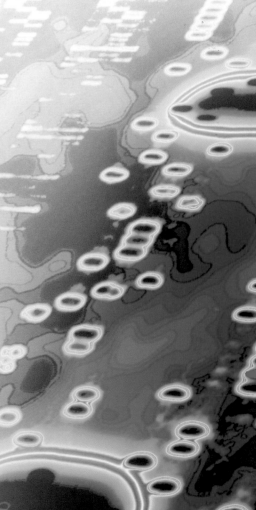

Below: A DNA autoradiogram is formed by fragmenting a DNA sample using enzymes, then separating the fragments under an electric current to form banding patterns.

234

Forensic expert witness Dr Henry Lee uses photographs to explain to the jury possible shoe imprints on the blood-stained jeans of murder victim Ron Goldman during the O.J. Simpson trial in 1995 in Los Angeles.

Blue Jeans

Imprint 1

Imprint 2

Imprint 3

A BETTER PICTURE

Image enhancement, as used by NASA to improve images sent from space, is now a common technique in forensic science. Videotape or photographs can be scanned into a computer and improved. Images of robbers' faces caught on security cameras are often of poor quality, making a positive identification impossible. In many recent cases, colour enhancement and other technologies have clarified the images and led to identifications. Other non-destructive photographic techniques are used to enhance impressions on hard surfaces and imprints in soft materials like mud, sand and snow. These techniques include filters and alternate lighting techniques like ultraviolet light, polarized light and infrared light.

NASA's Retinex Image Processing technology makes images brighter, sharper and clearer, as seen in this view of Jupiter's moon Io.

Advanced DNA Databases

Forensic scientists throughout the world are able to use databases to help solve cases that would have remained mysteries a few years ago.

The two major criminal databases are the Combined DNA Index System (CODIS) of the FBI in the US and the National DNA Database (NDNAD) of the Forensic Science Service in the UK.

CODIS has an impressive sharing system of DNA profiles kept in the FBI's National DNA Index System (NDIS), which numbered 4,398,639 in February 2007. CODIS, at that time, had produced more than 45,400 hits and assisted in more than 46,300 investigations. The system has a Forensic Index with DNA profiles from crime-scene evidence, and an Offender Index with DNA profiles of those convicted of violent crimes and sex offences. All of the profiles originate at the local level and are then sent to state offices and on to the FBI.

MATCHING THE EVIDENCE

Matches among the profiles of the Forensic Index can link crime scenes together and possibly identify serial offenders. After a match, police in various jurisdictions can co-ordinate their investigations and share leads. Matches made between the Forensic and Offender indexes provide the identity of the perpetrator(s). After CODIS identifies a potential match, DNA analysts in the laboratories contact each other to validate or reject a match.

CODIS began in 1990 as a pilot project. Four years later, the US Congress DNA Identification Act gave the FBI authority to establish a national DNA index for law

CODIS is in the FBI building at 935 Pennsylvania Avenue NW in Washington, DC. Officially the J. Edgar Hoover Building, it was occupied in 1975 after the bureau had spent its first 67 years in the US Department of Justice Building.

enforcement purposes. NDIS became operational in 1998.

KEEPING A RECORD

The Forensic Science Service, part of the Home Office, runs the UK's National DNA Database. NDNAD was established in 1995 and now contains about 3.6 million profiles, more than five per cent of the country's population. This is expected to climb to 4.25 million profiles by 2008.

The Criminal Justice and Police Act 2001 permitted police to take and retain DNA from anyone charged with a crime, but these had to be destroyed if the person was found to be innocent. Under the Criminal Justice Act 2003, however, the police may now retain the DNA of innocent suspects.

The majority of Britain's criminal population now have their DNA on record. Police receive more than 3500 DNA matches a month, which is double the figure received in 1998–1999.

A gloved hand holds a sample tube containing DNA above the graph that shows the results of this particular DNA analysis.

AUTOMATED FINGERPRINT IDENTIFICATION

In 1999, the FBI placed into service its Integrated Automated Fingerprint Identification System (IAFIS). In 2007 it had grown to a data resource of more than 43 million 10-print records. Some 60,000 queries are now received electronically each day, and 80 per cent are answered in less than 40 minutes. New technology is coming that will shorten this response time further still. Interpol, the International police force, has an experts group studying the Automated Fingerprint Identification System (AFIS) in order to inform member states on how to acquire and develop their own system.

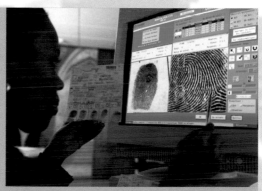

Computer technology has dramatically sped up the identification of criminals and victims through DNA profiles and fingerprint records.

DNA Database Failures

Despite their reputation for accuracy, DNA databases can in rare cases yield an incorrect result.

One wrongful arrest confirmed by the UK's Forensic Science Service involved Raymond Easton, who had given a blood sample 1995 after a minor domestic dispute. Four years later, police investigating a burglary asked for another blood sample

Easton was not worried, because he had been with his family on the night in question and he also had advanced Parkinson's disease. Yet the police returned to arrest him after the DNA database matched his sample to that left by the robber. The database's six genetic loci system supposedly had only one chance in 37 million of wrongly linking Easton to the DNA recovered.

Easton spent seven hours in a cell. Because of his situation, his lawyer successfully applied for a more sophisticated DNA test with 10 genetic loci. It was able to discriminate between Easton's DNA and that found at the scene, so the charges were dropped. For its part, the FSS upgraded its database to 10 loci.

In a different type of database failure, research by the American newspaper *USA Today* revealed that investigators failed to pursue potential suspects whose DNA on the FBI's CODIS system had matched evidence from crime scenes in nearly three dozen cases from 2001 to 2006. This happened because of backlogs of unsolved 'cold cases' or was a result of basic police mistakes. 'Once a mistake has been made,' warns Australia's Federal Privacy Commission Malcolm Crompton, 'it is very difficult to fix or to undo the damage.'

Right: A scientist examines a sample of DNA on a computer database.

A scientist uses a magnifying glass to study a series of DNA sequencing autoradiograms, or genetic fingerprints. He is determining the sequence of base pairs (cytosine, guanine, adenine and thymine) that form the code for a section of DNA.

'A SILENT PROBLEM'

The FBI has begun creating a database of DNA from unidentified corpses, with one source estimating the US has at least 40,000 cases. These include murder and accident victims, vagrants, and runaways. Some are buried in paupers' graves or kept in local crime laboratories. Reporting unidentified remains is not required of coroners and medical examiners, but some states like Nevada and Pennsylvania now require DNA to be taken before an unidentified body can be buried.

'It's a silent problem', said Michael Murphy, coroner in Clark County, Nevada. 'But these are also homicides that could be solved, accidents that could be cleared up, families whose questions could finally be put to rest.'

ESTABLISHING A EUROPEAN DNA DATABASE

No European DNA database exists, and the urgent need for one was realized in 1996 when an English schoolgirl was murdered in France. The perpetrator was caught in the US, helped by American DNA testing, and this brought changes to the French DNA database. The UK put forward a proposal for a European database in 2004, and the following year, seven European countries announced they would sign an agreement to allow access to each other's DNA and fingerprint databases. In 2007, EU ministers from all 27 of the member states informally said they would explore the possibility of exchanging DNA and fingerprint data.

A technician at the Sanger Centre in Cambrige loads samples into automated DNA sequencers used for the Human Genome Project.

In 2005 seven European countries announced that they would allow access to each other's DNA and fingerprint databases.

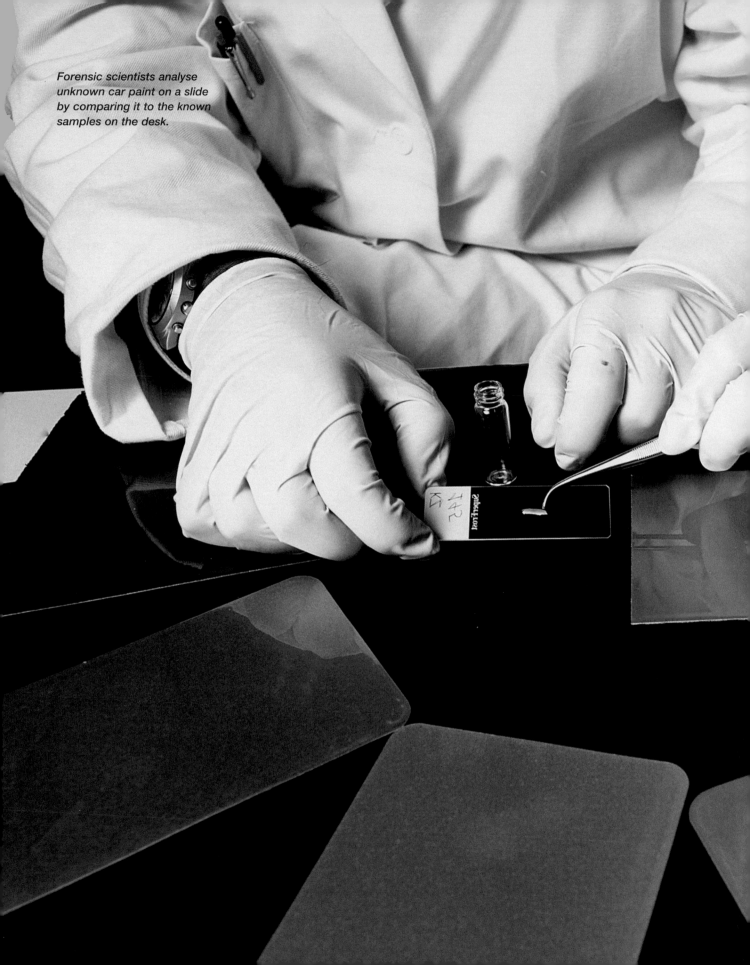

Forensic scientists analyse unknown car paint on a slide by comparing it to the known samples on the desk.

Chapter Thirteen

The Forensic Career

As the various forensic specialities have expanded, so have the opportunities for employment in this rewarding career, which serves the interests of society, justice, and public safety. The large umbrella of forensic science covers a fascinating assortment of jobs, from surgeon to fire investigator to administrator. All are involved in applying science to the law,

Forensic scientists from the Institute Recherche Criminelle in France join a policeman to investigate the scene of a crime in a forest.

so a good scientific background and an understanding of police work are both necessary.

An inquisitive nature and stamina are required, too. 'You also have to learn to use deductive and inductive logic', says Dr Henry C. Lee, the American recognized as one of the world's leading forensic scientists. 'You need to have curiosity. You can't have an eight-to-four attitude. You have to have that persistence.'

Forensic scientists are totally responsible for their examinations and results, but they work closely with police, lawyers and other investigators. The result of their expert opinions will often influence the judge and jury to the point of determining the outcome of a court case. On the other hand, forensic scientists may reduce the number of cases in the overloaded court system by proving that an issue does not merit a court hearing.

A forensic scientist uses powder to reveal fingerprints on a pane of glass at a crime scene. This will determine if a suspect was there.

Fact And Fiction

While slick television shows such as 'CSI' and 'Bones' glamorize the work of forensic teams, the hour-long format also gives the impression that investigators provide strong results after brief examinations.

In fact, a former supervisory scientist with the FBI Laboratory, Max Houck, has identified what he calls the 'CSI Effect', which gives juries unrealistic expectations about what forensic laboratories can do. 'Defence attorneys now worry about the CSI Effect, as well', he noted, 'because they think that the jurors come in and have this view of science as this juggernaut, this infallible objective method that is always right and spells doom for their client.'

However, reality is not so neatly programmed in laboratories, which

Above: On this 'CSI: Miami' episode, Adam Rodriguez portrays a forensic scientist investigating a suspicious accident of a man decapitated doing a daring car stunt.

Left: Fictional forensic science must create ever original storylines. Here on 'CSI: NY,' the actors (left to right) Hill Harper, Carmine Giovinazzo and Melina Kanakaredes, track a serial killer who uses codes on T-shirts as inspiration for murder.

are often understaffed and overworked. Many traditional labs are suffering because the demand for DNA services has concentrated money and talent in that field.

A GRUESOME JOB

Also, television does not depict the often bloody, gruesome and smelly conditions prevailing in the lab or at a crime scene, where investigators must sift through dirt and mud to find blood droplets, bullet fragments and other trace evidence.

'There are certainly unpleasant scenes at crime scenes,' said the US forensic scientist Dr John DeHaan, a fire and explosives expert in Vallejo, California. He himself once had to crawl through a tight space in a home past the rotting body of the victim. 'You're cold and wet, or you're hot, and you're out there examining blood spatter or shoveling ashes and thinking,

"Maybe Mom was right – maybe I should have been an accountant."'

Perhaps because of his humorous outlook, Dr DeHaan has persevered with his job for more than 30 years. The great majority of forensic experts are dedicated scientists, intrigued by their work of using intuition and high-tech science to find and convict criminals.

'CSI: Crime Scene' has popularized forensic science careers. Here it premiered its seventh season with a story about an aspiring dancer being killed backstage.

TELEVISION ERRORS

The basic science is normally correct in fictionalized forensic plots on television, but many liberties are taken. Some that have been pointed out by real laboratory workers are:

- Technicians in real labs do specific work and hand in the results. Unlike the TV version, they do not work outside the lab or talk with police investigators about the case, and most certainly never draw conclusions on the guilt of the suspect.

- In a real lab, only about half the crimes are solved by forensic evidence, while television always solves every crime.

- Television experiments always work on the first try, whereas in reality reruns are often required.

- In a real lab, investigators often find DNA and fingerprints without knowing to whom they belong, so no match is made. A television series always has a suspect.

- Television lab workers never spend any time analyzing the data as is needed, but just wait for a printout from a test that gives them an immediate, clear result.

Duties of a Forensic Scientist

The main function of a forensic scientist is to provide scientific and impartial evidence for use in courts of law, and this means they will work closely with the police and may be required to go to a crime scene, such as a murder or fire.

Forensic scientists and reporting officers may attend crime scenes and have some supervisory responsibility within the lab. Most work concerns using all forms of analysis to examine trace evidence and relate it to a suspect.

Forensic scientists who are reporting officers provide impartial scientific evidence for use in the courts.

OTHER FORENSICS STAFF

Assistant forensic scientists aid forensic scientists in biology- and chemistry-based analytical work, predominately based in the lab.

Forensic pathologists carry out routine coroners' autopsies and suspicious deaths autopsies. They

Left: A forensic artist uses a wire frame and wax to reassemble a human skull. The face may also be reconstructed.

also supervise the pathology lab or even the entire crime lab, such as the new Department of Forensic Medical Sciences in the UK's Forensic Science Service.

Forensic document experts looks at questioned documents to identify an individual by the handwriting or signature, or by the paper, ink, and indented impressions.

Forensic administrators review the development and implementation of leading technology, seek the legal and political context of forensic science, and study how to reduce error rates by reorganizing the existing processes.

INTERNATIONAL FORENSIC ORGANIZATIONS

The American Academy of Forensic Sciences (AAFS), founded in 1948, is headquartered in Colorado Springs, Colorado. It has members from 55 countries and all 50 US states. It publishes the *Journal of Forensic Sciences* and is committed to 'the promotion of education and the elevation of accuracy, precision and specificity in the forensic sciences'.

The Forensic Science Society, based in Harrogate, North Yorkshire, is an international professional body founded in 1959 with more than 2500 members from over 60 countries. It publishes the journal *Science & Justice* and arranges scientific conferences.

Most work concerns using all forms of analysis to examine trace evidence and relate it to a suspect.

Investigators deal with a large variety of objects. The scientist above is taking a blood sample from a hammer found at a murder scene in order to make a DNA analysis, while the forensic expert at the right is using a microscope to study the sole of a suspect's boot.

COMMON LABORATORY WORK

The UK's Forensic Science Service lists the following eight common tasks found in a forensic lab:

- Identification of blood, semen and other body fluids; the blood grouping of dried stains, and the use of DNA profiling to compare samples.

- Identification and comparison of textile fibres.

- Identification and comparison of plant and animal materials, including hairs.

- Analysis of blood and urine samples for their drug or alcohol content in driving offences.

- Analysis of body fluids and organs in cases of suspected poisoning.

- Identification of illegal drugs, such as amphetamine, heroin and cannabis. The purity of these drugs is often determined and samples can be compared.

- Comparison of materials used to package drugs.

- Examination of paint and glass fragments using microscopy, and physical and chemical methods.

245

Forensic Scientists In Court

Unlike the ordinary fact witness, the forensic scientist is an expert witness, whose evaluation of the scientific tests performed must be presented in everyday language anyone could understand.

Often, this does not come easily, and forensic training normally teaches how to rephrase complex science into simple terms.

A jury is normally in some awe when confronted by a scientist, and it is important that his or her qualifications are brought out in

questioning, including the number of years of experience in the field, the degrees received, participation in professional organizations and any

Opposing lawyers seek to find flaws in the forensic scientist's tests.

Dr Randall Alexander, an expert child-abuse witness for the prosecution, points to a doll representing six-year-old Tiffany Eunick and describes the deadly injuries she received in 2001 in Fort Lauderdale, Florida.

professional books or articles the scientist has published.

DISCREDITING SCIENTISTS

Facts in the testimony of a scientist are open to be challenged in court, with opposing attorneys seeking to find flaws in the scientific tests or the interpretation. It is not easy to discredit forensic facts or the science upon which they are based, but lawyers have had some successes. For this reason, the forensic scientist must be aware of the court's rules of evidence on the admissibility of opinions and conclusions. And throughout the testimony, a

forensic expert must maintain an impartial professionalism, no matter which side is helped or harmed by the presentation.

An expert in court is an impressive witness but, in reality, forensic scientists are required to appear in court in a very few number of cases. For most cases, they write up comprehensive reports of the forensic examinations. The side that has retained the scientist will present these, so, as with an oral testimony, they should be written in such a way that anyone could easily understand the report.

Left: Defense attorney Roger Diamond shows a bottle of herbal Ecstacy to expert prosecution witness Dr. Jo Ellen Dyer, a toxicologist, at the date rape trial of Max Factor heir, Andrew Luster, in 2003 in Ventura, California.

WRONGFUL TESTIMONY

If a forensic scientist becomes too eager to back up the police view of a case, the result can be a terrible miscarriage of justice. This happened in Chicago, Illinois in 1986 during the trial of two African–American defendants, Donald Reynolds and Billy Wardell, for the rape of a University of Chicago student and the attempted rape of another.

The testimony came in 1988 from the Chicago Police forensic serologist Pamela Fish. Fish testified that semen recovered from one victim could have come only from 38 percent of the male population, including Reynolds, when actually 80 percent of black males could have been the source. She also did not disclose to the jury that another Chicago Police crime lab analyst had examined hairs recovered from Reynolds and determined that they could not have come from either victim. The accused, who had been identified by the victims, were found guilty and given a total of 69 years in prison. The judge denied their request for DNA tests, but in 1996 new attorneys were able to ensure the tests were carried out, and these proved the men were innocent after spending 11 years behind bars.

Acquiring a Forensic Job

Media attention to forensic science in the court has created a rapidly expanding job market resulting in numerous well paying jobs being available to university graduates with degrees in the field.

This is the opinion of Loyola University in Chicago, which offers a major in forensic science, and it adds: 'Recent published studies report an ever-increasing demand for forensic scientists and estimates suggest that 10,000 new forensic scientists will be required in the next five years to sufficiently staff the nation's forensic laboratories.'

For its positions on offer, the

Forensic scientists in New York collect evidence at the scene of a murder. Everything of the remotest importance must be photographed and recorded.

UK's Forensic Science Service (FSS) recommends that a scientific qualification, often to degree level, is the best route, but even applicants with university degrees should gain paid laboratory experience.

PROFESSIONAL QUALIFICATIONS

Applicants for some specialist positions, such as a crime scene investigator who must have an

UNIVERSITY FORENSIC COURSES

The UK only offered three undergraduate courses at three universities in 1993, but by 2006 an explosion of courses saw more than 460 being offered by more than 60 universities and institutions of higher education. These included the Universities of the West of England at Bristol, Chester, Coventry, East London, Wales at Bangor, and at Lampeter, Greenwich, Manchester, Plymouth, Strathclyde and Worcester.

Among the many US universities with degree courses in forensic sciences are the University of Alabama at Birmingham; California State University, Sacramento; George Washington University in Washington, DC; the University of New Haven in Connecticut; and the University of Texas Southwestern Medical Center in Dallas. Courses at university level in Canada are offered at the University of Toronto and Laurentian University in Sudbury, (both of which are in Ontario), and at Mount Royal College in Calgary, Alberta.

WORK SATISFACTION

The American Academy of Forensic Sciences offers the following answer to the question, 'How much money will I make?'

'Income in the forensic sciences varies greatly depending upon your degree, your actual job, where you work, and how many hours you work. You may never "get rich" but you will have a good income. You will be satisfied with your job, knowing you are contributing to justice. Essentially every branch of forensic science offers opportunities for personal growth, advancement and increasing financial compensation.'

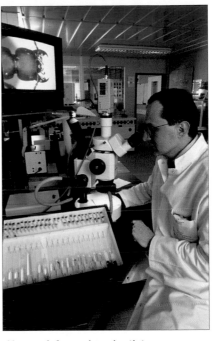

Above: A forensic scientist uses a microscope to examine a rove beetle found on a corpse. The beetle's head is shown on the monitor at upper left.

Association of Chief Police Officers certificate, must be already fully qualified when joining the FSS. A forensic photographer should have a minimum of a BTEC National Diploma in Photography or at least a year's professional photographic work experience.

IN-HOUSE TRAINING

All forensic laboratories have some in-house training programmes, and the FBI's Forensic Science Training Unit is widely considered outstanding. Mandatory classes are given to new scientists and technicians, with the New Agent Program providing instruction on crime scene evidence. The FBI also conducts a University Education Program that provides financial support for Laboratory personnel to earn advanced academic degrees and/or certifications.

Below: A pathologist prepares to perform an autopsy on a corpse. Autopsies are called for if a death is sudden or suspicious or to help identify a victim.

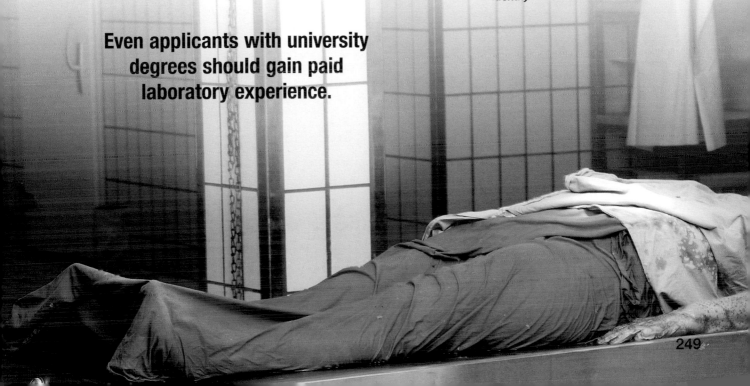

Even applicants with university degrees should gain paid laboratory experience.

Glossary

Abrasion: An injury in which the skin has been scraped off.

AFIS: Abbreviation for the Automated Fingerprint Identification System which scans fingerprints electronically and plots the positions of their ridge characteristics, comparing them with prints in a database.

Arches: Fingerprint ridges that rise above one another at their centre like an arch.

Autolysis: The bacterial and chemical breakdown of the body's cells and tissues that cause postmortem decomposition, or putrefaction.

Cadaveric spasm: A type of instant rigor mortis in which muscle stiffness occurs just after death because the muscles were being used with great exertion while dying.

CART: Abbreviation for the FBI's Computer Analysis and Response Team that examines computers during investigations.

CCTV: Abbreviation for a closed-circuit television surveillance camera used to record crimes being committed, to find lost persons, or to prevent crime.

Chain of custody: A list that records every official person who handles a piece of evidence. Those in the chain put their initials and the date on the evidence container.

CODIS: Abbreviation for the Combined DNA Index System of the FBI which is used to share DNA profiles kept in the FBI's National DNA Index System (NDIS) with law enforcement bodies.

Cold case: A old unsolved criminal case. Many are now being solved with the advent of DNA tests.

Comparison microscope: A microscope that has two compound light microscopes with an optical bridge, so two samples can be viewed in a single eyepiece. It is used to match trace evidence such as fibres and bullet casings.

Contamination: The act of ruining evidence by accidentally depositing outside trace evidence, including DNA, on items from a crime scene or suspect.

Continuity of evidence: An official record of the movement of evidence through a chain of authorities.

Contusion: A bruise in which the skin is not broken.

CPR: Abbreviation for the first aid method of cardio-pulmonary resuscitation, in which mouth-to-mouth resuscitation is combined with chest compressions.

CT scanner: Short for a computer tomography scanner that uses cross-sectional images to produce a three-dimensional image of a body structure. CT scans are used for computer facial reconstructions.

DNA: Deoxyribonucleic acid, constructed of a double helix like a twisted ladder formed into long strands called chromosomes. It carries unique inherited genetic information. Common forensic sources of DNA include samples of hair, blood, semen, saliva and skin.

ECG: Abbreviation of electroencephalograph, used to probe the criminal mind. Informally known as 'brain fingerprinting', an ECG test is conducted with the suspect wearing a headband having electronic sensors that measure electrical signal surges in the brain when something familiar is recognized.

E-FIT: An electronic facial identification technique that stores hundreds of facial features in a software program, like a computerized photofit program.

Electrophoresis: A process in which an electrical current is passed through a DNA sample to move it through a gel or narrow tube, separating the fragments into a series of bands. These are read by a detector and displayed on a graph.

Expert witness: A specialist witness, such as a forensic scientist, who testifies at a trial.

FISH: Abbreviation for the Forensic Information System for Handwriting, a database of handwriting samples.

FOA: Abbreviation for the first officer attending a crime scene.

Fracture: A break, crack, or shattering of a bone

Gas chromatography: An analytical technique of chromatography that identifies chemical compositions by measuring the speed of vaporized samples moving at different rates through a narrow tube.

Genome: The complete set of DNA within a cell. These regulate our genetic material used by forensic scientists to identify individuals.

Henry System: A system used for classifying 10-fingerprint collections, developed in 1899 by Sir Edward R. Henry with the British police in India.

Human Genome Project: A project that identified all of the 20,000 to 25,000 genes in human DNA. It was compiled in 2003, coordinated by the US Department of Energy and the National Institutes of Health.

IAFIS Abbreviation for the FBI's Integrated Automated Fingerprint Identification System. Police forces can submit samples to be compared to those on this computerized database.

Identikit: A facial identification technique that uses sketches.

Lab-on-a-chip: A portable micro-laboratory that speeds up DNA tests by automatically analyzing samples. All components are on a single chip.

Laceration: A cut that is deep enough to need stitches.

Latent fingerprints: Fingerprints that are invisible to the naked eye, but which can still be detected by such methods as an angled beam of ultraviolet light or a laser.

Locard's Exchange Principle: A principle by Dr Edmund Locard, a French police officer and forensic scientist, that any physical contact between a suspect and victim will result in physical evidence being exchanged between them.

Loops: Fingerprint patterns consisting of ridges that double back on themselves.

Magnetic resonance imaging (MRI): A brain scan that may be used to probe the criminal mind. It is focused on parts of the cerebral cortex where nerve endings are active.

Mass spectrometry: A technique used by toxicologists to identify chemical compositions. The instrument breaks a chemical down into its ions and accelerates them in a magnetic field that produces a unique spectrum.

Mitochondrial DNA (mtDNA): A type of DNA located in the mitochondrion of most cells. Since it lasts longer than nuclear DNA and comes only from the mother, mtDNA is used to trace ancestry.

Modus operandi (MO): The usual method of operation used by a perpetrator, such as the weapon used and the taking of 'trophy' items from victims.

NDNAD: Abbreviation for the National DNA Database of the Forensic Science Service in the UK. It has profiles of most of Britain's criminal population on record.

Nuclear DNA: The unique DNA that is inherited from each parent.

OPS: Abbreviation for optically pumped semiconductor, a laser that can find trace evidence in adverse conditions.

Polygraph: The formal name for a lie detector. It measures a person's stress level while a sequence of questions is asked. Tests are taken with a sphygmomanometer cuff around the arm of the suspect to measure pulse rates, electrodes on the fingers to detect electrical resistance in the skin, and two pneumographs strapped around the chest to measure heavy breathing caused by anxiety.

Postmortem: The medical examination that normally involves dissecting a body to determine the cause of death.

PCR: Abbreviation for polymerase chain reaction, a 'molecular photocopying' technique that amplifies specific regions of a DNA strand. The polymerase enzyme is used for copying DNA.

Phishing: A technique used by identity thieves who send out a great amount of e-mails that pretend to be from companies and organizations requesting personal information.

Professional witness: A professional person, such as a police officer or security guard, who testifies at a trial.

Photofit: A facial identification system that uses photographs.

Psychological stress evaluator: An instrument that measures stress in a suspect's voice based on the assumption that a voice will reach a higher pitch when the person is telling a lie.

Reenactment of a crime: The use of ordinary people or actors to recreate a crime.

Reconstruction of a crime: Determining the way a crime happened, pieced together using evidence at the crime scene.

Rigor mortis: A stiffening of the body that occurs about 30 minutes after death and continues for up to 18 hours.

Scanning electron microscope (SEM): A microscope that reveals exceptional details as samples are bombarded with electrons. It is used to identify trace evidence as well as pigments in art forgeries.

Skeletalization: The process of a body's soft tissues completely decomposing to leave only the bones.

SOCO: Scene of Crime Officer

Staged crime scene: A crime scene where the perpetrator has left false clues to mislead investigators.

Trace evidence: Small items of evidence from a crime scene or suspect, such as hairs, fabric, skin, and gunshot residue, often including fingerprints, footprints and tire prints.

Trauma: A wound or a physical or emotional shock to the body.

Whorls: Fingerprint patterns that resemble small whirlpools revolving around a point.

Witness of fact: A member of the general public who testifies at a trial.

Index

Index

Index

Picture Credits